THE ORIGINS OF
AMERICAN SLAVERY AND
RACISM

African Afro-American Studies Series

Darwin T. Turner, Editor

University of Michigan

THE ORIGINS OF AMERICAN SLAVERY AND RACISM

Edited by

Donald L. Noel

University of Wisconsin, Milwaukee

Charles E. Merrill Publishing Co.
A Bell & Howell Company
Columbus, Ohio

ISBN: 0-675-09145-4

Library of Congress Catalog Card Number: 71-182258

1 2 3 4 5 6 7 8 — 77 76 75 74 73 72

Printed in the United States of America

CONTRIBUTORS

JOSEPH BOSKIN is Professor of History and Afro-American Studies at Boston University. His publications include an edited book, *Urban Racial Violence in the Twentieth Century,* and the recently published *The Life and Death of Sambo: The Racial Stereotype in the Popular Culture.*

CARL N. DEGLER is Professor of History at Stanford University. The author of *Out of Our Past* and *Neither Black Nor White,* he has taught previously at New York University and Vassar College.

STANLEY M. ELKINS, Sydenham Clark Parsons Professor of History at Smith College, is the author of *Slavery: A Problem in American Institutional and Intellectual Life.* He formerly taught at the University of Chicago.

OSCAR HANDLIN is Professor of History and Director of the Charles Warren Center for Studies in American History at Harvard. His publications include *The Uprooted, The Newcomers,* and *Firebell in the Night.* MARY F. HANDLIN has collaborated with her husband on numerous publications including *Commonwealth* and *The Dimensions of Liberty.*

WINTHROP D. JORDAN is Professor of History at the University of California, Berkeley. He is the author of *White Over Black: Attitudes Toward the Negro, 1550-1812.*

GARY B. NASH is Associate Professor of History at the University of California, Los Angeles. He is the author of *Quakers and Politics,*

Pennsylvania 1681-1726 and co-editor of *The Great Fear: Race in the Mind of America.*

DONALD L. NOEL is Associate Professor of Sociology at the University of Wisconsin-Milwaukee. He received his Ph.D. from Cornell University and taught previously at the University of Washington and Ohio State University. He contributed to the volume *Strangers Next Door: Ethnic Relations in American Communities* (by Robin M. Williams, Jr.) and is co-author of a work in process on *Racial and Ethnic Differentiation in Sociological Perspective.*

CONTENTS

PREFACE

There is an abundance of readers on race relations at present, including several on the topic of slavery. Several of the latter are extremely valuable but others err, I believe, by trying to cover too broad a topic. While general readers are helpful, especially at the introductory level, increasingly there is a need for more sharply focused works. The intent in assembling the present reader is not to provide a general introduction to American slavery, much less to all slavery, but to explore a delimited aspect of slavery in the United States in depth. The focus is on the origin of American slavery and its relation to the ideology of racism.

Numerous issues in addition to that of origin provide useful topics for volumes on slavery. These include the processes by which a slave system is maintained, the processes by which it is altered and is replaced, the nature of the actual pattern of relations between masters and slaves, the effect of slavery on the personality of the slave, and many other issues. It is my conviction that each volume should focus on a topic sufficiently specific to enable thorough coverage of the significant questions generated by the topic.

A second shortcoming common to many readers is that they suffer from a severe lack of editorial integration. One often wonders if a particular reader is not simply a hasty compilation of articles thrown together helter-skelter in order to help the editor temporarily ease the pressures of "publish or perish." (I have just received a reader in which the editors' sole contribution is a two-page preface, a handful of discussion questions and a short bibliography!) While it is useful to have a number of broadly related articles from various sources pulled together in one volume, this hardly seems *sufficient* justification for a reader in this day of copying facilities. I am strongly inclined to the view that a reader should not be published unless it includes a considerable contribution by the editor(s) and, more to the point, a contribution which clearly reveals the unity of the reader and advances knowledge regarding the issues raised. Whether I have succeeded or failed in meeting these objectives, it is in these terms that I hope this reader will be judged.

I am indebted to Joseph Boskin, Carl N. Degler, Clyde Franklin, Nason E. Hall, Benjamin Quarles, Frank H. White, and Sidney M. Willhelm for encouragement and constructive criticism in the development of this reader. Needless to say, they are in no way responsible for the shortcomings of the finished product. I also wish to express my thanks to Virginia Lee Noel and Brooke Wickliffe for typing the manuscript, to the Yale University Press for permission to quote from *Slave Society in the British Leeward Islands at the End of the Eighteenth Century* by Elsa V. Goveia, and to Roger Ratliff for being a patient and congenial editor.

Milwaukee, Wisconsin

PART I

Slavery

The past two decades have witnessed a rich, scholarly productivity in the analysis of slavery in the Americas. This research has been explicitly comparative in some instances and focused on a particular society in others. The present reader primarily constitutes a contribution of the second type but in two respects it is also a contribution to comparative research. First, like all studies of single societies, it is indirectly comparative in that precise and reliable knowledge of individual societies is the indispensable foundation for comparative research. Second, the reader is focused on the emergence of slavery and racism in the United States[1] with an eye to formulating *generalizations* about the conditions under which these phenomena emerge and are interrelated. More specifically, our concern is to summarize what is known about the origins of American slavery and racism in order to formulate a theory of the emergence of systems of ethnic stratification in general and their relationship to the ideology of racism.

The basic issues raised in this volume — the origin of slavery and its relation to racism — may, at first consideration, seem far removed from the present day racial conflict in America. In one sense, this is clearly the case. Nevertheless, slavery, as Staughton Lynd has recently reminded us,[2] is a central theme in American history. As such, an understanding of slavery provides a very useful — indeed, required — background for an adequate analysis and understanding of contemporary race relations. The same factors which account for slavery's origin also explain the advent of Jim Crow segregation and, conversely, change in the values of these factors facilitates the emergence of protest groups which vigorously attack involuntary segregation and other contemporary forms of discrimination. Similarly, analysis of the relationship between slavery and racism sheds light on the more general problem of the relationship between social structure and ideology. In any era this is a very significant issue for those who seek change for they must decide whether genuine change is most effectively secured by concentrating their finite resources upon the structure of racial discrimination or upon the racist ideology undergirding and justifying this structure. The current struggle to achieve justice in the relations between blacks and whites has undoubtedly been a factor in stimulating much of the recent wave of research on slavery and, as Merton Dillon has suggested, the relationship is reciprocal — understanding the past makes "more comprehensible some of the events of recent times."[3]

The relationship between slavery and racism has often been dogmatically asserted but it has not been adequately researched. In contrast, the existent literature includes many valuable contributions regarding the development of seventeenth-century American race relations which culminated in the secure institutionalization of slavery. Four articles are selected from this literature to provide a general overview of the emergence of slavery. These articles conflict in some particulars but they provide the basic data from which the remaining two selections in part two attempt to derive insights and construct a more general explanation of the origin of slavery, American and otherwise. These articles also provide perceptive, albeit conflicting, leads regarding the relationship of slavery and racism. These leads are utilized, along with others drawn from the larger literature, in developing the concluding essay in part three on slavery and the rise of racism.

This introductory essay has two major purposes. First, it provides an overview of slavery primarily oriented toward explicating its essential nature and the diversity of forms which it has taken. This creates a basis for a brief consideration of possible variations in the relationship between slavery and racism as a function of variations in the form or the context of slavery. Second, this essay presents an analytic summary of four overlapping but distinct theories of the origin of slavery. This creates a reference point for assessing the articles presented in part two. The introduction also includes a brief overview of the central issues and contributions of these articles and those presented in part three.

The Nature of Slavery

Slavery is an institutional arrangement whereby some persons are, without just cause, coerced into perpetual servitude, defined as property (i.e., a thing, a commodity), and denied rights commonly accorded other members of society. There is widespread consensus that these components — perpetuity, property, and denial of rights — are part of slavery, but they are not uniformly specified as the defining characteristics. Davis, for example, omits perpetuity and stresses coercion as a third essential feature.[4] Certainly, coercion is intimately involved with slavery and it may differentiate slavery from indenture (although perpetuity is a more efficient differentium), but it clearly ignores the reality of coercion inherent in many other forms of servitude. If slavery is invariably involuntary, debt bondage and serfdom may be said to be voluntary only in a very technical sense — i.e., a "voluntary" response to involuntary conditions (e.g., the threat of starvation) imposed by the absence of economic alternatives. In any event, coercion is implied by each of the three defining characteristics and especially by perpetuity, for "even if each person could alienate himself, he could not alienate his children. . . ."[5]

Given the acknowledged difficulties "in comprehending the historical varieties of slavery or in clearly distinguishing the institution from other types of involuntary servitude" within the bounds of a single definition,[6] it is most feasible to consider perpetuity, property, and denial of rights as equally essential (i.e., defining) characteristics of slavery. Clearly no one of the three can stand alone as a basis for differentiating slavery from all other forms of servitude. At the extreme slavery is so distinct that a single criterion—property—may be sufficient, but there are points where slavery overlaps other servile statuses to such an extent that it can only be distinguished by applying two or all three defining criteria. Thus, Finley speaks of "a spectrum of statuses between the two extremes of absolute rightlessness and of absolute freedom to exercise all rights at all times" and elsewhere raises the question of whether the Roman slave with a *peculium* was more or less free than the technically free debt-bondsman.[7] The question is unanswerable but the criteria of perpetuity and, to a lesser degree, of property provide a basis for distinguishing the two even if that of freedom does not. The villein, on the other hand, is distinguishable from the slave less in terms of perpetuity than in the retention of a larger bundle of rights. This, too, blurs in the case of the slave with a *peculium* and hence the slave – serf distinction is generally made in terms of the property criterion. However, the villein was in his legal status alienable property like the slave — i.e., "the villein was a chattel who could be sold apart from the manor and whose labor was unregulated by law."[8] Slaves then can be distinguished from other serviles only by a combination of readier alienability, fewer opportunities for change of status, and generally fewer rights. In short, slaves are the most deprived and oppressed class of serviles.

A multidimensional definition of slavery is also necessitated by the fact that no single dimension or criterion can uniformly subsume the other criteria across all the varied historical forms of slavery. The primary controversy regarding the defining characteristics concerns the alleged hierarchical relation between the authority and property criteria. M. G. Smith exemplifies those who view authority as the more basic criterion while Magnus Mörner represents those who give priority to property.[9] The broader issue underlying this controversy is whether slavery is to be conceived primarily as an economic or as a social institution. The position here is that neither authority nor property can invariably subsume the other since slavery may be primarily economic or primarily social (i.e., a power relation) dependent upon the broader social structure in which it is located. Clarification of this requires a classification of slavery in terms of the institution's overall centrality and primary function in the larger society.

The primary axis of classification turns on the distinction between societies in which slavery is only an incidental part of the institutional fabric and those in which slavery is the pivot of the entire institutional structure and value system. Finley calls the former "slaveowning" societies while the latter are "genuine" slave societies.[10] The *sine qua non* of the genuine slave society is a high degree of dependence upon slave labor to provide a substantial proportion of the productive labor force. In time this dependence has a significant impact upon the polity and other vital institutional sectors of the society.[11] By contrast, slaves form only a small and insignificant part of the labor force in the incidental slave society. The second axis of classification divides each of these types of slave society into two subtypes according to whether the primary function of slavery is economic or social. These subtypes may be designated the utilitarian and assimilative forms of incidental slavery and the exploitative and paternalist forms of genuine slavery.

Africa and the ancient world, excluding Greece and Rome, provide numerous examples of incidental slave societies. In a few of these societies (e.g., the Ibo of West Africa) slaves were very harshly and negatively defined, but "even where slaves were economically valuable . . . other factors mitigated the definition of a slave as an impersonal thing or object."[12] In general, African slaves were not chattel but were provided opportunities for mobility and thus were "in a state of continuously merging with, and becoming indistinguishable from, the free members of the society."[13] In short, economic exploitation and an ideology of inferiority were the exception in African slavery while assimilation and other social functions (primarily familial) were the rule.

This form of slavery is so different from that institutionalized in the new world that it is questionable whether it should even be classified under the same rubric.[14] The characteristically secondary nature of the economic function of African slaves deemphasizes, but does not deny, the property criterion, while the assimilative function undercuts the perpetuity criterion. If we emphasize the authority criterion, however, these societies clearly qualify as slave societies for African slaves generally, with some very significant exceptions, had sharply restricted political rights. In stressing the authority criterion — i.e., "complete subordination of slaves to the will of their masters" — Smith cautions that couching our definition of slavery in terms of property is a trap which leads "to the treatment of the institution primarily or even wholly in economic terms."[15] This bias leads to neglect of variations in the "purity of strictly economic motivations in the recruitment and administration of slaves" and also obscures highly significant differences between slave systems as regards the property, racial and personal components of slave status.[16]

Even in the genuine slave societies of the new world slavery was not uniformly a preeminently economic institution. Societies which introduce slavery in order to further rational economic goals do not necessarily grant priority to this goal throughout their entire history. The economic irrationality of slaveholders in instances where rational economic behavior required significant alteration of the established pattern of race relations has been widely acknowledged. Genovese, for example, emphasizes that the emergent values of the planter class, symbolized by slavery *as a way of life,* absorbed their economic interests and directed them into channels compatible with slavery.[17] The outcome of the developmental process by which an exploitative slave economy was converted into a paternalist slave society (i.e., a society in which slavery was no longer predominantly an economic institution) is perhaps best summarized by Goveia.

> There is a profound irony in the determined resistance of the British West Indian colonies to any form of basic change in their slave system. For the growing density of the slave populations concentrated on their sugar estates and the increasing expense of their traditional methods of agriculture under the slave system were among the most important factors contributing to the lack of competitive efficiency which was already affecting the economic fortunes of most of these territories by the end of the eighteenth century. By that time, however, the West Indians could no longer afford to regard slavery simply as the economic expedient for supplying labour which it had been originally. The slave system had become more than an economic enterprise which could be abandoned when it ceased to be profitable. It had become the very basis of organised society throughout the British West Indies, and therefore it was believed to be an indispensable element in maintaining the existing social structure and in preserving law and order in the community. The idea of a society in which Negroes were released from their subordination and allowed legal equality with whites was so antithetical to the principles on which the slave society rested that it seemed to threaten complete social dissolution and chaos.[18]

Although economic benefits ultimately ceased to be the exclusive or even the primary focus of slavery, the slave's status as property remained a critical feature of the institution inasmuch as slaves were the specific form of property which "carried the badges of honor, prestige and power."[19]

Finley neatly harmonizes the property and authority elements by defining slavery in terms of total lack of authority for which "the idea of property is juristically the key — hence the term 'chattel slave.' "[20] This equation of property and total rightlessness not only subsumes property under authority but also denies the reality of systems in which slaves exercise authority. Yet such systems do exist and the independent variability of the property and authority components indicates that neither criterion can be subsumed under the other.[21] The property criterion can no more be discarded because the economic function of the slave is sometimes superceded by noneconomic considerations than the authority criterion can be because slaves sometimes exercise authority. In short, both must be retained as defining characteristics of slavery while recognizing that the significance of each may vary from one slave system to another.

Perpetuity, the third criterion of slavery, has been less controversial and is, perhaps because of this, the least explicitly acknowledged and emphasized of the institution's defining characteristics. Many definitions do not include perpetuity, unless it is inferred from the property criterion, but it is clearly implied by others and emphasized by some. Smith implies perpetuity in his definition and subsequently refers to "the hereditary nature of the slave status. . . ."[22] Jordan brings perpetuity front and center when he speaks of "the two kinds of perpetuity" — lifetime and hereditary — as "the twin essence of slavery. . . ."[23] Similarly, Degler refers to lifetime servitude and inheritable status as "the two attributes of true slavery. . . ."[24] Palmer and Elkins also stress service for life as the basic feature of slavery.[25]

Manumission, as a possible avenue of escape from perpetual servitude, raises a very significant distinction between the individual status of slave and the institution of slavery. While manumission was a scheduled process in some incidental slave societies, few — if any — slave societies ever institutionalized manumission as a *right* of the occupants of the slave status.[26] Rather, slave societies simply differed in the nature and number of barriers erected to impede manumission and in the prospects for manumission as an indirect outgrowth of the denial or acknowledgment of other rights (e.g., the right of slaves to hire themselves out).[27] Freedom, in short, was a benefit to be bestowed by the master, not a right to be claimed by the slave.

The three defining characteristics constitute an ideal-typical portrait of slavery. In real societies each of the three is a variable and never realized to the full degree implied by the ideal portrait. The authority criterion posits the total subordination of slaves to their masters; slaves are chattel — beings utterly without rights. Nevertheless, they are typically accorded, even invested with, some rights of personhood in all slave societies, including American society. Similarly, the extent to which slaves are defined and treated as property is variable between societies, although recent research indicates that the extent of this variation has been greatly exaggerated at least among new world slave systems. Finally, recent research indicates that slavery was often a transitory, one-generation phenomenon in African slave societies, and even in societies where slavery was the keystone of the institutional structure the ever-present possibility of manumission meant that slavery was not a uniformly perpetual status. Still, the pattern is clear and the variations are generally acknowledged as just that — variations on a common social form reflecting differences in the function of slavery and in the environing institutional structure.

Slavery and Racism.   In the Western world slavery is generally thought to be associated with racism and indeed the two have frequently exhibited a significant functional relationship — namely, the relationship between a social structure and its sustaining ideology. As an ideology, racism does not refer to attitudes of prejudice nor to discriminatory behavior. Rather its referent is a set of values which justifies supersubordination and is rooted in a biogenetic conception of group superiority-inferiority. Ultimately, such an ideology played a crucial role in the integration of American slave society.[28] Goveia stresses the comparable role of racism in the British Leeward Islands, but racism has not played a uniformly important integrative role in all slave societies. Indeed, racism rarely exists in incidental slave societies and is highly variable in genuine slave societies. This suggests that its significance and strength, if not its appearance, is a function of the nature of the slave system and of other elements of the environing sociocultural matrix. Finley states the matter clearly:

> Slavery is not an autonomous system; it is an institution embedded in a social structure. It is no longer the same institution when the structure is significantly altered, *and ideas about slavery have to be examined structurally too.*[29]

Certainly one of the key ideas that has developed with slavery in the genuine slave societies of the new world is that of the biogenetic inferiority of black people — in short, racism. The contextual factors of possible relevance to the development of this definition of blacks are numerous and include such varied factors as: the extent of the colony's freedom from the mother country, the prior recognition of unfree statuses in law and custom, the availability of labor and the ratio of slave and other forms of unfree labor to free labor, the size of the organizational unit of slavery as an economic enterprise, the occupational and social differentiation and distribution of the slave and free population, the ratio of and extent of contact between slaves and nonslaves, and the nature of the dominant religious beliefs and the ratio of clergy to total population. The ongoing debate regarding the relative significance of this myriad of structural variables has largely reduced them to two general types —

the idealist and the materialist.[30] Advocates of the idealist position do not entirely ignore material factors but they stress the critical role of the church, the state, and historic legal codes as key determinants of the recognition or denial of the common humanity of white and black. In contrast the materialists stress the advent of a large scale plantation economy, heavily dependent upon slave labor, and certain demographic variables as the critical factors in the emergent definition of the blacks.

Both of these positions are oversimplifications of a very complex reality. For example, the differences in the legal frameworks of new world slavery have been greatly exaggerated and, in any event, the codes regulating master-slave relations were as often honored in the breach as in the adherence. On the other hand, cultural definitions and values are not an automatic reflection of economic interests.[31] Since the institution of slavery was in actual fact far more similar than different throughout the new world, Davis suggests that the differing attitudes toward race may be primarily a function of "economic and social structures which defined the relations between colored freedmen and the dominant white society."[32] This is consistent with the thesis that the emergence of a flexible, multi-category racial system is primarily a function of a shortage of free whites to occupy essential but poorly rewarded interstitial positions in the economic and social structure.[33] In those societies where a shortage of whites necessitated the emergence of a free colored population to fill these positions, racism was stunted. Certainly it was not absent in such societies[34] but this hypothesis suggests that racism therein was characterized by a slower rate of development, a lesser degree of institutionalization, and a more rapid decline in the post-abolition period.

The aforementioned variations in the environing sociocultural structure were undoubtedly critical to the meaning of race and the justifications of slavery, but "the ideological and material attachment to slavery grew strong even where it was a peripheral institution. . . ."[35] Nevertheless, despite the invariably tenacious attachment to slavery, its abolition generated protracted conflict only where a pervasive class interest was at stake. This was not a narrowly economic class interest but an expression of a total world view with its own appropriate morality.[36] Where this world view emerged, racism became a central facet of the society's value system. The planter elite in such a society — the paternalist slave society — held values antithetical to capitalism because the maintenance of slavery as a way of life had replaced a concern with profit as the central motif, the *raison d'etre* of the society.[37] Thus, as slave society evolved from an exploitative to a paternalist form, racism played an ever more important role in integrating the society.

Theories of the Origin of Slavery

While there have been few efforts to state a systematic theory of the origin of slavery, there are a number of contributions which provide partial theories and a foundation upon which a more comprehensive theory can be constructed. In particular, contributions by Nieboer, Schermerhorn, Antonovsky, and Wagley and Harris are useful. Although not necessarily conceived by their authors as explanations for the origin of slavery, these contributions identify one or more of the necessary and sufficient conditions for the emergence of stable, ethnically stratified societies.

H. J. Nieboer, writing at the turn of the century, viewed slavery as the outcome of two major, interrelated factors: a scarcity of unskilled labor and an abundance of other resources, especially land. This places such a high premium on free labor that slavery emerges because coercion is the only way to secure the necessary or desired labor force.[38] This explanation is appealing in its simplicity and the causal factors identified are highly significant, but it is only a partial explanation inasmuch as it leaves several crucial questions unanswered. First, the theory does not adequately explain why slavery emerges rather than serfdom or some other form of servitude.[39] These alternative institutional arrangements for procuring labor were also dependent on force albeit in a less harsh and restrictive manner. Second, Nieboer acknowledges that his key factors do not in themselves constitute sufficient conditions for the emergence of either slavery or serfdom.[40] Third, his emphasis on the economic aspects of slavery is so marked that he all but disavows any intent to explain noneconomic forms of slavery so common in incidental slave societies.[41] Finally, even given an assumption that slaves must necessarily be outsiders,[42] Nieboer provides few clues to explain which groups will be selected for enslavement.

The fact that the Indians in English America were so easily accessible made them a logical target for enslavement, but why were Africans selected in preference to both Indians and non-English Europeans? One element in the answer to this question is provided by consideration of the power of the enslaving group relative to that of various prospective target groups. The Indians and the European out-groups were for a variety of reasons in a better power position relative to the English colonists than were the Africans. The emergence of any system of ethnic stratification requires that one group have the capacity to impose its will upon the other by fair means or foul, violence or guile. This, of course, is generally accomplished by one group's possession of greater power.

Antonovsky has incorporated differential power into his theory of the origin of discrimination and has simultaneously broadened Nieboer's thesis by stressing competition, which may take noneconomic forms, rather than the availability of labor and other purely economic resources. "Thus scarcity, shared goals, and unequal power are the necessary conditions" for the emergence and persistence of discrimination.[43] Here again the precise structural form which discrimination takes (e.g., debt peonage, segregation, or slavery) is not explained although we might expect the form institutionalized to be more oppressive the more intense the competition and the greater the power differential. Nevertheless, Antonovsky's analysis takes us beyond Nieboer both by generalizing the impelling force for enslavement and by emphasizing an additional variable — unequal power — which significantly influences the choice of a target.

Schermerhorn also stresses the importance of power relations in establishing the social frame within which minority groups are or are not precipitated and discrimination does or does not take place.[44] Since power is rarely equal, he hypothesizes that encounters between distinct groups will lead to dominance by one group and that power will tend to be coercive to the extent that the values of the groups involved are incongruent. In short, he introduces a cultural element as a means of explaining variations in the structural form of ethnic stratification. He emphasizes, however, that "power is the primary concept . . . with the value variable accounting for variations in acculturative forms within the power framework."[45] Subsequently, Schermerhorn has moderated his emphasis on the primacy of power in favor of a more balanced appraisal and he has also elaborated the analysis of value congruence by considering the issues of legitimation and of common or discrepant definitions of the appropriate goals for subordinate ethnic groups to pursue.[46] His introduction of values raises the possibility that cultural elements other than shared goals (e.g., land or labor) may influence the form and span of ethnic stratification.

Wagley and Harris have also pursued this line of thought. They maintain that interaction between dominant and subordinate ethnic groups is invariably competitive and marked by conflict *and* that this enduring structural reality is shaped and sustained by the particular historical and cultural circumstances which provide the setting for group interaction.[47] Institutionalized patterns of conflict and cohesiveness vary between different pairs of groups in any society, but subordinate groups are especially set apart by two features: ethnocentrism and endogamy. Wagley and Harris view these as the key structural components of majority-minority relations but stress that competition is an additional requisite for the emergence of conflict. Given these elements the outcome of the resultant conflict between groups is crucially affected by the total environ-

mental conditions which must be adapted to and by "the degree of culturally induced preparedness of the minority for protecting and advancing
itself against the exploitation and hostility to which it may become
subject."[48]

This formulation is very useful but needlessly constrained by several
weaknesses. First, the authors undercut much of the formulation's potential utility for analyzing the *emergence* of ethnic stratification by assuming super-subordination and proceeding from there. This assumption is
reflected in their statement that the structural components of majority-
minority relations are those aspects "which derive from the nature of
minorities and majorities as distinctive kinds of social groups."[49] Second,
by explicitly considering adaptive capacity only in terms of the minority
and the sociocultural conditions to be adapted to only in terms of the
majority, they distract our attention from the interaction process which
underlies the formation and maintenance of ethnic stratification.[50] This
also obscures the fact that in regards to ethnic stratification adaptive
capacity is primarily *relative* to that of other groups participating in the
same arena. Finally, Wagley and Harris identify ethnocentrism as a structural component when it should be viewed as a cultural component closely
related to structural elements such as endogamy and other forms of
social segregation. While this distinction may be unimportant for some
purposes, the relative causal importance of structural and cultural variables is of great moment — hence, accurate identification is essential —
as regards social theory and its implications for social change.[51]

Despite these shortcomings, the contribution by Wagley and Harris
is of the first order both for its comparative context and detail and for
its identification of significant variables — in particular, ethnocentrism
and adaptive capacity — not stressed by other authors. When these variables are combined with competition and power, the conceptual tools
for constructing an explanation of the origin of slavery are at hand. The
building blocks are supplied by field work and historical research. In
part two we will draw upon this research as a foundation for a theory
of the origin of systems of ethnic stratification in general.

Overview of Parts II and III

Part two includes six articles, each with a critical introductory note to
clarify their present articulation and to promote a clearer grasp of the
contribution of each to a complete understanding of the origin of slavery
by highlighting relevant points, issues, or criticisms. The first two essays, by the Handlins and Elkins, focus on the status of blacks in the
seventeenth-century American colonies. Their common concern is to
delineate the initial status of blacks, to describe the changes in this status

as reflected in practice and in law during the seventeenth century, and to suggest factors which might explain these changes in legal and/or actual status.

The essays by Degler and Jordan share these concerns to a very considerable extent, but they also break new ground at least in terms of emphasis. Degler is critical of a number of points advanced by the Handlins and also introduces a new focus of discussion by emphasizing the causal relation between discrimination, prejudice, and slavery. Jordan retains this dual focus by providing additional evidence regarding the status of blacks in the seventeenth century and by drawing independent conclusions regarding the relation of slavery and prejudice. Because of their dual focus these essays are particularly valuable background for the concluding essay in part three of this reader.

The essays by Boskin and Noel which conclude part two are of a different order. They are not intended as additional, original researches regarding the status of blacks in early America but as critical theoretical assessment and generalization of the historical research already done. Boskin evaluates the explanations provided by the preceding authors and suggests the necessity for certain additional lines of study if we are to understand the process by which slavery emerged and was institutionalized. Noel organizes a set of concepts which describe the necessary and sufficient conditions for the emergence of any system of ethnic stratification. The resulting theory is used as a framework for analyzing and explaining the emergence of slavery in the American colonies.

Finally, two essays on the origin of American racism constitute part three of this volume. In the first, Nash analyzes the sociological basis of divergences in attitudes toward and ideas about Africans and Indians in Colonial America. Noel's concluding essay is a threefold attempt to clarify the long-standing controversy regarding the causal relation between slavery and racism. First, a number of concepts essential to an analysis of the relationship are carefully distinguished. Second, earlier analyses are criticized on the grounds that their failure to distinguish concepts made it logically impossible to view slavery as the cause of racism. Third, the essay suggests a tentative theory of the origin of racism and some historical analyses necessary to an adequate test of this theory.

Notes

1. Although it is undeniably ethnocentric, reference will hereafter be made to American slavery, as opposed to slavery in the Americas, in order to avoid the cumbersome "slavery in the mainland North American colonies which subsequently became the United States of America."

2. Staughton Lynd, *Class Conflict, Slavery, and the United States Constitution* (Indianapolis: Bobbs-Merrill, 1967), esp. ch. 6.

3. Merton Dillon, "The Abolitionists: A Decade of Historiography, 1959–1969," *Journal of Southern History* 35 (1969): 500-522.

4. David B. Davis, *The Problem of Slavery in Western Culture* (New York: Cornell University Press, 1966), p. 31.

5. Jean-Jacques Rousseau, *The Social Contract,* ed. L. G. Crocker (New York: Washington Square Press, 1967), p. 12.

6. Davis, p. 35.

7. Moses I. Finley, "Slavery," *International Encyclopedia of the Social Sciences* 14 (1968): 307-13 and "Between Slavery and Freedom," *Comparative Studies in Society and History* 6 (1964): 233-49. Finley states (p. 243) that "a significant proportion of the industrial and business activity in Rome and other cities was carried on by slaves acting independently, controlling and managing property known as a *peculium.*"

8. Davis, p. 34. He immediately adds that "by custom and economic circumstance the serf was in fact bound to the soil. There was no market for a mobile labor force. . . ."

9. See M. G. Smith, *The Plural Society in the British West Indies* (Berkeley: University of California Press, 1965), esp. ch. 6 and Magnus Mörner, "The History of Race Relations in Latin America: Some Comments on the State of Research," *Latin American Research Review* 1 (1966): 17-44 (esp. p. 30). Also see Mörner's *Race Mixture in the History of Latin America* (Boston: Little, Brown and Co., 1967), ch. 8.

10. Finley, "Slavery," esp. p. 308. See also the excellent review article by Arnold A. Sio, "Society, Slavery and the Slave," *Social and Economic Studies* 16 (1967): 330-44 (esp. p. 337). While Finley's distinction between slaveowning and genuine slave societies is apt, in this essay we will distinguish genuine and incidental slave societies to avoid confusion attendant upon the fact that all slave societies are, in fact, slaveowning.

11. The extent to which slavery affected all segments of the genuine slave society is nowhere better expressed than in the classic by Frank Tannenbaum, *Slave and Citizen: The Negro in the Americas,* Vintage Book (New York: Random House, 1963), esp. pp. 116-17.

12. Arthur Tuden and Leonard Plotnicov, eds., *Social Stratification in Africa,* (New York: Macmillan Co., 1970), p. 13. They acknowledge, however, that "some slaves were regarded as only and purely economic commodities. . . . They were totally de-humanized and were no more a part of any social system than any item of trade or wealth."

13. *Ibid.,* pp. 9, 13-15, and 47-58. Also see Ronald Cohen, "Introduction to Slavery in Africa," *Transaction,* January-February, 1967, pp. 44-46; Eugene D. Genovese, *The Political Economy of Slavery* (New York: Random House, 1965), ch. 3; A. Norman Klein, "West African Unfree Labor Before and After the Rise of the Atlantic Slave Trade," pp. 87-95 in Laura Foner and Eugene D. Genovese, eds., *Slavery in the New World* (Englewood Cliffs, N.J.: Prentice-Hall, 1969); and Smith, p. 121.

14. See Genovese, p. 77 and Smith, p. 128.

15. *Ibid.,* p. 120.

16. *Ibid.,* p. 121 and Arnold A. Sio, "Interpretations of Slavery: The Slave Status in the Americas," *Comparative Studies in Society and History* 7 (1965): 289-308.

17. "The slaveholders simply could not accept the idea that the cash nexus offered a permissible basis for human relations." Genovese, esp. pp. 28-31 (quotation at p. 30). Also see Smith, pp. 122 and 140-48 and Stanley M. Elkins, *Slavery: A Problem in American Institutional and Intellectual Life* (Chicago: University of Chicago Press, 1968), pp. 249-50.

18. Elsa V. Goveia, *Slave Society in the British Leeward Islands at the End of the Eighteenth Century* (New Haven: Yale University Press, 1965), p. 329. This process bears a definite relation to the development of racism which will be examined shortly.

19. Genovese, p. 28.

20. Finley, "Slavery," p. 307. Tuden and Plotnicov (pp. 11-12) accord the two criteria equal significance by defining slavery as "the legal institutionalization of persons as property."

21. *Ibid.*, pp. 9 and 14 and Davis, p. 50 (esp. n. 40). Sio's "Interpretations . . ." demonstrates the independent variability of the property and authority criteria in that the racial component of American slavery greatly affected the legal rights of slaves, by comparison with their Roman counterparts, while scarcely affecting their status as property.

22. Smith, pp. 120 and 123.

23. Winthrop Jordan, *White Over Black* (Chapel Hill: University of North Carolina Press, 1968), p. 73.

24. Carl N. Degler, "Slavery and the Genesis of American Race Prejudice," *Comparative Studies in Society and History* 2 (1959): 49-66 (quotation at p. 53).

25. Paul C. Palmer, "Servant Into Slave: The Evolution of the Legal Status of the Negro Laborer in Colonial Virginia," *South Atlantic Quarterly* 65 (1966): 355-70 (esp. p. 359) and Elkins, pp. 38 and 40.

26. Finley implies in "Slavery" (p. 307) that a "claim to eventual manumission" may have existed in some slave societies, but Davis (pp. 56-57) suggests that manumitting was always "on the terms of the master class." Later Davis notes that some Spanish slaves could force their masters "to accept payment for freedom" (p. 267n). Also see Mörner, *Race Mixture . . .*, p. 42.

27. See Tannenbaum, esp. pp. 53-61 and 65-71; Davis, esp. pp. 262-73; and Carl N. Degler, "Slavery in Brazil and the United States: An Essay in Comparative History," *American Historical Review* 75 (1970): 1004-28.

28. Sio, "Society, . . .," pp. 338-39.

29. M. I. Finley, "The Idea of Slavery" (Review of D. B. Davis, *The Problem of Slavery in Western Culture),* in Foner and Genovese, pp. 256-61 (quotation at p. 260; emphasis added).

30. This debate is the focus of Foner and Genovese's excellent reader cited in footnote 13.

31. This is well illustrated by the quotation from Goveia on p. 7 but see also the essay by Eugene D. Genovese, "Materialism and Idealism in the History of Negro Slavery in the Americas" in Foner and Genovese, pp. 238-55; Smith, esp. pp. 140-56; and Davis, esp. ch. 8 and pp. 150-59.

32. *Ibid.*, p. 262. Also see H. Hoetink, *The Two Variants in Caribbean Race Relations* (New York: Oxford University Press, 1967), esp. pp. 31 and 34 and Mörner, "The History of Race. . .," p. 34.

33. Marvin Harris, *Patterns of Race in the Americas* (New York: Walker and Company, 1964), ch. 7. This interpretation is challenged by Peter Dodge, "Com-

parative Racial Systems in the Greater Caribbean," *Social and Economic Studies* 16 (1967): 249-61.

34.   Relevant here is Boxer's widely quoted comment that "one race cannot systematically enslave members of another on a large scale for over three centuries without acquiring a conscious or unconscious feeling of racial superiority." C. R. Boxer, *Race Relations in the Portuguese Colonial Empire, 1415–1825* (New York: Oxford University Press, 1963), p. 56.

35.   Eugene D. Genovese, *The World the Slaveholders Made* (New York: Random House, 1969), p. 65.

36.   Neither a mechanical economic interpretation of slavery nor a cultural determinist interpretation is adequate. Each must be supplemented via recognition of the complex interplay of economic and cultural forces. See esp. *ibid.,* p. 65 and Genovese, "Materialism and Idealism. . .," pp. 244 and 248-49.

37.   See Sio, "Society. . .," esp. p. 339.

38.   H. J. Nieboer, *Slavery as an Industrial System* (Martinus Nijhoff, 1900), esp. pp. 169-73, 254-60, 387-90, and 419-26.

39.   Indeed, Nieboer partially tests his theory by the analysis of medieval villeinage and directly acknowledges that abundant resources are vital to the explanation of serfdom as well as slavery. *Ibid.,* pp. 348-87 and esp. pp. 350-51, 389 (incl. n. 1) and 423. The emergent form of servitude may be partly a function of the degree of abundance of resources — that is, the more abundant, the more severe and coercive the institutionalized labor arrangement must be in order to secure sufficient laborers.

40.   *Ibid.,* pp. 257 and 389n. He does give considerable attention to a series of relatively specific secondary causes. See pp. 258-59 and 390-417.

41.   Nieboer mentions noneconomic forms of slavery but in a context which implies that such forms are generally to be explained by secondary causes of which militarism seems to be the most important. *Ibid.,* pp. 259, 419, and 427-28.

42.   Nieboer does not make this assumption (e.g., see p. 420), but Finley asserts that "the slave is an outsider: that alone permits not only his uprooting but also his reduction from a person to a thing which can be owned. Insiders en masse cannot be so totally transformed; no community could survive that." See "Slavery," p. 308. Klein (p. 91) shows, however, that in at least one African society the most oppressed slave status was occupied exclusively by "insiders." Finley's point is perhaps valid for genuine slave societies — indeed, he qualifies his observation by reference to insiders "en masse" — but even here it depends on the meaning of outsider for internal minorities may clearly be a target for enslavement. See Finley, "Between Slavery and Freedom," p. 239 and Hubert M. Blalock, Jr., *Toward A Theory of Minority-Group Relations* (New York: John Wiley, 1967), pp. 47-48.

43.   Aaron Antonovsky, "The Social Meaning of Discrimination," *Phylon* 21 (1960): 81-95 (quotation at p. 82). Antonovsky does not explicitly use the concept competition, but it is generally defined as interaction between two or more social units seeking *shared, scarce goals.*

44.   R. A. Schermerhorn, "Power as a Primary Concept in the Study of Minorities," *Social Forces* 35 (1956): 53-56.

45.   *Ibid.,* esp. pp. 55 and 56.

46.   R. A. Schermerhorn, *Comparative Ethnic Relations* (New York: Random House, 1970), esp. chs. 1 and 2. E. K. Francis also stresses the importance of values and other sociocultural similarities and differences in "Variables in the

Formation of So-Called 'Minority Groups,'" *American Journal of Sociology* 60 (1954): 6-14.

47.   Charles Wagley and Marvin Harris, *Minorities in the New World* (New York: Columbia University Press, 1958), esp. pp. 253-56.

48.   *Ibid.,* p. 256. The present writer would prefer to say *each group's* "degree of culturally induced preparedness . . . for protecting and advancing itself" but Wagley and Harris assume prior establishment of dominance. They use minority and majority with the traditional social science meaning of subordinate and dominant groups.

49.   *Ibid.,* p. 256; see footnote 48 (above). Their analysis of the formation of minority groups (i.e., the emergence of ethnic stratification) is confined to a discussion of migration and the development and expansion of the state (see esp. pp. 240-53). As regards the interaction process in which dominant and subordinate groups are generated, see Tamotsu Shibutani and Kian M. Kwan, *Ethnic Stratification* (New York: Macmillan Co., 1965), esp. chs. 6 and 8.

50.   Wagley and Harris, pp. 256 and 264. Adaptive capacity is their label for the (minority) group's culturally induced ability, or inability, to take care of itself within the arena of competition. The latter is their label for the dominant group imposed sociocultural conditions to which the minority must adapt. They acknowledge (p. 264) that "the separation of these two aspects of the historical-cultural relations between minority and majority is somewhat artificial." More than that, it is misleading and wholly unnecessary.

51.   The conclusion that slavery — or its descendant, segregation — generated and maintained the ideology of racism requires a very different program of action to secure equality than would be the case if the reverse conclusion were reached. The complicating fact of reciprocal causation requires that we determine the primary direction of causality and the degree of one-sidedness in the relationship, whether between slavery and racism or ethnocentrism and endogamy, and gear our action program accordingly.

PART II

The Origin of American Slavery

THE ORIGINS OF NEGRO SLAVERY

Oscar and Mary F. Handlin

The article by Oscar and Mary Handlin initiated the modern effort to clarify seventeenth-century white-black stratification. The Handlins review the traditional English forms of servitude and argue that blacks in the mainland British colonies were initially defined and treated as indentured servants. It does not necessarily follow, of course, that their treatment was identical to that accorded white servants, but the Handlins' thesis is that slavery emerged from the interaction between American conditions and old world institutions of servitude.[1] The initial indentured status was continually modified by new world conditions until it culminated in the equation of black with chattel slave. The strength of their supporting analysis consists of their identification of the major socio-cultural conditions which account for the blacks' descent to slavery. These conditions are: a marked scarcity of cheap labor, the rejection of blacks as a culturally *and* racially alien group, and the weak power position of blacks attendant upon their involuntary "migration" to the new world. A theory of the origin of slavery and of systems of ethnic stratification in general is implicit in this case analysis.

Subsequent research has confirmed the Handlins' analysis in some particulars and corrected it in others. For example, Towner presents data which indicate that the power position of the group to which the individual servant belonged was intimately related to the path pursued in seeking redress for grievances.[2] Conversely, the Handlins' denial that the emergence of American slavery was influenced by that already existent in the West Indies has been convincingly challenged.[3] However, the main thrust of the Handlins' essay remains solidly grounded. Regardless of available models (e.g., nearby Barbados) it would not have been profitable or feasible for slavery to supplant the traditional English system of servitude in the absence of the conditions described

21

by the Handlins. Sociologically, their essay is a classic. Their identification of the sociocultural conditions essential to the emergence of ethnic stratification is unsurpassed by later work.

Notes

1. Evidence that the British heritage "was spent in different ways by the colonial heirs, depending on varying conditions encountered in the New World" is provided by Winthrop D. Jordan, "American Chiaroscuro: The Status and Definition of Mulattos in the British Colonies," *William and Mary Quarterly* 19 (1962): 183-200.

2. Lawrence W. Towner, " 'A Fondness For Freedom': Servant Protest in the Puritan Society," *William and Mary Quarterly* 19 (1962): 201-19 (esp. p. 213).

3. See especially Sidney M. Greenfield, "Slavery and the Plantation in the New World: The Development and Diffusion of a Social Form," *Journal of Inter-American Studies* 11 (1969): 44-57; Winthrop D. Jordan, "The Influence of the West Indies on the Origins of New England Slavery," *William and Mary Quarterly* 18 (1961): 243-50; and M. Eugene Sirmans, "The Legal Status of the Slave in South Carolina, 1670–1740," *Journal of Southern History* 28 (1962): 462-73.

In the bitter years before the Civil War, and after, men often turned to history for an explanation of the disastrous difference that divided the nation against itself. It seemed as if some fundamental fault must account for the tragedy that was impending or that had been realized; and it was tempting then to ascribe the troubles of the times to an original separateness between the sections that fought each other in 1861.

The last quarter century has banished from serious historical thinking the ancestral cavaliers and roundheads with whom the rebels and Yankees had peopled their past. But there is still an inclination to accept as present from the start a marked divergence in the character of the labor force, free whites in the North, Negro slaves in the South. Most commonly, the sources of that divergence are discovered in geography. In the temperate North, it is held, English ways were transposed intact. But the soil and climate of the South favored the production of staples, most efficiently raised under a regime of plantation slavery.

Reprinted from *Race and Nationality in American Life* by Oscar Handlin, by permission of Atlantic-Little, Brown and Co. (Complete with footnotes as in original publication in *William and Mary Quarterly* 7 [1950]: 199-222.) Copyright © by Oscar Handlin.

In this case, however, it is hardly proper to load nature with responsibility for human institutions. Tropical crops and climate persisted in the South after 1865 when its labor system changed, and they were there before it appeared.[1] Negro slavery was not spontaneously produced by heat, humidity, and tobacco. An examination of the condition and status of seventeenth-century labor will show that slavery was not there from the start, that it was not simply imitated from elsewhere, and that it was not a response to any unique qualities in the Negro himself. It emerged rather from the adjustment to American conditions of traditional European institutions.

By the latter half of the eighteenth century, slavery was a clearly defined status. It was

> that condition of a natural person, in which, by the operation of law, the application of his physical and mental powers depends . . . upon the will of another . . . and in which he is incapable . . . of . . . holding property [or any other rights] . . . except as the agent or instrument of another. In slavery, . . . the state, in ignoring the personality of the slave, . . . commits the control of his conduct . . . to the master, together with the power of transferring his authority to another.[2]

Thinking of slavery in that sense, the Englishmen of 1772 could boast with Lord Mansfield that their country had never tolerated the institution; simply to touch the soil of England made men free.[3] But the distinction between slave and free that had become important by the eighteenth century was not a significant distinction at the opening of the seventeenth century. In the earlier period, the antithesis of "free" was not "slave" but unfree; and, within the condition of unfreedom, law and practice recognized several gradations.

The status that involved the most complete lack of freedom was villeinage, a servile condition transmitted from father to son. The villein was limited in the right to hold property or make contracts; he could be bought and sold with the land he worked or without, and had "to do all that that the Lord will him command"; while the lord could "rob, beat, and chastise his Villain at his will."[4] It was true that the condition had almost ceased to exist in England itself. But it persisted in Scotland well into the eighteenth century. In law the conception remained important enough to induce Coke in 1658/9 to give it a lengthy section; and the analogy with villeinage served frequently to define the terms of other forms of servitude.[5]

For law and practice in the seventeenth century comprehended other forms of involuntary bondage. The essential attributes of villeinage were fastened on many men not through heredity and ancient custom, as in the case of the villein, but through poverty, crime, or mischance. A debtor, in cases "where there is not sufficient distresse of goods" could be "sold at an outcry." Conviction for vagrancy and vagabondage, even the mere absence of a fixed occupation, exposed the free-born Englishman, at home or in the colonies, to the danger that he might be bound over to the highest bidder, his labor sold for a term. Miscreants who could not pay their fines for a wide range of offenses were punished by servitude on "publick works" or on the estates of individuals under conditions not far different from those of villeinage. Such sentences, in the case of the graver felonies, sometimes were for life.[6]

The sale by the head of a household of members of his family entailed a similar kind of involuntary servitude. A husband could thus dispose of his wife, and a father of his children. Indeed, reluctance to part with idle youngsters could bring on the intercession of the public authorities. So, in 1646, Virginia county commissioners were authorized to send to work in the public flaxhouse two youngsters from each county, kept at home by the "fond indulgence or perverse obstinacy" of their parents. Orphans, bastards, and the offspring of servants were similarly subject to disposal at the will of officials.[7]

Moreover servitude as an estate was not confined to those who fell into it against their wills. It also held many men who entered it by agreement or formal indenture, most commonly for a fixed span of years under conditions contracted for in advance, but occasionally for life, and frequently without definite statement of terms under the assumption that the custom of the country was definite enough.[8]

Early modification in the laws regulating servitude did not, in England or the colonies, alter essentially the nature of the condition.[9] Whether voluntary or involuntary, the status did not involve substantially more freedom in law than villeinage. It was not heritable; but servants could be bartered for a profit, sold to the highest bidder for the unpaid debts of their masters, and otherwise transferred like movable goods or chattels. Their capacity to hold property was narrowly limited as was their right to make contracts.[10] Furthermore, the master had extensive powers of discipline, enforced by physical chastisement or by extension of the term of service. Offenses against the state also brought on punishments different from those meted out to free men; with no property to be fined, the servants were whipped.[11] In every civic, social, and legal attribute, these victims of the turbulent displacements of the sixteenth and seventeenth centuries were set apart. Despised by every other order, without apparent means of rising to a more favored place, these men, and their children, and their children's children seemed mired in a hard, degraded life.[12] That they formed a numerous element in society was nothing to lighten their lot.

The condition of the first Negroes in the continental English colonies must be viewed within the perspective of these conceptions and realities of servitude. As Europeans penetrated the dark continent in search of gold and ivory, they developed incidentally the international trade in Blacks. The Dutch in particular found this an attractive means of breaking into the business of the Spanish colonies, estopped by the policy of their own government from adding freely to their supply of African labor. In the course of this exchange through the West Indies, especially through Curacao, occasional small lots were left along the coast between Virginia and Massachusetts.[13]

Through the first three-quarters of the seventeenth century, the Negroes, even in the South, were not numerous; nor were they particularly concentrated in any district.[14] They came into a society in which a large part of the population was to some degree unfree; indeed in Virginia under the Company almost everyone, even tenants and laborers, bore some sort of servile obligation.[15] The Negroes' lack of freedom was not unusual. These newcomers, like so many others, were accepted, bought and held, as kinds of servants.[16] They were certainly not well off. But their ill-fortune was of a sort they shared with men from England, Scotland, and Ireland, and with the unlucky aborigines held in captivity. Like the others, some Negroes became free, that is, terminated their period of service. Some became artisans; a few became landowners and the masters of other men.[17] The status of Negroes was that of servants; and so they were identified and treated down to the 1660's.[18]

The word, "slave" was, of course, used occasionally. It had no meaning in English law, but there was a significant colloquial usage. This was a general term of derogation. It served to express contempt; "O what a rogue and peasant slave am I," says Hamlet (Act II, Scene 2). It also described the low-born as contrasted with the gentry; of two hundred warriors, a sixteenth-century report said, eight were gentlemen, the rest slaves.[19] The implication of degradation was also transferred to the low kinds of labor; "In this hal," wrote More (1551), "all vyle seruice, all slauerie . . . is done by bondemen."[20]

It was in this sense that Negro servants were sometimes called slaves.[21] But the same appelation was, in England, given to other non-English servants — to a Russian, for instance.[22] In Europe and in the American colonies, the term was, at various times and places, applied indiscriminately to Indians, mulattoes, and mestizos, as well as to Negroes.²³ For that matter, it applied also to white Englishmen. It thus commonly described the servitude of children; so, the poor planters complained, "Our children, the parents dieinge" are held as "slaues or drudges" for the discharge of their parents' debts.²⁴ Penal servitude too was often referred to as slavery; and the phrase, "slavish servant" turns up from time to time. Slavery had no meaning in law; at most it was a popular description of a low form of service.²⁵

Yet in not much more than a half century after 1660 this term of derogation was transformed into a fixed legal position. In a society characterized by many degrees of unfreedom, the Negro fell into a status novel to English law, into an unknown condition toward which the colonists unsteadily moved, slavery in its eighteenth- and nineteenth-century form. The available accounts do not explain this development because they assume that this form of slavery was known from the start.

Can it be said, for instance, that the seventeenth-century Englishman might have discovered elsewhere an established institution, the archetype of slavery as it was ultimately defined, which seemed more advantageous than the defined English customs for use in the New World? The internationally recognized "slave trade" has been cited as such an institution.²⁶ But when one notes that the Company of Royal Adventurers referred to their cargo as "Negers," "Negro-Servants," "Servants . . . from Africa," or "Negro Person," but rarely as slaves, it is not so clear that it had in view some unique or different status.²⁷ And when one remembers that the transportation of Irish servants was also known as the "slave-trade," then it is clear that those who sold and those who bought the Negro, if they troubled to consider legal status at all, still thought of him simply as a low servant.²⁸

Again, it has been assumed that Biblical and Roman law offered adequate precedent. But it did not seem so in the perspective of the contemporaries of the first planters who saw in both the Biblical and Roman institutions simply the equivalents of their own familiar forms of servitude. King James's translators rendered the word, "bond-servant"; "slave" does not appear in their version.²⁹ And to Coke the Roman *servus* was no more than the villein ("and this is hee which the civilians call servus").³⁰

Nor did the practice of contemporary Europeans fall outside the English conceptions of servitude. Since early in the fifteenth century, the Portuguese had held Moors, white and black, in "slavery," at home, on the Atlantic islands, and in Brazil. Such servitude also existed in Spain and in Spanish America where Negroes were eagerly imported to supply the perennial shortage of labor in the Caribbean sugar islands and the Peruvian mines. But what was the status of such slaves? They had certain property rights, were capable of contracting marriages, and were assured of the integrity of their families. Once baptised it was almost a matter of course that they would become free; the right to manumission was practically a "contractual arrangement." And once free, they readily inter-married with their former masters. These were no chattels, devoid of personality. These were human beings whom chance had rendered unfree, a situation completely comprehensible within the degrees of unfreedom familiar to the English colonist. Indeed when Bodin wishes to illustrate the condition of such "slaves," he refers to servants and apprentices in England and Scotland.[31]

Finally, there is no basis for the assertion that such a colony as South Carolina simply adopted slavery from the French or British West Indies.[32] To begin with, the labor system of those places was not yet fully evolved.[33] Travelers from the mainland may have noted the advantages of Negro labor there; but they hardly thought of chattel slavery.[34] The Barbadian gentlemen who proposed to come to South Carolina in 1663 thought of bringing "Negroes and other servants." They spoke of "slaves" as did other Englishmen, as a low form of servant; the "weaker" servants to whom the Concessions referred included "woemen children slaves."[35] Clearly American slavery was no direct imitation from Biblical or Roman or Spanish or Portuguese or West Indian models. Whatever connections existed were established in the eighteenth and nineteenth centuries when those who justified the emerging institution cast about for possible precedents wherever they might be found.

If chattel slavery was not present from the start, nor adopted from elsewhere, it was also not a response to any inherent qualities that fitted the Negro for plantation labor. There has been a good deal of speculation as to the relative efficiency of free and slave, of Negro, white, and Indian, labor. Of necessity, estimates of which costs were higher, which risks — through mortality, escape, and rebellion — greater, are inconclusive.[36] What is conclusive is the fact that Virginia and Maryland planters did not think Negro labor more desirable. A preference for white servants persisted even on the islands.[37] But when the Barbadians could not get those, repeated representations in London made known their desire for Negroes.[38] No such demands came from the continental colonies.[39] On the contrary the calls are for skilled white labor with the preference for those most like the first settlers and ranging down from Scots and Welsh to Irish, French, and Italians.[40] Least desired were the unskilled, utterly strange Negroes.[41]

It is quite clear in fact that as late as 1669 those who thought of large-scale agriculture assumed it would be manned not by Negroes but by white peasants under a condition of villeinage. John Locke's constitutions for South Carolina envisaged an hereditary group of servile "leetmen"; and Lord Shaftsbury's signory on Locke Island in 1674 actually attempted to put that scheme into practice.[42] If the holders of large estates in the Chesapeake colonies expressed no wish for a Negro labor supply, they could hardly have planned to use black hands as a means of displacing white, whether as a concerted plot by restoration courtiers to set up a new social order in America,[43] or as a program for lowering costs.[44]

Yet the Negroes did cease to be servants and became slaves, ceased to be men in whom masters held a proprietary interest and became chattels, objects that were the property of their owners. In that transformation originated the southern labor system.

Although the colonists assumed at the start that all servants would "fare alike in the colony," the social realities of their situation early gave rise to differences of treatment.[45] It is not necessary to resort to racist assumptions to account for such measures; these were simply the reactions of immigrants lost to the stability and security of home and isolated in an immense wilderness in which threats from the unknown were all about them. Like the millions who would follow, these immigrants longed in the strangeness for the company of familiar men and singled out to be welcomed those who were most like themselves. So the measures regulating settlement spoke specifically in this period of differential treatment for various groups. From time to time, regulations applied only to "those of our own nation," or to the French, the Dutch, the Italians, the Swiss, the Palatines, the Welsh, the Irish, or to combinations of the diverse nationalities drawn to these shores.[46]

In the same way the colonists became aware of the differences between themselves and the African immigrants. The rudeness of the Negroes' manners, the strangeness of their languages, the difficulty of communicating to them English notions of morality and proper behavior occasioned sporadic laws to regulate their conduct.[47] So Bermuda's law to restrain the insolencies of Negroes "who are servents" (that is, their inclination to run off with the pigs of others) was the same in kind as the legislation that the Irish should "straggle not night or dai, as is too common with them."[48] Until the 1660's the statutes on the Negroes were not at all unique. Nor did they add up to a decided trend.[49]

But in the decade after 1660 far more significant differentiations with regard to term of service, relationship to Christianity, and disposal of children, cut the Negro apart from all other servants and gave a new depth to his bondage.

In the early part of the century duration of service was of only slight importance. Certainly in England where labor was more plentiful than the demand, expiration of a term had little meaning; the servant was free only to enter upon another term, while the master had always the choice of taking on the old or a new servitor. That situation obtained even in America as long as starvation was a real possibility. In 1621, it was noted, "vittles being scarce in the country noe man will tacke servants."[50] As late as 1643 Lord Baltimore thought it better if possible to hire labor than to risk the burden of supporting servants through a long period.[51] Under such conditions the number of years specified in the indenture was not important, and if a servant had no indenture the question was certainly not likely to rise.[52]

That accounts for the early references to unlimited service. Thus Sandys's plan for Virginia in 1618 spoke of tenants-at-half assigned to the treasurer's office, to "belong to said office for ever." Again, those at Berkeley's Hundred were perpetual "after the manner of estates in England."[53] Since perpetual in seventeenth-century law meant that which had "not any set time expressly allotted for [its] . . . continuance," such provisions were not surprising.[54] Nor was it surprising to find instances in the court records of Negroes who seemed to serve forever.[55] These were quite compatible with the possibility of ultimate freedom. Thus a colored man bought in 1644 "as a Slave for Ever," nevertheless was held "to serve as other Christians servants do" and freed after a term.[56]

The question of length of service became critical when the mounting value of labor eased the fear that servants would be a drain on "vittles" and raised the expectation of profit from their toil. Those eager to multiply the number of available hands by stimulating immigration had not only to overcome the reluctance of a prospective newcomer faced with the trials of a sea journey; they had also to counteract the widespread reports in England and Scotland that servants were harshly treated and bound in perpetual slavery.[57]

To encourage immigration therefore, the colonies embarked upon a line of legislation designed to improve servants' conditions and to enlarge the prospect of a meaningful release, a release that was not the start of a new period of servitude, but of life as a freeman and landowner.[58] Thus Virginia, in 1642, discharged "publick tenants from their servitudes, who, like one sort of villians anciently in England" were attached to the lands of the governor; and later laws provided that no person was to "be adjudged to serve the collonie hereafter."[59] Most significant were the statutes which reassured prospective newcomers by setting limits to the terms of servants without indentures, in 1638/9 in England, in 1642/3 in Virginia.[60] These acts seem to have applied only to voluntary immigrants "of our own nation."[61] The Irish and other aliens, less desirable, at first received longer terms.[62] But the realization that such discrimination retarded "the peopling of the country" led to an extension of the identical privilege to all Christians.[63]

But the Negro never profited from these enactments. Farthest removed from the English, least desired, he communicated with no friends who might be deterred from following. Since his coming was involuntary, nothing that happened to him would increase or decrease his numbers. To raise the status of Europeans by shortening their terms would ultimately increase the available hands by inducing their compatriots to emigrate; to reduce the Negro's term would produce an immediate loss and no ultimate gain. By midcentury the servitude of Negroes seems generally lengthier than that of whites; and thereafter the consciousness dawns that the Blacks will toil for the whole of their lives, not through any particular concern with their status but simply by contrast with those whose years of labor are limited by statute. The legal position of the Negro is, however, still uncertain; it takes legislative action to settle that.[64]

The Maryland House, complaining of that ambiguity, provoked the decisive measure; "All Negroes and other slaves," it was enacted, "shall serve Durante Vita."[65] Virginia reached the same end more tortuously. An act of 1661 had assumed, in imposing penalities on runaways, that *some* Negroes served for life.[66] The law of 1670 went further; "all servants not being christians" brought in by sea were declared slaves for life.[67]

But slavery for life was still tenuous as long as the slave could extricate himself by baptism. The fact that Negroes were heathens had formerly justified their bondage, since infidels were "perpetual" enemies of Christians.[68] It had followed that conversion was a way to freedom. Governor Archdale thus released the Spanish Indians captured to be sold as slaves to Jamaica when he learned they were Christians.[69] As labor rose in value this presumption dissipated the zeal of masters for proselytizing. So that they be "freed from this doubt" a series of laws between 1667 and 1671 laid down the rule that conversion alone did not lead to a release from servitude.[70] Thereafter manumission, which other servants could demand by right at the end of their terms, in the case of Negroes lay entirely within the discretion of the master.[71]

A difference in the status of the offspring of Negro and white servants followed inevitably from the differentiation in the length of their terms. The problem of disposing of the issue of servants was at first general.

Bastardy, prevalent to begin with and more frequent as the century advanced, deprived the master of his women's work and subjected him to the risk of their death. Furthermore the parish was burdened with the support of the child. The usual procedure was to punish the offenders with fines or whippings and to compel the servant to serve beyond his time for the benefit of the parish and to recompense the injured master.[72]

The general rule ceased to apply once the Negro was bound for life, for there was no means of extending his servitude. The most the outraged master could get was the child, a minimal measure of justice, somewhat tempered by the trouble of rearing the infant to an age of usefulness.[73] The truly vexing problem was to decide on the proper course when one parent was free, for it was not certain whether the English law that the issue followed the state of the father would apply. Maryland, which adopted that rule in 1664, found that unscrupulous masters instigated intercourse between their Negro males and white females which not only gave them the offspring, but, to boot, the service of the woman for the life of her husband. The solution in Virginia which followed the precedent of the bastardy laws and had the issue follow the mother seemed preferable and ultimately was adopted in Maryland and elsewhere.[74]

By the last quarter of the seventeenth century, one could distinguish clearly between the Negro slave who served for life and the servant for a period. But there was not yet a demarcation in personal terms: the servant was not yet a free man, nor the slave a chattel. As late as 1686, the words slave and servant could still be conflated to an extent that indicated men conceived of them as extensions of the same condition. A Frenchman in Virginia in that year noted, "There are degrees among the slaves brought here, for a Christian over 21 years of age cannot be held a slave more than five years, but the negroes and other infidels remain slaves all their lives."[75]

It was the persistence of such conceptions that raised the fear that "noe free borne Christians will ever be induced to come over servants" without overwhelming assurance that there would be nothing slavish in their lot. After all Pennsylvania and New York now gave the European newcomer a choice of destination.[76] In Virginia and Maryland there was a persistent effort to make immigration more attractive by further ameliorating the lot of European servants. The custom of the country undoubtedly moved more rapidly than the letter of the law. "Weake and Ignorant" juries on which former servants sat often decided cases against masters.[77] But even the letter of the law showed a noticeable decline in the use of the death penalty and in the power of masters over men. By 1705 in some colonies, white servants were no longer transferable; they could not be whipped without a court order; and they were protected against the avaricious unreasonable masters who attempted to force them into new contracts "some small tyme before the expiration of their tyme of service."[78]

Meanwhile the condition of the Negro deteriorated. In these very years, a startling growth in numbers complicated the problem. The Royal African Company was, to some extent, responsible, though its operations in the mainland colonies formed only a very minor part of its business. But the opening of Africa to free trade in 1698 inundated Virginia, Maryland, and South Carolina with new slaves.[79] Under the pressure of policing these newcomers the regulation of Negroes actually grew harsher.

The early laws against runaways, against drunkenness, against carrying arms or trading without permission had applied penalties as heavy as death to all servants, Negroes and whites.[80] But these regulations grew steadily less stringent in the case of white servants. On the other hand fear of the growing number of slaves, uneasy suspicion of plots and conspiracies, led to more stringent control of Negroes and a broad view of the master's power of discipline. Furthermore the emerging difference in treatment was calculated to create a real division of interest between Negroes on the one hand and whites on the other. Servants who ran away in the company of slaves, for instance, were doubly punished, for the loss of their own time and for the time of the slaves, a provision that discouraged such joint ventures. Similarly Negroes, even when freed, retained some disciplinary links with their less fortunate fellows. The wardens continued to supervise their children, they were not capable of holding white servants, and serious restrictions limited the number of manumissions.[81]

The growth of the Negro population also heightened the old concern over sexual immorality and the conditions of marriage. The law had always recognized the interest of the lord in the marriage of his villein or neife and had frowned on the mixed marriage of free and unfree. Similarly it was inclined to hold that the marriage of any servant was a loss to the master, an "Enormious offense" productive of much detriment "against the law of God," and therefore dependent on the consent of the master.[82] Mixed marriages of free men and servants were particularly frowned upon as complicating status and therefore limited by law.[83]

There was no departure from these principles in the early cases of Negro-white relationships.[84] Even the complicated laws of Maryland in 1664 and the manner of their enactment revealed no change in attitude. The marriage of Blacks and whites was possible; what was important was the status of the partners and of their issue.[85] It was to guard against the complications of status that the laws after 1691 forbade "spurious" or illegitimate mixed marriages of the slave and the free and punished violations with heavy penalties.[86] Yet it was also significant that by then the prohibition was couched in terms, not simply of slave and free man, but of Negro and white. Here was evidence as in the policing regulations of an emerging demarkation.

The first settlers in Virginia had been concerned with the difficulty of preserving the solidarity of the group under the disruptive effects of migration. They had been enjoined to "keepe to themselves" not to "marry nor give in marriage to the heathen, that are uncircumcised."[87] But such resolutions were difficult to maintain and had gradually relaxed until the colonists included among "themselves" such groups as the Irish, once the objects of very general contempt. A common lot drew them together; and it was the absence of a common lot that drew these apart from the Negro. At the opening of the eighteenth century, the Black was not only set off by economic and legal status; he was "abominable," another order of man.

Yet the ban on intermarriage did not rest on any principle of white racial purity, for many men contemplated with equanimity the prospect of amalgamation with the Indians.[88] That did not happen, for the mass of Redmen were free to recede into the interior while those who remained sank into slavery as abject as that of the Blacks and intermarried with those whose fate they shared.[89]

Color then emerged as the token of the slave status; the trace of color became the trace of slavery. It had not always been so; as late as the 1660's the law had not even a word to describe the children of mixed marriages. But two decades later, the term mulatto is used, and it serves, not as in Brazil, to whiten the Black, but to affiliate through the color tie the offspring of a spurious union with his inherited slavery.[90] (The compiler of the Virginia laws then takes the liberty of altering the texts to bring earlier legislation into line with his own new notions.[91]) Ultimately the complete judicial doctrine begins to show forth, a slave cannot be a white man, and every man of color was descendent of a slave.[92]

The rising wall dividing the legal status of the slave from that of the servant was buttressed by other developments which derogated the qualities of the Negro as a human being to establish his inferiority and thus completed his separation from the white. The destruction of the black man's personality involved, for example, a peculiar style of designation. In the seventeenth century many immigrants in addition to the Africans — Swedes, Armenians, Jews — had brought no family names to America. By the eighteenth all but the Negroes had acquired them. In the seven-

teenth century, Indians and Negroes bore names that were either an
approximation of their original ones or similar to those of their masters,—
Diana, Jane, Frank, Juno, Anne, Maria, Jenny. In the eighteenth century
slaves seem increasingly to receive classical or biblical appelations, by
analogy with Roman and Hebrew bondsmen.[93] Deprivation by statute
and usage of other civic rights, to vote, to testify, to bring suit, even if
free, completed the process. And after 1700 appear the full slave codes,
formal recognition that the Negroes are not governed by the laws of
other men.[94]

The identical steps that made the slave less a man made him more a
chattel. All servants had once been reckoned property of a sort; a runaway was guilty of "Stealth of ones self."[95] Negroes were then no different from others.[96] But every law that improved the condition of the white
servant chipped away at the property element in his status. The growing
emphasis upon the consent of the servant, upon the limits of his term,
upon the obligations to him, and upon the conditional nature of his
dependence, steadily converted the relationship from an ownership to
a contractual basis. None of these considerations applied to the Negro;
on the contrary considerations of consent and conditions disappeared
from his life. What was left was his status as property — in most cases
a chattel though for special purposes real estate.[97]

To this development there was a striking parallel in the northern colonies. For none of the elements that conspired to create the slave were
peculiar to the productive system of the South. The contact of dissimilar
peoples in an economy in which labor was short and opportunity long
was common to all American settlements. In New England and New
York too there had early been an intense desire for cheap unfree hands,
for "bond slaverie, villinage or Captivitie," whether it be white, Negro,
or Indian.[98] As in the South, the growth in the number of Negroes had
been slow until the end of the seventeenth century.[99] The Negroes were
servants who, like other bondsmen, became free and owners of land.
But there too, police regulations, the rules of marriage, and the development of status as property turned them into chattel slaves.[100]

A difference would emerge in the course of the eighteenth century, not
so much in the cities or in the Narragansett region where there were substantial concentrations of Blacks, but in the rural districts where hand-
fuls of Negroes were scattered under the easy oversight of town and
church. There the slave would be treated as an individual, would become
an equal, and acquire the rights of a human being. Men whose minds
would be ever more preoccupied with conceptions of natural rights and
personal dignity would find it difficult to except the Negro from their
general rule.[101]

But by the time the same preoccupations would fire imaginations in the South, the society in which the slave lived would so have changed that he would derive no advantage from the eighteenth-century speculations on the nature of human rights. Slavery had emerged in a society in which the unit of active agriculture was small and growing smaller; even the few large estates were operated by sub-division among tenants.[102] After 1690, however, South Carolinians (and still later Georgians) turned from naval stores and the fur trade to the cultivation of rice, cotton, and indigo. In the production of these staples, which required substantial capital equipment, there was an advantage to large-scale operations. By then it was obvious which was the cheapest, most available, most exploitable labor supply. The immense profits from the tropical crops steadily sucked slaves in ever growing numbers into the plantation. With this extensive use, novel on the mainland, the price of slaves everywhere rose sharply, to the advantage of those who already held them. The prospect that the slaveowner would profit not only by the Negroes' labor, but also by the rise in their unit value and by their probable increase through breeding, accounted for the spread of the plantation to the older tobacco regions where large-scale production was not, as in the rice areas, necessarily an asset.[103]

The new social and economic context impressed indelibly on the Negro the peculiar quality of chattel with which he had been left, as other servants escaped the general degradation that had originally been the common portion of all. Not only did the concentration of slaves in large numbers call for more rigid discipline, not only did the organization of the plantation with its separate quarters, hierarchy of overseers, and absentee owners widen the gulf between black and white, but the involvement of the whole southern economy in plantation production created an effective interest against any change in status.[104]

Therein, the southern mainland colonies also differed from those in the West Indies where the same effective interest in keeping the black man debased was created without the prior definition of his status. The actual condition of the Negro differed from island to island, reflecting variations in the productive system, in the labor supply, and in economic trends. But with surprising uniformity, the printed statutes and legislative compilations show no concern with the problems of defining the nature of his servitude. The relevant laws deal entirely with policing, as in the case of servants.[105] A similar unconcern seems to have been characteristic of the French, for the most important aspects of the royal *Code noir* issued from Paris in 1685 were entirely disregarded.[106]

The failure to define status may have been due, in the islands which changed hands, to contact with the Spaniards and to the confusion attendant upon changes of sovereignty. More likely it grew out of the manner in which the Negroes were introduced. Places like the Barbados and St. Christopher's were at the start quite similar to Virginia and Maryland, societies of small farmers, with a labor force of indentured servants and *engagées*. The Negroes and the sugar plantation appeared there somewhat earlier than on the continent because the Dutch, English, and French African companies, anxious to use the islands as entrepots from which their cargoes would be re-exported to Latin America, advanced the credit not only for purchase of the Blacks, but also for sugar-making equipment. But the limited land of the islands meant that the plantation owner and the yeoman competed for the same acres, and in the unequal competition the farmer was ultimately displaced.[107]

The planter had no inveterate preference for the Negro, often expressed a desire for white labor. But the limits to the available land also prevented him from holding out the only inducements that would attract servants with a choice — the prospect of landed freedom. From time to time desultory laws dealt with the term of service, but these showed no progression and had no consequences. The manumitted were free only to emigrate, if they could, or to hang about, hundreds of them "who have been out of their time for many years . . . [with] never a bit of fresh meat bestowed on them nor a dram of rum."[108] The process of extending the rights of servants, which on the mainland was the means of defining the status of the slave, never took place on the islands.

The term, slave, in the West Indies was at the start as vague as in Virginia and Maryland; and when toward mid-century it narrowed down to the plantation Negroes as sugar took hold through the stimulus of the Africa traders, it does not seem to have comprehended more than the presumption of indefinite service.[109] To Europeans, any service on the islands continued to be slavery. For whatever distinctions might be drawn among various groups of them, the slavish servants remained slavish servants. All labor was depressed, Negro and white, "domineered over and used like dogs." That undoubtedly affected emigration from the islands, the decline of white population, the relationships of Blacks and whites, the ultimate connotation of the term slave, the similarities in practice to villeinage, the savage treatment by masters and equally savage revolts against them, the impact of eighteenth-century humanitarianism, and the direction of emancipation.[110]

The distinctive qualities of the southern labor system were then not the simple products of the plantation. They were rather the complex outcome of a process by which the American environment broke down the traditional European conceptions of servitude. In that process the weight of the plantation had pinned down on the Negro the clearly-defined status of a chattel, a status left him as other elements in the population achieved their liberation. When, therefore, Southerners in the eighteenth century came to think of the nature of the rights of man they found it inconceivable that Negroes should participate in those rights. It was more in accord with the whole social setting to argue that the slaves could not share those rights because they were not fully men, or at least different kinds of men. In fact to the extent that Southerners ceased to think in terms of the seventeenth century degrees of freedom, to the extent that they thought of liberty as whole, natural, and inalienable, they were forced to conclude that the slave was wholly unfree, wholly lacking in personality, wholly a chattel.

Only a few, like St. George Tucker and Thomas Jefferson, perceived that here were the roots of a horrible tragedy that would some day destroy them all.[111]

Notes

1.   See, in general, Lewis Cecil Gray, *History of Agriculture in the Southern United States to 1860* (New York, 1941), I, 302 ff.

2.   Summarized in John Codman Hurd, *Law of Freedom and Bondage in the United States* (Boston, 1858), I, 42, 43.

3.   William Blackstone, *Commentaries . . .*, edited by St. George Tucker (Philadelphia, 1803), I, 126, 423. For Somerset's Case, see Hurd, *Law of Freedom and Bondage*, I, 189 ff.; also *ibid.*, I, 185 ff.

4.   [Thomas Blount], *Les Termes de la Ley; or, Certain Difficult and Obscure Words and Terms of the Common Laws and Statutes . . . Explained* (London, 1685), 648-652; Hurd, *Law of Freedom and Bondage,* I, 136.

5.   Edward Coke, *First Part of the Institutes of the Laws of England; or, a Commentary upon Littleton . . .*, edited by Charles Butler (Philadelphia, 1853), Bk. II, Ch. II, Sections 172-212; James Paterson, *Commentaries on the Liberty of the Subject and the . . . Security of the Person* (London, 1877), I, 492; Jacob D. Wheeler, *Practical Treatise on the Law of Slavery . . .* (New York, 1837), 256, 257; Tucker's Appendix to Blackstone, *Commentaries,* I, 43n; Gray, *History of Agriculture,* I, 343 ff.

6.   See *Maryland Archives* (Baltimore, 1883 ff.), I, 69 (1638/9), 152 ff. (1642), 187 (1642), 192 (1642); William Waller Hening, *Statutes at Large Being a Collection of all the Laws of Virginia . . .* (New York, 1823 ff.), I, 117; Gray, *History of Agriculture,* I, 343; John H. Lefroy, *Memorials of the Discovery and Early Settlement of the Bermudas or Somers Islands, 1518-1685* (London, 1877), I, 127.

7.   See Hening, *Statutes,* I, 336; also Paterson, Commentaries, I, 495; Gray, *History of Agriculture,* I, 343; Susie M. Ames, *Studies of the Virginia Eastern Shore in the Seventeenth Century* (Richmond, 1940), 78 ff.; *infra,* 212.

8.   Paterson, *Commentaries,* I, 494; *infra,* 209.

9.   See Gray, *History of Agriculture,* I, 343 ff.

10. *Maryland Archives,* I, 69 (1638/9); Hening, *Statutes,* I, 245, 253, 274, 439, 445; Ames, *Eastern Shore,* 77; *infra,* 214.

11. See, for instance, Hening, *Statutes,* I, 167, 189, 192.

12. Philip Alexander Bruce, *Institutional History of Virginia . . .* (New York, 1910), II, 614.

13. See Elizabeth Donnan, ed., *Documents Illustrative of the History of the Slave Trade to America* (Washington, 1930 ff.), I, 83 ff., 105, 106, 151; Gray, *History of Agriculture,* I, 352.

14. Philip Alexander Bruce, *Social Life of Virginia in the Seventeenth Century* (Richmond, 1907), 14; James M. Wright, *Free Negro in Maryland 1634-1860* (New York, 1921), 13.

15. See Gray, *History of Agriculture,* I, 314 ff.

16. This fact was first established by the work of James Curtis Ballagh, *History of Slavery in Virginia* (Baltimore, 1902), 9 ff., 28 ff. and John Henderson Russell, *Free Negro in Virginia 1619-1865* (Baltimore, 1913), 23 ff. Their conclusions were accepted by Ulrich B. Phillips, *American Negro Slavery* (New York, 1918), 75; although they ran counter to the position of Philip Alexander Bruce, *Economic History of Virginia in the Seventeenth Century* (New York, 1907), II, 52 ff. They were not seriously disputed until the appearance of Ames, *Eastern Shore,* 100 ff. Miss Ames's argument, accepted by Wesley Frank Craven, *Southern Colonies in the Seventeenth Century 1607-1689* (Baton Rouge, 1949), 402, rests on scattered references to "slaves" in the records. But these are never identified as Negroes; the reference is always to "slaves," to "Negroes or slaves," to "Negroes and slaves," or to "Negroes and other slaves," just as there are many more frequent references to "Negroes and servants" (for the meaning of "slave" in these references, see *infra,* 204). Miss Ames also argues that the free Negroes referred to by Russell may have been manumitted. But unless she could prove—and she cannot—that Englishmen in Virginia had a previous conception of slavery as a legal status within which the Negro fell, it is much more logical to assume with Russell that these were servants who had completed their terms. For the same reasons we cannot accept the unsupported assumptions of Wright, *Free Negro in Maryland,* 21-23.

17. Marcus W. Jernegan, "Slavery and the Beginnings of Industrialism in the American Colonies," *American Historical Review,* XXV (1920), 227, 228; Ames, *Eastern Shore,* 106, 107.

18. In such a work as [Nathaniel Butler], *Historye of the Bermudaes or Summer Islands,* edited by J. Henry Lefroy (London, 1882), for instance, the term "slave" is never applied to Negroes (see pp. 84, 99, 144, 146, 211, 219, 242). For disciplinary and revenue laws in Virginia that did not discriminate Negroes from other servants, see Hening, *Statutes,* I, 174, 198, 200, 243, 306 (1631-1645). For wills (1655-1664) in which "Lands goods & chattels cattle monys negroes English servts horses sheep household stuff" were all bequeathed together, see *Lancaster County Records,* Book 2, pp. 46, 61, 121, 283 (cited from Beverley Fleet, ed., *Virginia Colonial Abstracts* [Richmond, 1938 ff.]).

19. *State Papers Henry VIII, Ireland,* II, 448; also III, 594 (under Sklaw); see also Shakespeare's *Coriolanus,* Act IV, Scene 5.

20. Thomas More, *Utopia* (Oxford, 1895), 161, 221, 222.

21. See Russell, *Free Negro,* 19.

22. Paterson, *Commentaries,* I, 492.

23. See Bruce, *Institutional History,* I, 673; Ames, *Eastern Shore,* 72 ff.; E. B. O'Callaghan, ed., *Documents Relative to the Colonial History of the State of New York* (Albany, 1856 ff.), III, 678.

24. Butler, *Historye of the Bermudaes,* 295, 296. See also Lorenzo Johnston Greene, *Negro in Colonial New England 1620-1776* (New York, 1942), 19, *n.* 25; Arthur W. Calhoun, *Social History of the American Family* (Cleveland, 1917), I, 82; and also the evidence cited by Richard B. Morris, *Government and Labor in Early America* (New York, 1946), 339, 340.

25. See Abbot Emerson Smith, *Colonists in Bondage* (Chapel Hill, 1947), 158, 186; *Maryland Archives,* I, 41; Gray, *History of Agriculture,* I, 359; Butler, *Historye of the Bermudaes,* 295; Morris, *Government and Labor,* 346. Some of the earliest Negroes in Bermuda and Virginia seem thus to have been held as public servants, perhaps by analogy with penal servitude (Ballagh, *Slavery in Virginia,* 29).

26. See, for example, Craven, *Southern Colonies,* 219.

27. Donnan, *Documents,* I, 128-131, 156, 158, 163, 164. For continued use of the term, "Negro Servants" by the Royal African Company, see *ibid.,* I, 195.

28. John P. Prendergast, *Cromwellian Settlement of Ireland* (London, 1865), 53*n,* 238; Patrick Francis Moran, *Historical Sketch of the Persecutions Suffered by the Catholics of Ireland under the Rule of Cromwell and the Puritans* (Dublin, 1907), 343-346, 356, 363.

29. See, for example, Genesis, XIV, 14, XXX, 43; Leviticus, XXV, 39-46; Exodus, XXI, 1-9, 16. See also the discussion by Roger Williams (1637), *Massachusetts Historical Society Collections,* Fourth Series, VI (1863), 212.

30. Coke, *First Institute upon Littleton,* 116a, §172.

31. I. [Jean] Bodin, *Six Bookes of a Commonweale,* translated by Richard Knolles (London, 1606), 33. For the Portuguese and Spanish situations, see Jose Antonio Saco, *Historia de la esclavitud desde los tiempos mas remotos hasta nuestros dias* (2d ed., Habana, 1937), III, 266-277; Donnan, *Documents,* I, 15, 16, 29 ff.; Frank Tannenbaum, *Slave and Citizen the Negro in the Americas* (New York, 1947), 43 ff., 55; Gray, *History of Agriculture,* I, 110, 304-306; Marcus W. Jernegan, *Laboring and Dependent Classes in Colonial America, 1607-1783* (Chicago, 1931), 25.

32. See, for example, Edward McCrady, *History of South Carolina under the Proprietary Government 1670-1719* (New York, 1897), 357; Gray, *History of Agriculture,* I, 322.

33. See *infra, n.*105.

34. *Massachusetts Historical Society Collections,* Fourth Series, VI, 536 ff.

35. *Collections of the South Carolina Historical Society,* V (1897), II, 32, 42, 43.

36. For material relevant to these questions, see Lucien Peytraud, *L'Esclavage aux antilles françaises avant 1789* (Paris, 1897), 20 ff.; Gray, *History of Agriculture,* I, 362-370; Bruce, *Social Life,* 16; Ulrich B. Phillips, *Life and Labor in the Old South* (Boston, 1929), 23; Ralph B. Flanders, *Plantation Slavery in Georgia* (Chapel Hill, 1933), 9, 10; Ballagh, *Slavery in Virginia,* 51; Wright, *Free Negro in Maryland,* 21; E. Franklin Frazier, *Negro in the United States* (New York, 1949), 29 ff.; Donnan, *Documents,* I, 174.

37. See C. S. S. Higham, *Development of the Leeward Islands under the Restoration 1660-1688* (Cambridge, 1921), 143, 165.

38. Donnan, *Documents,* I, 91, 92, 115-118.

39. Craven, *Southern Colonies,* 25. There is no evidence to support T. J. Wertenbaker's statement that the demand for Negro slaves remained active in Virginia after 1620 and that if England had early entered the slave trade, Virginia and Maryland "would have been from the first inundated with black workers." See *Planters of Colonial Virginia* (Princeton, 1922), 31, 125; *First Americans 1607-1690* (New York, 1929), 23.

40.   William Berkeley, *A Discourse & View of Virginia* (London, 1663), 4, 5, 7, 8; *Virginia Historical Register*, I, 63; Phillips, *Life and Labor*, 44; T. J. Wertenbaker, *Patrician and Plebeian in Virginia* (Charlottesville, Va., 1910), 137 ff.

41.   Ballagh, *Slavery in Virginia*, 14; McCrady, *South Carolina*, 383; Alexander S. Salley, Jr., ed., *Narratives of Early Carolina 1650-1708* (New York, 1910), 60.

42.   Locke also anticipated a lower form of labor to be performed by Negro slaves. But while the leetmen would be held only by the lords of manors, any freeman would have power to hold slaves. See John Locke, *First Set of the Fundamental Constitutions of South Carolina*, articles 22-26, 101 (a draft is in *Collections of the South Carolina Historical Society*, V, 93 ff.); also Gray, *History of Agriculture*, I, 323-325.

43.   William E. Dodd, "The Emergence of the First Social Order in the United States," *American Historical Review*, XL (1935), 226, 227.

44.   See Wertenbaker, *Planters*, 86 ff.; Wertenbaker, *Patrician*, 144 ff.; Wertenbaker, *First Americans*, 42 ff. In addition it might well be questioned whether large producers in a period of falling prices would have driven out the small producer who operated with little reference to conditions of prices and costs. See *Maryland Archives*, II, 45, 48 (1666); Gray, *History of Agriculture*, I, 231, 232, 276.

45.   Hening, *Statutes*, I, 117.

46.   See *Maryland Archives*, I, 328, 331, 332 (1651), III, 99 (1641), 222 (1648); Gray, *History of Agriculture*, I, 87, 88; Higham, *Leeward Islands*, 169 ff.

47.   See Bruce, *Social Life*, 139, 152; Bruce, *Institutional History*, I, 9.

48.   Lefroy, *Memorials*, I, 308; Smith, *Colonists in Bondage*, 172. For the dangers of reading Negro law in isolation, see the exaggerated interpretation of the act of 1623, Craven, *Southern Colonies*, 218.

49.   That there was no trend is evident from the fluctuations in naming Negroes slaves or servants and in their right to bear arms. See Hening, *Statutes*, I, 226, 258, 292, 540; Bruce, *Institutional History*, II, 5 ff., 199 ff. For similar fluctuations with regard to Indians, see Hening, *Statutes*, I, 391, 518.

50.   Charles M. Andrews, *Colonial Period of American History* (New Haven, 1934 ff.), I, 137.

51.   *Maryland Archives*, III, 141. See also the later comment on the Barbados by Berkeley, *Discourse*, 12; and the complaint of Thomas Cornwallis that the cost of maintaining many servants was "never defrayed by their labor," *Maryland Archives*, I, 463.

52.   That the practice of simply renewing expired terms was common was shown by its abuse by unscrupulous masters. See *infra*, n. 71, n. 78.

53.   Gray, *History of Agriculture*, I, 316, 318 ff.

54.   We have discussed the whole question in "Origins of the American Business Corporation," *Journal of Economic History*, V (1945), 21 ff. See also Smith, *Colonists in Bondage*, 108.

55.   Russell, *Free Negro*, 34.

56.   Helen Tunnicliff Catterall, *Judicial Cases Concerning American Slavery and the Negro* (Washington, 1926 ff.), I, 58.

57.   *Collections of the South Carolina Historical Society*, V, 152; Wertenbaker, *Planters*, 60; Higham, *Leeward Islands*, 169; Jeffrey R. Brackett, *Negro in Maryland* (Baltimore, 1889), 23.

58.   *Maryland Archives*, I, 52, 97 (1640).

59. Hening, *Statutes,* I, 259, 459; Gray, *History of Agriculture,* I, 316, 346.

60. *Maryland Archives,* I, 37, 80, 352 (1654); Hening, *Statutes,* I, 257.

61. *Maryland Archives,* I, 80, 402-409 (1661), 453 (1662); Hening, *Statutes,* I, 411. The Maryland act specifically excluded "slaves."

62. See Virginia acts of 1654/5 and 1657/8, Hening, *Statutes,* I, 411, 441, 471.

63. *Ibid.,* I, 538, II, 113, 169, 297. The provision limiting the effectiveness of the act to Christians is not surprising in view of contemporary attitudes. See the act of the same year excluding Quakers, *ibid.,* I, 532. For later adjustments of term, see *Maryland Archives,* II, 147 (1666), 335 (1671).

64. For an example of such uncertainty, see the case of "Degoe the negro servant" (Virginia, 1665), *Lancaster County Record Book,* Book 2, p. 337; also Craven, *Southern Colonies,* 219. It is instructive to note how that question was evaded by ninety-nine year terms in Bermuda as late as 1662. See Lefroy, *Memorials,* II, 166, 184.

65. *Maryland Archives,* I, 526 ff., 533; Wright, *Free Negro in Maryland,* 21; Brackett, *Negro in Maryland,* 28.

66. Hening, *Statutes,* II, 26, 116; Catterall, *Judicial Cases,* I, 59.

67. Hening, *Statutes,* II, 283; it was reenacted more stringently in 1682, *ibid.,* II, 491. See also McCrady, *South Carolina,* 358.

68. See Saco, *Historia de la esclavitud,* III, 158 ff.; Hurd, *Law of Freedom and Bondage,* I, 160; Donnan, *Documents,* I, 3, 4.

69. John Archdale, *A New Description of the Province of Carolina* (1707), in Salley, *Narratives,* 300. For English law on the question, see Gray, *History of Agriculture,* I, 359.

70. Catterall, *Judicial Cases,* I, 57; Hening, *Statutes,* II, 260; Locke, *Constitutions,* Article 101; *Maryland Archives,* I, 526, II, 265, 272; Ballagh, *Slavery in Virginia,* 46-48; Russell, *Free Negro,* 21; Wright, *Free Negro in Maryland,* 22; Hurd, *Law of Freedom and Bondage,* I, 210; Brackett, *Negro in Maryland,* 29.

71. For the feudal derivation of manumission, see Coke, *First Institute upon Littleton,* I, 137b, §204. For the application to servants see Bodin, *Six Bookes,* 33; Hening, *Statutes, II,* 115 (1661/2). The requirement for manumission of servants in Virginia, to some extent, seems to have become a means of protection against labor-starved masters who coerced their servants into new contracts just before the old expired. See Hening, *Statutes,* II, 388 (1676/7).

72. *Maryland Archives,* I, 373 (1658), 428, 441 (1662); Hening, *Statutes,* I, 438, II, 114 (1661/2), 168 (1662), 298 (1672), III, 139; Bruce, *Institutional History,* I, 45-50, 85, 86; Calhoun, *American Family,* I, 314. Women were always punished more severely than men, not being eligible for benefit of clergy. See Blackstone, *Commentaries,* I, 445n.

73. Ballagh, *Slavery in Virginia,* 38 ff.; Greene, *Negro in New England,* 290 ff.

74. See Coke, *First Institute upon Littleton,* I, 123a, §187; *Maryland Archives,* I, 526-533; Wright, *Free Negro in Maryland,* 21, 22, 27; Wheeler, *Practical Treatise,* 3, 21; Russell, *Free Negro,* 19, 21; Greene, *Negro in New England,* 182 ff.

75. [Durand], *A Frenchman in Virginia Being the Memoirs of a Huguenot Refugee in 1686,* edited by Fairfax Harrison, (Richmond, 1923), 95 ff. For laws conflating servant and slave, see Brackett, *Negro in Maryland,* 104. This contradicts the assumption of Catterall, *Judicial Cases,* I, 57, that the status of Negroes was completely fixed by 1667.

76. The agitation against transportation of felons was also evidence of the desire to supply that assurance. See *Maryland Archives,* I, 464; Hening, *Statutes,* II, 509 ff., 515 (1670); Ballagh, *Slavery in Virginia,* 10; Phillips, *Life and Labor,* 25. The attractiveness of rival colonies may account for the low proportion of servants who took up land in Maryland. See Abbot Emerson Smith, "The Indentured Servant and Land Speculation in Seventeenth Century Maryland," *American Historical Review,* XL (1935), 467 ff.; Gray, *History of Agriculture,* I, 88, 348.

77. See the complaint of Thomas Cornwallis, *Maryland Archives,* I, 463 ff.

78. See Hening, *Statutes,* II, 117, 156, 157, 164 (1661/2), 388 (1676/7), 464 (1680); Maryland Archives, II, 30 (1666), 351 (1674); Smith, *Colonists in Bondage,* 110, 228, 233; Bruce, *Economic History,* II, 11 ff.

79. See Donnan, *Documents,* I, 86, 87; Gray, *History of Agriculture,* I, 352-355; Bruce, *Economic History,* II, 85; Salley, *Narratives,* 204; Higham, *Leeward Islands,* 162 ff.; Craven, *Southern Colonies,* 401; Russell, *Free Negro,* 29; Hening, *Statutes,* II, 511 ff.

80. See Hening, *Statutes,* I, 401, 440; *Maryland Archives,* I, 107 ff. (1641), 124 (1642), 193 (1642), 500 (1663); McCrady, *South Carolina,* 359.

81. *Maryland Archives,* I, 249 (1649), 348 (1654), 451 (1662), 489 (1663), II, 146 (1666), 224 (1669), 298 (1671), 523 (1676); Hening, *Statutes,* II, 116, 118 (1661/2), 185, 195 (1663), 239 (1666), 266 (1668), 270, 273 (1669), 277, 280 (1670), 299 (1672), 481 (1680), 492 (1682), III, 86 ff., 102 (1691), 179 (1699), 210 (1701), 269, 276, 278 (1705); Thomas Cooper and David J. McCord, eds., *Statutes at Large of South Carolina* (Columbia, 1836 ff.), VII, 343 ff.; Brackett, *Negro in Maryland,* 91 ff.; Phillips, *Life and Labor,* 29; Russell, *Free Negro,* 10, 21, 51, 138 ff.; Bruce, *Social Life,* 138; Bruce, *Economic History,* II, 120 ff.; Ames, *Eastern Shore,* 99; also Addison E. Verrill, *Bermuda Islands* (New Haven, 1902), 148 ff.

82. See Hening, *Statutes,* I, 252, 433, 438; *Maryland Archives,* I, 73, 97 (1638/9), 428, 442 ff. (1662), II, 396 (1674). For English law, see Coke, *First Institute upon Littleton,* 135b, 136a, §202; *ibid.,* 139b, 140a, §209.

83. Hening, *Statutes,* II, 114 (1661/2); Jernegan, *Laboring and Dependent Classes,* 55, 180.

84. Hening, *Statutes,* I, 146, 552.

85. See *supra,* 213; Wright, *Free Negro in Maryland,* 28-31.

86. Hening, *Statutes,* III, 86-87, 453 (1705); Brackett, *Negro in Maryland,* 32 ff., 195 ff.; Russell, *Free Negro,* 124; Craven, *Southern Colonies,* 402. For the use of "spurious" in the sense of illegitimate see the quotations, Calhoun, *American Family,* I, 42.

87. *Ibid.,* I, 323.

88. Almon W. Lauber, *Indian Slavery in Colonial Times* (New York, 1913), 252.

89. See Hening, *Statutes,* I, 167, 192, (1631/2), 396, 415 (1655/6), 455, 456, 476 (1657/8), II, 340, 346 (1676); *Maryland Archives,* I, 250 (1649); Catterall, *Judicial Cases,* I, 69, 70; Lauber, *Indian Slavery,* 105-117, 205, 287; Brackett, *Negro in Maryland,* 13; Craven, *Southern Colonies,* 367 ff.; Ballagh, *Slavery in Virginia,* 34, 47-49; McCrady, *South Carolina,* 189, 478; Greene, *Negro in New England,* 198 ff.; Peytraud, *L'Esclavage,* 29; Gray, *History of Agriculture,* I, 361.

90. By 1705, a mulatto was a person with a Negro great grandparent. See Hening, *Statutes,* III, 252; also Ballagh, *Slavery in Virginia,* 44; Tannenbaum, *Slave and Citizen,* 8.

91. See Hening, *Statutes,* II, iii, 170. For other alterations to insert "slave" where it had not originally been, see *ibid.,* II, 283, 490.

92. Catterall, *Judicial Cases,* II, 309, 338; Wheeler, *Practical Treatise,* 3, 12.

93. *Lancaster County Record Book,* Book 3, p. 285; Catterall, *Judicial Cases,* II, 7, 8; Greene, *Negro in New England,* 201; Calhoun, *American Family,* I, 190; Bruce, *Institutional History,* I, 673.

94. No earlier laws covered the same ground. See *Maryland Archives,* II, 523 ff. (1676); Hening, *Statutes,* III, 298, 447, 453 (1705); *Statutes of South Carolina,* VII, 343 ff.; Craven, *Southern Colonies,* 217; Morris, *Government and Labor,* 501; Russell, *Free Negro,* 117-119, 125 ff.

95. *Maryland Archives,* I, 72; Morris, *Government and Labor,* 432; Smith, *Colonists in Bondage,* 234.

96. Thus the inclusion of the Negroes among the Virginia tithables was at first a recognition of their status as personalities rather than as property. The tax was not intended to be discriminatory, but to apply to all those who worked in the fields, white and black. The first sign of discrimination was in 1668 when white but not Negro women were exempt. See Hening, *Statutes,* I, 144, 241, 292, 356, 361, 454, II, 84, 170, 267, 296; Russell, *Free Negro,* 21; Bruce, *Institutional History,* II, 458, 546 ff. For other difficulties in treating Negroes as chattels see Hening, *Statutes,* II, 288.

97. See *Maryland Archives,* II, 164 (1669); Hurd, *Law of Freedom and Bondage,* I, 179; Hening, *Statutes,* III, 333 (1705); Gray, *History of Agriculture,* I, 359; Brackett, *Negro in Maryland,* 28.

98. *Massachusetts Historical Society Collections,* Fourth Series, VI, 64 ff.; Greene, *Negro in New England,* 63, 65, 125.

99. *Ibid.,* 73 ff., 319.

100. For an abstract of legislation, see Hurd, *Law of Freedom and Bondage,* I, 254-293. See also Greene, *Negro in New England,* 126-139, 169, 170, 178, 184, 208 ff.; George Elliott Howard, *History of Matrimonial Institutions* (Chicago, 1904), II, 225, 226; Calhoun, *American Family,* I, 65, 210; J. H. Franklin, *From Slavery to Freedom* (New York, 1947), 89-98; Ellis L. Raesly, *Portrait of New Netherland* (New York, 1945), 104, 161, 162.

101. Greene, *Negro in New England,* 86, 103 ff., 140; Calhoun, *American Family,* I, 82.

102. See Ames, *Eastern Shore,* 16, 17, 30 ff., 37 ff.; McCrady, *South Carolina,* 189; Werkenbaker, *Planters,* 45, 52 ff.; Phillips, *Life and Labor,* 34; Craven, *Southern Colonies,* 210 ff.

103. Flanders, *Plantation Slavery,* 20; Gray, *History of Agriculture,* I, 120, 278, 349.

104. [Durand], *Frenchman in Virginia,* 112 ff.; Phillips, *Life and Labor,* 47; Salley, *Narratives,* 207, 208.

105. See *Montserrat Code of Laws from 1668 to 1788* (London, 1790), 8, 16, 38; *Acts of Assembly Passed in the Island of Nevis from 1664, to 1739, Inclusive* (London, 1740), 9, 10, 11, 17, 25, 28, 37, 46, 75; *Acts of Assembly Passed in the Island of Barbadoes from 1648 to 1718* (London, 1721), 22, 101, 106, 137 ff.; *Acts of Assembly Passed in the Island of Jamaica from the Year 1681 to the Year 1768, Inclusive* (Saint Jagoe de la Vesga, 1769), I, 1, 57; [Leslie], *New History of Jamaica* (2d ed., London, 1740), 204 ff., 217 ff. There seem to have been two minor exceptions. The question of slave status was implicitly touched on in the laws governing in-

heritance and the sale of property for debt (*Acts of Barbadoes*, 63, 147) and in early orders affecting term of service. See *Calendar of State Papers, Colonial*, I, 202; [William Duke], *Some Memoirs of the First Settlement of the Islands of Barbados* . . . (Barbados, 1741), 19.

106.   Peytraud, *L'Esclavage*, 143 ff., 158 ff., 208 ff.

107.   See Peytraud, *L'Esclavage*, 13-17; Gray, *Southern Agriculture*, I, 303-309; Donnan, *Documents*, I, 92, 100, 108-111, 166, 197, 249 ff.; Vincent T. Harlow, *History of Barbados 1625-1685* (Oxford, 1926), 42.

108.   Smith, *Colonists in Bondage*, 294.

109.   See Richard Ligon, *True & Exact History of the Island of Barbados* . . . (London, 1657), 43-47; [Charles C. de Rochefort], *History of the Caribby-Islands* . . . , translated by John Davies (London, 1666), 200 ff.

110.   Smith, *Colonists in Bondage*, 294. For examples of servant legislation, see *Acts of Barbadoes*, 22 ff., 80 ff., 145 ff., 150, 168, 204 ff. (1661-1703). See also Peytraud, *L'Esclavage*, 38, 135 ff.; Donnan, *Documents*, I, 97; Morris, *Government and Labor*, 503; Leslie, *New History of Jamaica*, 89, 148 ff.; Morgan Godwyn, *Negro's and Indian's Advocate* (London, 1680), 12 ff.; Frank W. Pitman, "Slavery on British West India Plantations in the Eighteenth Century," *Journal of Negro History*, XI (1926), 610 ff., 617; William L. Mathieson, *British Slavery and Its Abolition, 1823-1838* (London, 1926), 44, 50 ff.

111.   See the eloquent discussion in Tucker's appendix to Blackstone, *Commentaries*, I, 35 ff.

THE DYNAMICS OF UNOPPOSED CAPITALISM

Stanley M. Elkins

The selection by Elkins refocuses the Handlins' thesis by emphasizing the capitalistic framework within which economic and political forces conducive to the origin of slavery unfolded. The slim margin of profit per unit of production which dictated economies of scale in commercial agriculture also forestalled the profitable use of free labor in a society where productive land was readily available. That is, it was not the scarcity of labor *per se* which heightened the pressures for resort to slave labor, but the fact that uncoerced laborers would seek out their own land (thus further heightening the demand for labor) unless recompensed at a rate which budding enterpreneurs could ill afford.[1] Elkins stresses that the emerging planter-capitalists caught in this economic squeeze were able to institute slavery as a solution to their problem because there simply was no effective opposition to their interests. Accordingly, the planters utilized their power in the service of their interests by institutionalizing that mode of organizing the labor force which provided laborers at the lowest cost.

The thesis that emerging capitalism was the prime factor in the origin of American slavery can be challenged on the grounds that American slavery was basically precapitalist. Thus, Genovese argues that rational, innovative solutions to the economic problems confronting society are thwarted in a society founded on slavery.[2] However, this incisive analysis of the inefficiency of slavery does not in itself undermine the capitalistic interpretation of slavery's *origin*. Genovese's critique of slavery is addressed to a different question — the question of maintenance rather than of origin — and a different time period than Elkin's essay. Genovese's analysis is focused on the mature nineteenth-century slave society in which the planter elite held values antithetical to capitalism precisely because the maintenance of slavery had replaced the maximization of

45

profit as the *raison d'etre* of the society. "Slavery . . . *increasingly* came to be seen as the very foundation of a proper social order. . . ."[3] This is entirely compatible with Elkins's analysis which seeks to explain the origin of the American slave economy in the middle and late seventeenth century. Indeed, Elkins himself acknowledges the highly significant non-rational and irrational features of nineteenth-century American slavery without jeopardizing his thesis.[4]

In contrast to the Handlins, Elkins implies that instances of indenture and subsequent freedom constitute "exceptions" to the general practice (i.e., automatic slavery) even for the earliest blacks. Palmer leans the other way in stating: "That *some* Virginia Negroes served for life in the 1640's and 1650's is certain; it is just as certain that *many* did not."[5] Palmer provides evidence that some of the free Negroes in the Virginia of 1670 were manumitted slaves while others were released after fulfilling the terms of their indenture. We simply don't know whether indenture or slavery was the common practice initially and, in light of the generally acknowledged scarcity of evidence, it is perhaps safest to conclude that "in this ill-defined period there were no automatic guarantees for the Negroes, one way or the other."[6]

Notes

1. The problem would have remained acute regardless of the rate of increase in the number of potential laborers so long as productive land was plentiful. This position reflects an earlier thesis regarding the decisive importance of abundant resources. See H. J. Nieboer, *Slavery as an Industrial System* (Martinus Nijhoff, 1900), esp. pp. 387-90.

2. Eugene D. Genovese, *The Political Economy of Slavery,* Vintage Book (New York: Random House, 1967), esp. chap. 1 and pp. 264-70.

3. *Ibid.,* p. 8 (emphasis added).

4. *Slavery,* 2d ed. (1968), pp. 249-50.

5. Paul C. Palmer, "Servant into Slave: The Evolution of the Legal Status of the Negro Laborer in Colonial Virginia," *South Atlantic Quarterly* 65 (1966): 355-70: Quotation (emphasis added) at p. 358; see also pp. 363 and 369-70.

6. Joseph Boskin, "The Origins of American Slavery: Education as an Index of Early Differentiation," *Journal of Negro Education* 35 (1966): 125-33 (quotation at p. 126n).

How had Negro slavery in the United States come into being? There was nothing "natural" about it; it had no necessary connection with either tropical climate or tropical crops: in Virginia and Maryland, where the institution first appeared and flourished, the climate was hardly tropical, and the staple crop—tobacco—might have been grown as far north as Canada. It had nothing to do with characteristics which might have made the Negro peculiarly suited either to slavery or to the labor of tobacco culture. Slavery in past ages had been limited to no particular race, and the earliest planters of colonial Virginia appear to have preferred a laboring force of white servants from England, Scotland, and Ireland, rather than of blacks from Africa. Nor was it a matter of common-law precedent, for the British colonists who settled the areas eventually to be included in the United States brought with them no legal categories comparable to that of "slave," as the term would be understood by the end of the seventeenth century. "Slavery," considered in the abstract as servile bondage, had existed elsewhere for centuries; indeed, the natives of Africa had known it intimately. Yet nothing was inherent, even in the fact of *Negro* slavery, which should compel it to take the form that it took in North America. Negro slavery flourished in Latin America at that same period, but there the system was strikingly different. In certain altogether crucial respects slavery as we know it was not imported from elsewhere but was created in America—fashioned on the spot by Englishmen in whose traditions such an institution had no part. American slavery was unique, in the sense that, for symmetry and precision of outline, nothing like it had ever previously been seen.

An important essay by Oscar and Mary Handlin has focused new attention upon these facts.[1] Although the first shipload of twenty Negroes had arrived in Virginia in 1619, it was not until the 1660's that the key item in the definition of their status — term of servitude — was clearly fixed in law. It was apparently possible for the earliest Negroes to fall into the various servant categories long familiar to the common law of England, none of which in a practical sense included perpetual and inherited chattel bondage.[2] The bulk of agricultural laborers coming into the colonies at this period were white servants whose terms, as time went on, were to become more and more definitely fixed by indenture, and the Negroes, so far as the law was concerned, could be regarded as "servants" like the rest; there was no articulated legal structure in the colonies to impede their becoming free after a term of service and entering society as artisans and holders of property. Indeed, it was still assumed that the profession of Christianity should itself make a difference in

Reprinted from *Slavery: A Problem in American Institutional and Intellectual Life* by Stanley M. Elkins (Chicago: University of Chicago Press, 1968), pp. 37-52, by permission of The University of Chicago Press.

status.[3] Manumission, moreover, for whatever reason, was a practice common enough to be taken for granted and was attended by no special legal restrictions.[4]

Yet all this began changing drastically with the 1660's. The very need for new colonists to people the country, and the very preference of planters for English-speaking whites rather than African savages as laborers, had already set into motion a trend to define in law the rights of white servants. To encourage the immigration of such servants and to counteract homeward-drifting rumors of indefinite servitude under desperate conditions, it was becoming more and more the practice to fix definite and limited terms of indenture—five or six years—as a guaranty that a clear future awaited the white man who would cast his lot with the colonies. The Negro, as the Handlins put it, "never profited from these enactments. Farthest removed from the English, least desired, he communicated with no friends who might be deterred from following. Since his coming was involuntary, nothing that happened to him would increase or decrease his numbers."[5] In short, every improvement in the status of the white servant, in widening the gulf between his condition and that of the Negro, served to dramatize the deepening significance of color and in effect to depress the black ever closer to a state of perpetual slavery. This tendency was ultimately recognized by the legislatures of Maryland and Virginia, and they were led to embody in law what had already become fact. "All negroes or other slaves within the province [according to a Maryland law of 1663], and all negroes and other slaves to be hereafter imported into the province, shall serve *durante vita;* and all children born of any negro or other slave, shall be slaves as their fathers were for the term of their lives."[6] Such was the first legal step whereby a black skin would itself ultimately be equatable with "slave."

Now there is not much doubt that in actual practice the Negro in Virginia and Maryland had become a slave long before this time. There were precedents in English colonial practice—if not quite in law—that might have been drawn from Barbados any time after the 1630's.[7] In all likelihood the delay in defining Negro status may be ascribed to the fact that their numbers prior to the 1660's were never very great and hardly warranted special legislation.[8] But there is much significance simply in the fact that a state of legal indeterminacy existed for some forty years. During that period there are just enough examples of Negro suits for freedom, Negro ownership of property (with the legal incidents thereof), and so on, to convince one that even so small a margin between automatic lifetime slavery and something else made all the difference— considering what plantation slavery, both in law and in fact, would be a generation later.[9] It meant a precious margin of space, not to be discounted, for the conservation of traditional human rights. However, once the initial step had been taken, and once Negroes began arriving in appreciable numbers — as they did in the years following the Restoration — there was, as it turned out, little to impede the restless inclination of the law to remove ambiguities. A further course of legislation in the colonies — to which by then had been added the Carolinas — was inaugurated in the period roughly centering upon the turn of the seventeenth century; this legislation began suppressing, with a certain methodical insistence, whatever rights of personality still remained to the Negro slave. It was thus that most of the features marking the system of American slavery, as the nineteenth century knew it, had been stamped upon it by about the middle of the eighteenth.

Yet before reviewing in greater detail the legal aspects of this servitude, we should note that the most vital facts about its inception remain quite unaccounted for. The reasons for its delay have been satisfactorily explained — but why did it occur at all? Why should the drive to establish such a status have got under way when it did? What was the force behind it, especially in view of the prior absence of any sort of laws defining slavery? We may on the one hand point out the lack of any legal structure automatically compelling the Negro to become a slave, but it is only fair, on the other, to note that there was equally little in the form of such a structure to prevent him from becoming one. It is not enough to indicate the simple process whereby the interests of white servants and black were systematically driven apart: what was its dynamic? Why should the status of "slave" have been elaborated, in little more than two generations following its initial definition, with such utter logic and completeness to make American slavery unique among all such systems known to civilization?[10]

Was it the "motive of gain"? Yes, but with a difference. The motive of gain, as a psychic "fact," can tell us little about what makes men behave as they do; the medieval peasant himself, with his virtually marketless economy, was hardly free from it. But in the emergent agricultural capitalism of colonial Virginia we may already make out a mode of economic organization which was taking on a purity of form never yet seen, and the difference lay in the fact that here a growing system of large-scale staple production for profit was free to develop in a society where no prior traditional institutions, with competing claims of their own, might interpose at any of a dozen points with sufficient power to retard or modify its progress. What happens when such energy meets no limits?[11]

Here, even in its embryonic stages, it is possible to see the process whereby capitalism would emerge as the principal dynamic force in American society. The New World had been discovered and exploited by a European civilization which had always, in contrast with other world cultures, placed a particularly high premium on personal achievement, and it was to be the special genius of Englishmen, from Elizabeth's time onward, to transform this career concept from its earlier chivalric form into one of economic fulfilment — from "glory" to "success." Virginia was settled during the very key period in which the English middle class forcibly reduced, by revolution, the power of those standing institutions — the church and the crown — which most directly symbolized society's traditional limitations upon personal success and mobility. What the return of the crown betokened in 1660 was not so much "reaction" as the fact that all society had by then somehow made terms with the Puritan Revolution. Virginia had proven a uniquely appropriate theater for the acting-out of this narrower, essentially modern ideal of personal, of *economic,* success. Land in the early days was cheap and plentiful; a ready market for tobacco existed; even the yeoman farmer could rise rapidly if he could make the transition to staple production; and above all there was a quick recognition of accomplishment, by a standard which was not available in England but which was the only one available in Virginia: success in creating a plantation.[12]

The decade of the 1660's, inaugurated by the restoration of the Stuart monarchy, marked something of a turning point in the fortunes of the colony not unrelated to the movement there and in Maryland to fix irrevocably upon the Negro a lifetime of slavery. It was during this decade that certain factors bearing upon the colony's economic future were precipitated. One such factor was a serious drop in tobacco prices, brought on not only by overproduction but also by the Navigation Acts of 1660 and 1661,[13] and the market was not to be fully restored for another twenty years. This meant, with rising costs and a disappearing margin of profit, that commercial production on a small-scale basis was placed under serious disabilities. Another factor was the rise in the slave population. Whereas there had been only about 300 in 1650, by 1670 there were, according to Governor Berkeley, 2,000 slaves in a servant population of 8,000. This was already 25 per cent of the servants, and the figure was even more significant for the future, since the total white servant population in any given period could never be counted on to exceed their average annual immigration multiplied by five or six (the usual term in years, of their indenture), while the increase of slaves over the the same period would be cumulative.[14] Such a development would by now be quite enough to stimulate the leaders of the colony — virtually all planters — to clarify in law once and for all the status of lifetime Negro servitude. The formation in 1662 of a Royal Company of Adventurers for the importation of Negroes symbolized the crown's expectation that a labor force of slaves would be the coming thing in the colonies.[15]

It was thus in a period of relatively hard times that it became clear, if the colony of Virginia were to prosper, that capitalism would be the dynamic force in its economic life. "Success" could no longer be visualized as a rise from small beginnings, as it once could, but must now be conceived as a matter of substantial initial investments in land, equipment, and labor, plus the ability to undertake large annual commitments on credit. With the fall in tobacco prices, and with the tiny margin of profit that remained, the yeoman farmer found it difficult enough to eke out a bare living, let alone think of competing with the large planter or of purchasing slaves' or servants' indentures.[16] Success was still possible, but now its terms were clearer, and those who achieved it would be fewer in numbers. The man who managed it would be the man with the large holdings — the man who could command a substantial force of laborers, white or black — who could afford a sizable yearly investment in the handling of his crop: in short, the capitalist planter.

The period beginning in the 1680's and ending about 1710 marked still a new phase. It saw, now under conditions of comparative prosperity, the full emergence of the plantation as the basic unit of capitalist agriculture. By about 1680 the market for Virginia and Maryland tobacco had been restored, though it is important to note that this was accompanied by no great rise in prices. It was rather a matter of having recaptured the European market by flooding it with cheap tobacco and underselling competitors. Returning prosperity, therefore, meant something far more concrete to the man with resources, who could produce tobacco in large enough amounts to make a slim profit margin worthwhile, than to the one whose productivity was limited by the acreage which he and his family could work. These years also witnessed the initial exploitation of the Carolinas, a process which moved much more directly toward large agricultural units than had been the case in Virginia.[17] The acceleration of this development toward clarifying the terms of commercial production — large plantations and substantial investments — had a direct connection with the widening of the market for slaves during this same period. Hand in hand with large holdings went slaves — an assumption which was now being taken more or less for granted. "A rational man," wrote a South Carolina colonist in 1682, "will certainly inquire, 'when I have Land, what shall I doe with it? What commoditys shall I be able to produce, that will yield me money in other countrys, that I may be inabled to buy Negro-slaves, (without which a planter can never doe any great matter)?' "[18] The point had clearly passed when white servants could realistically, on any long-term appraisal, be considered preferable to Negro slaves. Such appraisals were now being made in terms of capitalized earning power, a concept appropriate to large operations rather than small, to long-term rather than short-term planning.

It was, of course, only the man of means who could afford to think in this way. But then he is the one who most concerns us — the man responsible for Negro slavery. Determined in the sixties and seventies to make money despite hard times and low prices, and willing to undertake the investments which that required, he could now in the eighties reap the fruits of his foresight. His slaves were more valuable than ever — a monument to his patience and planning. What had made them so? For one thing he, unlike the yeoman farmer, had a large establishment for training them and was not pressed by the need, as he would have been with white servants on limited indenture, to exploit their *immediate* labor. The labor was his permanently. And for another thing, the system was by now just old enough to make clear for the first time the full meaning of a second generation of native-born American Negroes. These were the dividends: slaves born to the work and using English as their native tongue.[19] By the 1690's the demand for slaves in the British colonies had become so great, and the Royal African Company so inefficient in supplying them, that in 1698 Parliament revoked the company's monopoly on the African coast and threw open the traffic to independent merchants and traders. The stream of incoming slaves, already of some consequence, now became enormous, and at the same time the annual flow of white servants to Virginia and the Carolinas dropped sharply. By 1710 it had become virtually negligible.[20]

What meaning might all this have had for the legal status of the Negro? The connection was intimate and direct; with the full development of the plantation there was nothing, so far as his interests were concerned, to prevent unmitigated capitalism from becoming unmitigated slavery. The planter was now engaged in capitalistic agriculture with a labor force entirely under his control. The personal relationship between master and slave — in any case less likely to exist on large agricultural units than on smaller ones — now became far less important than the economic necessities which had forced the slave into this "unnatural" organization in the first place. For the plantation to operate efficiently and profitably, and with a force of laborers not all of whom may have been fully broken to plantation discipline, the necessity of training them to work long hours and to give unquestioning obedience to their masters and overseers superseded every other consideration. The master must have absolute power over the slave's body, and the law was developing in such a way as to give it to him at every crucial point. Physical discipline was made virtually unlimited[21] and the slave's chattel status unalterably fixed.[22] It was in such a setting that those rights of personality traditionally regarded between men as private and inherent, quite apart from the matter of lifetime servitude, were left virtually without defense. The integrity of the family was ignored, and slave marriage was deprived of any legal or moral standing.[23] The condition of a bondsman's soul — a matter of much concern to church and civil authority in the Spanish colonies — was here very quickly dropped from consideration. A series of laws enacted between 1667 and 1671 had systematically removed any lingering doubts whether conversion to Christianity should make a difference in status: henceforth it made none.[24] The balance, therefore, involved on the one side the constant pressure of costs, prices, and the problems of management, and on the other the personal interests of the slave. Here, there were no counterweights: those interests were unsupported by any social pressures from the outside; they were cherished by no customary feudal immunities; they were no concern of the government (the king's main interest was in tobacco revenue); they could not be sustained by the church, for the church had little enough power and influence among its own white constituencies, to say nothing of the suspicion its ministers aroused at every proposal to enlarge the church's work among the blacks.[25] The local planter class controlled all those public concerns which most affected the daily life of the colony, and it was thus only in matters of the broadest and most general policy that this planter domination was in any way touched by bureaucratic decisions made in London. The emergent institution of slavery was in effect unchallenged by any other institutions.[26]

The result was that the slave, utterly powerless, would at every critical point see his interests further depressed. At those very points the drive of the law — unembarrassed by the perplexities of competing interests — was to clarify beyond all question, to rationalize, to simplify, and to make more logical and symmetrical the slave's status in society. So little impeded was this pressure to define and clarify that all the major categories in law which bore upon such status were very early established with great thoroughness and completeness.

Notes

1. See Oscar and Mary F. Handlin, "Origins of the Southern Labor System," *William and Mary Quarterly,* 3d Series, VII (April, 1950), 199-222.

2. The state of villeinage, which had once flourished in England during the Middle Ages, had many of the attributes which later characterized plantation slavery. Yet one crucial aspect of slavery—the legal suppression of the personality—was never present in villeinage. The status of villein, moreover, had by the seventeenth century become virtually extinct in England.

3. This assumption, having its roots in tradition, was still persistent enough throughout most of the seventeenth century that, as late as the 1690's, colonial assemblies felt the necessity to declare, in legal enactments, that baptism did not confer on the slave the right to be manumitted. See John Codman Hurd, *The Law of Freedom and Bondage in the United States* (Boston: Little, Brown, 1858), I, 232, 250, 297, 300-301.

4. The implications of the Handlin thesis are sufficient for the limited purposes for which it is being used here. To the extent that the Handlins appear to argue that an indentured status was automatically assumed in this period, in the absence of automatic legal guaranties of slavery, to that extent is their essay quite misleading. Insofar as they point, on the other hand, to a condition legally indeterminate — with practice still sufficiently blurred as to allow a number of exceptions, unthinkable a generation later, to automatic slavery — they do no violence to what is known about the period.

This very indeterminacy has sustained a minor debate going back more than fifty years. James C. Ballagh in 1902 first challenged the accepted notion that slavery in Virginia dated from 1619. The parcel of twenty Negroes sold in that year to the Virginians from a Dutch ship were not held as slaves, Ballagh insisted, but rather as servants, and Virginia law did not recognize out-and-out slavery until more than forty years later. John H. Russell, writing in 1913, accepted Ballagh's position. While admitting that lifetime servitude in Virginia existed long before it was given statutory recognition, he agreed that without a prior system of slavery or a slave code it was "plausible that the Africans became servants who, after a term of service varying from two to eight years, were entitled to freedom." Russell cited examples of Negroes who sued for their freedom or who became independent landowners. The Ballagh-Russell thesis — accepted by Ulrich Phillips — was not questioned until Susie Ames's *Studies of the Virginia Eastern Shore* appeared in 1940. Miss Ames held that there was not enough evidence to support Ballagh and Russell, and that Russell's examples may simply have been of manumitted slaves (in other words, if Negroes were not automatically considered as indentured servants — which she thought doubtful — then they must have been automatically considered as slaves: it had to be one thing or the other). Wesley Frank Craven in 1949 gave further support to Miss Ames's position; in his opinion it was likely that "the trend from the first was toward a sharp distinction between . . . [the Negro] and the white servant." The Handlins, taking issue with Miss Ames, in effect brought the argument back to Ballagh and Russell — not asserting flatly (for Miss Ames and Mr. Craven were at least right about the scarcity of evidence) but calling it "much more logical to assume with Russell that these were servants who had completed their terms." And there the argument rests. See James C. Ballagh, *History of Slavery in Virginia* (Baltimore: John Hopkins, 1902), pp. 9-10, 27-31; John H. Russell, *The Free Negro in Virginia, 1619-1865* (Baltimore: Johns Hopkins, 1913), pp. 23-31; Ulrich B. Phillips, *American Negro Slavery* (New York: D. Appleton & Co., 1918), p. 75; Susie M. Ames, *Studies of the Virginia Eastern Shore in the Seventeenth Century* (Richmond, Va.: Dietz, 1940), pp. 100-106; Wesley Frank Craven, *The Southern Colonies in the Seventeenth Century, 1607-1689* (Baton Rouge: Louisiana State University, 1949), pp. 218-19. See also n. 7 below.

5. Handlin and Handlin, "Origins of the Southern Labor System," p. 211.

6. Quoted in Hurd, *Law of Freedom and Bondage,* I, 249. A Virginia act of the year before had assumed and implied lifetime slavery. It provided special punishments for servants who ran away in the company of "negroes who are incapable of making satisfaction by addition of a time." Helen T. Catterall, *Judicial Cases concerning American Slavery and the Negro* (Washington: Carnegie Institution, 1926 ff.), I, 59. The matter was made explicit when in 1670 it was enacted that

"all servants not being Christians, imported into this colony by shipping, shall be slaves for their lives. . . ." Hurd, *Law of Freedom and Bondage,* I, 233.

7. It should be noted that the Handlins do rule out rather too hastily the possibility of the Virginians' adapting the status of slavery from the West Indies, claiming as they do that Negroes there were still regarded as "servants" as late as 1663. Their assertion is not entirely correct. There were, indeed, few Negroes in the West Indies prior to the 1630's, and there was no slave code there until 1663. But by 1636, Negroes were already coming into Barbados in great enough numbers that the governor's council felt it necessary in that year, law or no law, to issue a regulation declaring that all Negroes or Indians landed on the island would be considered as slaves, bound to work there for the rest of their lives. See Sir Harry Johnston, *The Negro in the New World* (London: Methuen & Co., 1910), p. 211; Vincent Harlow, *A History of Barbados* (Oxford: Clarendon, 1926), pp. 309-10. Even in the Spanish colonies, lifetime servitude had been familiar for nearly a century.

Some kind of statutory recognition of slavery in the American colonies occurred as follows: Massachusetts, 1641; Connecticut, 1650; Virginia, 1661; Maryland, 1663; New York and New Jersey, 1664; South Carolina, 1684; and Rhode Island, 1700. The apparent significance of this chronology diminishes, however, when it is noted that although enactments in the Northern colonies recognized the legality of lifetime servitude, no effort was made to require all Negroes to be placed in that condition. The number of Negroes, moreover, was so small that in Massachusetts it was not until 1698 that any effort was made to consider the important problem of slave children's status. See Ballagh, *Slavery in Virginia,* pp. 35, 39.

8. See n. 14 below.

9. Russell, *Free Negro in Virginia,* pp. 24-39.

10. The common-law tradition actually worked in more than one direction to help perfect the legal arrangements of slavery. Not only was there little in the common law, simply as law, to prevent the Negro from being compelled into a state of slavery, but the very philosophy of the common law would encourage the colonial courts to develop whatever laws appeared necessary to deal with unprecedented conditions.

11. Ever since the time of Marx and Engels (and indeed, before), the idea of "Capitalism" has been a standard tool in the analysis of social behavior. Up to a point this tool is useful; it can throw light on changes in behavior patterns at the point where capitalistic methods and habits in a society begin to supersede feudal ones. In Europe it made some sense. Here is how Engels argued: "According to this conception," he wrote in *Anti-Dühring,* "the ultimate causes of all social changes and political revolutions are to be sought, not in the minds of men, in their increasing insight into eternal truth and justice, but in changes in mode of production and exchange; they are to be sought not in the *philosophy* but in the *economics* of the epoch concerned." But then this idea cannot tell us much about the differences between two societies, *both* capitalist, but in one of which the "means of production" have changed into capitalistic ones and in the other of which the means of production were never anything *but* capitalistic and in which no other forces were present to resist their development.

12. Despite the relative mobility of English society since Tudor times, personal achievement and status still inhered in any number of preferable alternatives to trade and production. But the openness of Virginia lay in the fact that purely capitalistic incentives were being used to get people to come there. No nobles, with their retinues of peasants, migrated to the colony; indeed, there was little reason why the ideal of "making good" should in itself hold many attractions for an aristocracy already established. But for others there were rewards for risk-taking

which were simply not available in England. True, Virginia did develop its own aristocracy, but it had to be a created one, based on terms peculiar to the new country, and—at least as a basis for aspirations—theoretically open to everyone. At any rate, the standards for joining it were not primarily chivalric: to be a "gentleman" one must first have been a successful planter.

13. These acts embodied the Puritan mercantilist policy which Cromwell had never been able to enforce but which had been taken over by the Restoration government. Their general purpose was that of redirecting colonial trade (much of which had been engrossed by the Dutch during the Civil War) through the hands of English merchants. Their immediate effects on tobacco, before the market could readjust itself, was, from the viewpoint of colonial planters, most unfavorable. By limiting the sale of Virginia tobacco to England and requiring that it be transported in English ships, the Navigation Acts cut off Virginia's profitable trade with the Dutch and temporarily crippled its profitable foreign markets. This, according to Thomas J. Wertenbaker, was the basic cause for the serious drop in tobacco prices. See *Planters of Colonial Virginia* (Princeton: Princeton University Press, 1922), pp. 85-87, 90.

14. "40,000 persons, men, women, and children, of which 2,000 are black slaves, 6,000 Christian servants for a short time. Gov. Berkeley." Evarts B. Greene and Virginia D. Harrington, *American Population before the Federal Census of 1790* (New York: Columbia University Press, 1932), p. 36. This figure may be looked at two ways. From the standpoint of *later* populations, one may call attention to its smallness. But consider how it must have appeared to the man looking back to a time only two decades before, when the number of Negroes was negligible. Now, in 1670, with Negroes constituting a full quarter of the servant population (a proportion which gave every promise of increasing), they become a force to be dealt with. By now, men would take them into account as a basis for future calculations in a way which previously they had never needed to do. The very laws demonstrate this. Moreover, Negroes had accumulated in large enough parcels in the hands of the colony's most powerful men to develop in these men deep vested interests in the Negroes' presence and a strong concern with the legal aspects of their future. Among the land patents of the sixties, for example, may already be seen Richard Lee with eighty Negroes, Carter of Corotoman with twenty, the Scarboroughs with thirty-nine, and numerous patents listing fifteen or more. Philip Alexander Bruce, *Economic History of Virginia in the Seventeenth Century* (New York: Macmillan, 1907), II, 78.

15. The subsequent increase of slaves in Virginia was not largely the work of this company. But its formation under royal protection, coming at the time it did, appears to form part of a general pattern of expectations regarding the future state of labor in the plantation colonies. This, taken together with the drop in tobacco prices and coincident with the Navigation Acts and the first general laws on perpetual servitude, all coming at once, seem to add up to something: profitable enterprise, when possible at all, would henceforth as never before have to be conceived in terms of heavily capitalized investment, and more and more men were recognizing this.

16. This had not always been so; the aspirations of a farmer in, say, 1649, with prices at 3 pence a pound, could include a wide range of possibilities. But now, with the price at one-fourth of that figure and costs proportionately much greater than formerly, he could hardly think of the future realistically in terms of becoming a planter. See Lewis Cecil Gray, *History of Agriculture in the Southern States to 1860* (Washington: Carnegie Institution, 1933), I, 263. Now this does not mean that after 1660 the yeoman farmer invariably faced destitution. A great deal depended on how such a farmer conceived his future. The man who made his living from diversified subsistence farming and who planted tobacco as an extra-money crop would undoubtedly suffer less from a drop in prices than the heavily capitalized

planter. However if this same farmer hoped to emulate "his predecessors of the earlier period in saving money, purchasing land . . . and becoming a substantial citizen, the task was well nigh impossible of accomplishment." Wertenbaker, *Planters of Colonial Virginia,* p. 97. See also *ibid.,* pp. 96-100, for an extended discussion of the effects of this depression on the yeomanry as a class.

17.   The Carolina proprietors had a far clearer notion of the terms on which money was to be made from their colony than had been true of the London Company of sixty years before with regard to Virginia. They appear at the very outset to have fostered the establishment of large estates, and a number of such estates set up in the 1670's and 1680's were organized by Barbados men with first-hand plantation experience. See Gray, *History of Agriculture,* I, 324-25; also J. P. Thomas, "Barbadians in Early South Carolina," *South Carolina Historical Magazine,* XXXI (April, 1930), 89. Although a dominant staple was not to emerge until some time later, with rice and indigo, it seems to have been conceived in terms of large units to a degree never envisaged at a comparable stage in the development of Virginia. One index of this is quickly seen in the composition of the laboring population there; a little over a generation after the first settlements the ratio of Negro slaves to whites in the total population could be safely estimated at about one to one, whereas the same ratio would not be attained in Virginia until late in the eighteenth century. Greene and Harrington, *American Population,* pp. 124, 137.

18.   Quoted in Gray, *History of Agriculture,* I, 352.

19.   This is another point of view from which to consider the 1671 figure (cited in n. 14 above) on the Virginia slave population. The difference between the 300 Negroes of 1650 and the 2,000 of 1670 is substantial—nearly a sevenfold increase. According to Berkeley's testimony the importations over the previous seven years had not been more than two or three cargoes. If this were true, it would be safe to estimate that a significant number of that 2,000 must already have been native-born American Negroes. As for the period to which the above paragraph has reference—fifteen or twenty years later—the number of native-born must by then have increased considerably.

20.   Greene and Harrington, *American Population,* pp. 136-37; Gray, *History of Agriculture,* I, 349-50.

21.   As early as 1669 a Virginia law had declared it no felony if a master or overseer killed a slave who resisted punishment. According to the South Carolina code of 1712, the punishment for offering "any violence to any christian or white person, by striking, or the like" was a severe whipping for the first offense, branding for the second, and death for the third. Should the white man attacked be injured or maimed, the punishment was automatically death. The same act provided that a runaway slave be severely whipped for his first offense, branded for his second, his ears cut off for the third, and castrated for the fourth. It is doubtful whether such punishments were often used, but their very existence served to symbolize the relationship of absolute power over the slave's body. Hurd, *Law of Freedom and Bondage,* I, 232; Thomas Cooper and D. J. McCord (eds.), *Statutes at Large of South Carolina* (Columbia, S.C., 1836-41), VII, 357-59.

22.   Slaves in seventeenth-century Virginia had become, as a matter of actual practice, classed on the same footing as household goods and other personal property. The code of 1705 made them a qualified form of real estate, but that law was in 1726 amended by another which declared that slaves were "to pass as chattels." Bruce, *Economic History,* II, 99; Hurd, *Law of Freedom and Bondage,* I, 242. The South Carolina code of 1740 made them "chattels personal, in the hands of their owners and possessors and their executors, administrators and assigns, to all intents, constructions and purposes whatsoever. . . ." *Ibid.,* I, 303.

23.   Bruce (*Economic History,* II, 108) describes a will, written about 1680, in which a woman "bequeathed to one daughter, . . . a negress and the third child

to be born of her; to a second daughter, . . . the first and second child to be born of the same woman."

24. See Handlin and Handlin, "Origins of the Southern Labor System," p. 212. The Maryland law of 1671 could leave no possible doubt in this matter, declaring that any Christianized slave "is, are and shall att all tymes hereafter be adjudged Reputed deemed and taken to be and Remayne in Servitude and Bondage and subject to the same Servitude and Bondage to all intents and purposes as is hee shee they every or any of them was or were in and Subject vnto before such his her or their Becomeing Christian or Christians or Receiving of the Sacrament of Baptizme any opinion or other matter or thing to the Contrary in any wise Notwithstanding." William Hand Browne (ed.), *Archives of Maryland* (Baltimore, 1884), II, 272. See also n. 3 above.

25. What this meant to the Negro is admirably reflected in a book by Morgan Godwyn, an Anglican minister who served in the 1670's both in Barbados and in Virginia. Godwyn's book, *The Negro's and Indian's Advocate,* was a plea for the care of the Negro's soul. He attacked the planters for keeping religion from the slaves, for "not allowing their children *Baptism;* nor suffering them upon better terms than direct *Fornication,* to live with their Women, (for Wives, I may not call them, being never married). And accounting it Foppish, when Dead, to think of giving them *Christian,* or even decent Burial; that so their pretence for Brutifying them, might find no Contradiction" (p. 37). In Godwyn's eyes the planters were men "who for the most part do know no other God but money, nor Religion but Profit" (Preface). He quotes one Barbadian who "openly maintained . . . that Negroes were beasts, and had no more souls than beasts, and that religion did not concern them. Adding that they [his fellow Barbadians] went *not* to those parts to save souls, or propagate religion, but to get Money" (p. 39). Even the care of white souls in the colonies appears to have occupied a rather low order of concern. The Attorney-General of England in 1693 objected strenuously to the erection of a college in Virginia, though he was reminded of the need to educate young men for the ministry and was begged to consider the souls of the colonists. "Souls! Damn your souls," he replied, "make tobacco." Quoted in Wertenbaker, *Planters of Colonial Virginia*, p. 138. It is doubtful that the planters of Virginia were quite so brutal as the Barbadians in their attitude toward the Negro or in the management of their plantations, but even in Virginia Godwyn found that the idea of teaching religion to the Negro slave was thought "so idle and ridiculous, so utterly needless and unnecessary, that no Man can forfeit his Judgement more, than by any proposal looking or tending that way" (p. 172). That such an attitude had not changed by the eighteenth century is suggested by a piece in the *Athenian Oracle* of Boston in 1707 in which the writer declared, "Talk to a *Planter* of the *Soul* of a *Negro,* and he'll be apt to tell ye (or at least his actions speak it loudly) that the Body of one of them may be worth twenty pounds; but the Souls of an Hundred of them would not yield him one Farthing." Quoted in Marcus W. Jernegan, "Slavery and Conversion in the American Colonies," *American Historical Review,* XXI (April, 1916), 516.

26. For the control exercised over colonial institutional life by this planter elite, see Craven, *Southern Colonies,* pp. 153, 159, 170-72, 274-78; Philip A. Bruce, *Institutional History of Virginia in the Seventeenth Century* (New York: Putnam, 1910), I, 468; and George M. Brydon, *Virginia's Mother Church, and the Political Conditions under Which It Grew* (Richmond: Virginia Historical Society, 1947), I, 94-96, 232.

SLAVERY AND THE GENESIS OF AMERICAN RACE PREJUDICE

Carl N. Degler

Degler emphasizes that the *practice* of slavery preceded the law and traces the evolution from *de facto* to *de jure* slavery in the process of documenting his thesis that blacks were never fully equal to whites, bond or free, in the colonies. His analysis effectively challenges the Handlins' argument that blacks were defined and treated like white servants until the 1660s. He does not assert that any major proportion of blacks were immediately defined as slaves, but he does give evidence that in general their status was clearly inferior to that of white servants and that some were defined as slaves at least as early as 1640. That others were defined as indentured servants and released at the expiration of their indenture as late as the 1670s does not deny the existence of racially discriminatory practices almost from the beginning. The basis of this early status ambiguity is revealed by Phillips's comment that "the first comers were slaves in the hands of their maritime sellers; but they were not fully slaves in the hands of their Virginia buyers, for there was neither law nor custom then establishing the institution of slavery in the colony."[1]

Degler makes another significant contribution by raising the question of the causal relationship between slavery and prejudice. He tentatively concludes that the latter preceded and generated the former but he is justifiably criticized by Ruchames for vacillating on this point.[2] This vacillation stems from his failure to distinguish carefully prejudice from discrimination, ethnocentrism, and the ideology of racism.[3] This conceptual imprecision prevents accurate causal analysis and, accordingly, the precise differentiation of these concepts is a primary focus of concern of the concluding essay in this volume.

Two additional weaknesses in Degler's analysis should be mentioned. First, he is not sufficiently critical of Tannenbaum's thesis regarding Iberian slavery. Other writers have pointed out that the celebrated

Iberian code protecting the rights of slaves was perhaps more honored in the breach than in the adherence and, indeed, Degler himself in a later article shows that the differences between British and Iberian slavery have been grossly exaggerated.[4] Nonetheless, his general point regarding variations in the causal relation between slavery and prejudice or slavery and racism as a function of the structural context is well taken. Second, Degler's criticism of the Handlins in regard to the changing status of white servants seems misdirected. The bulk of the evidence suggests that their status did improve steadily in the last half of the seventeenth century. Failure to acknowledge this leads Degler to grossly underestimate the importance of the economic motive in the origin of slavery. He simply overlooks the fact that the institutionalization of slavery as a method of assuring abundant cheap labor was critically important to individual planters and to other major "users" of black labor well before black labor became vitally important to the economic well-being of any colony, North or South, as a whole.

The heated exchange between Degler and the Handlins (see note 3) points up additional needed corrections of specific points in both articles. Degler has elaborated some aspects of his analysis in his excellent book, *Out of Our Past* (New York: Harper and Row, 1959), but the strengths and weaknesses of the analysis are essentially the same as in the present selection.

Notes

1.   Ulrich B. Phillips quoted in Louis Ruchames, "Introduction: The Sources of Racial Thought in Colonial America" in *Racial Thought in America* (Amherst: University of Massachusetts Press, 1969), p. 22.

2.   *Ibid.,* pp. 13, 14.

3.   This conceptual difficulty is discussed in a subsequent exchange of letters to the editor by Degler and the Handlins in *Comparative Studies in Society and History* 2 (1959-1960): 488-95.

4.   Carl N. Degler, "Slavery in Brazil and the United States: An Essay in Comparative History," *American Historical Review* 75 (1970): 1004-28.

Over a century ago, Tocqueville named slavery as the source of the American prejudice against the Negro. Contrary to the situation in antiquity, he remarked: "Among the moderns the abstract and transient fact of slavery is fatally united with the physical and permanent fact of color." Furthermore, he wrote, though "slavery recedes" in some portions of the United States, "the prejudice to which it has given birth is immovable."[1] More modern observers of the American past have also stressed this causal connection between the institution of slavery and the color prejudice of Americans.[2] Moreover, it is patent to anyone conversant with the nature of American slavery, particularly as it functioned in the nineteenth century, that the impress of bondage upon the character and future of the Negro in the United States has been both deep and enduring.

But if one examines other societies which the Negro entered as a slave, it is apparent that the consequences of slavery have not always been those attributed to the American form. Ten years ago, for example, Frank Tannenbaum demonstrated that in the Spanish and Portuguese colonies in South America, slavery did not leave upon the freed Negro anything like the prejudicial mark which it did in the United States.[3] He and others[4] have shown that once the status of slavery was left behind, the Negro in the lands south of the Rio Grande was accorded a remarkable degree of social equality with the whites. In the light of such differing consequences, the role of slavery in the development of the American prejudice against the Negro needs to be reexamined, with particular attention paid to the historical details of origins.

I

Tannenbaum showed that in the Portuguese and Spanish colonies there were at least three historical forces or traditions which tended to prevent the attribution of inferiority to the Negro aside from the legal one of slavery. One was the continuance of the Roman law of slavery in the Iberian countries, another was the influence of the Roman Catholic Church, and the third was the long history—by Anglo-American standards—of contacts with darker-skinned peoples in the course of the Reconquest and the African explorations of the fifteenth and sixteenth centuries. Roman law, at least in its later forms, viewed slavery as a mere accident, of which anyone could be the victim. As such it tended to forestall the identification of the black man with slavery, thus permitting the Negro to escape from the stigma of his degraded status once he ceased to be a slave. The same end, Tannenbaum showed, was served by the Roman Church's insistence upon the equality of all Christians and by the long familiarity of the Iberians with Negroes and Moors.

Reprinted from *Comparative Studies in Society and History* 2 (October 1959): 49-66, by permission of Cambridge University Press.

In North America, of course, none of these forces was operative—a fact which partly explains the differing type of slavery and status for Negroes in the two places. But this cannot be the whole explanation since it is only negative. We know, in effect, what were the forces which permitted the slave and the Negro in South America to be treated as a human being, but other than the negative fact that these forces did not obtain in the North American colonies, we know little as to why the Negro as slave or freedman, occupied a degraded position compared with that of any white man. A more positive explanation is to be found in an examination of the early history of the Negro in North America.

It has long been recognized that the appearance of legal slavery in the laws of the English colonies was remarkably slow. The first mention does not occur until after 1660—some forty years after the arrival of the first Negroes. Lest we think that slavery existed in fact before it did in law, two historians have assured us recently that such was not the case. "The status of Negroes was that of servants," Oscar and Mary Handlin have written, "and so they were identified and treated down to the 1660's."[5] This late, or at least, slow development of slavery[6] complicates our problem. For if there was no slavery in the beginning, then we must account for its coming into being some forty years after the introduction of the Negro. There was no such problem in the history of slavery in the Iberian colonies, where the legal institution of slavery came in the ships with the first settlers.

The Handlins' attempt to answer the question as to why slavery was slow in appearing in the statutes is, to me, not convincing. Essentially their explanation is that by the 1660's, for a number of reasons which do not have to be discussed here, the position of the white servant was improving, while that of the Negroes was sinking to slavery. In this manner, the Handlins contend, Negro and white servants, heretofore treated alike, attained different status. There are at least two major objections to this argument. First of all, their explanation, by depending upon the improving position of white servants as it does, cannot apply to New England, where servants were of minor importance. Yet the New England colonies, like the Southern, developed a system of slavery for the Negro that fixed him in a position of permanent inferiority. The greatest weakness of the Handlins' case is the difficulty in showing that the white servant's position was improving during and immediately after the 1660's.

Without attempting to go into any great detail on the matter, several acts of the Maryland and Virginia legislatures during the 1660's and 1670's can be cited to indicate that an improving status for white servants was at best doubtful. In 1662, Maryland restricted a servant's travel without a pass to two miles beyond his master's house;[7] in 1671 the same colony lengthened the time of servants who arrived without indenture from four to five years.[8] Virginia in 1668 provided that a runaway could be corporally punished and also have additional time exacted from him.[9] If, as these instances suggest, the white servant's status was not improving, then we are left without an explanation for the differing status accorded white and Negro servants after 1660.

Actually, by asking why slavery developed late in the English colonies we are setting ourselves a problem which obscures rather than clarifies the primary question of why slavery in North America seemed to leave a different mark on the Negro than it did in South America. To ask why slavery in the English colonies produced discrimination against Negroes after 1660 is to make the tacit assumption that prior to the establishment of slavery there was none. If, instead, the question is put, "Which appeared first, slavery or discrimination?" then no prejudgment is made. Indeed, it now opens a possibility for answering the question as to why the slavery in the English colonies, unlike that in the Spanish and Portuguese, led to a caste position for Negroes, whether free or slave. In short, the recent work of the Handlins and the fact that slavery first appeared in the statutes of the English colonies forty years after the Negro's arrival, have tended to obscure the real possibility that the Negro was actually *never* treated as an equal of the white man, servant or free.

It is true that when Negroes were first imported into the English colonies there was no law of slavery and therefore whatever status they were to have would be the work of the future. This absence of a status for black men, which, it will be remembered was not true for the Spanish and Portuguese colonies, made it possible for almost any kind of status to be worked out. It was conceivable that they would be accorded the same status as white servants, as the Handlins have argued; it was also possible that they would not. It all depended upon the reactions of the people who received the Negroes.

It is the argument of this paper that the status of the Negro in the English colonies was worked out within a framework of discrimination; that from the outset, as far as the available evidence tells us, the Negro was treated as an inferior to the white man, servant or free. If this be true, then it would follow that as slavery evolved as a legal status, it reflected and included as a part of its essence, this same discrimination which white men had practised against the Negro all along and before any statutes decreed it. It was in its evolution, then, that American colonial slavery differed from Iberian, since in the colonies of Spain and Portugal, the legal status of the slave was fixed before the Negro came to the Americas. Moreover, in South America there were at least three major traditional safeguards which tended to protect the free Negro against being treated as an inferior. In summary, the peculiar character of slavery in the English colonies as compared with that in the Iberian, was the result of two circumstances. One, that there was no law of slavery at all in the beginning, and two, that discrimination against the Negro antedated the legal status of slavery. As a result, slavery, when it developed in the English colonies, could not help but be infused with the social attitude which had prevailed from the beginning, namely, that Negroes were inferior.

II

It is indeed true as the Handlins in their article have emphasized that before the seventeenth century the Negro was rarely called a slave. But this fact should not overshadow the historical evidence which points to the institution without employing the name. Because no discriminatory title is placed upon the Negro we must not think that he was being treated like a white servant; for there is too much evidence to the contrary. Although the growth of a fully developed slave law was slow, unsteady and often unarticulated in surviving records, this is what one would expect when an institution is first being worked out.[10] It is not the same however, as saying that no slavery or discrimination against the Negro existed in the first decades of the Negro's history in America.

As will appear from the evidence which follows, the kinds of discrimination visited upon Negroes varied immensely. In the early 1640's it sometimes stopped short of lifetime servitude or inheritable status — the two attributes of true slavery — in other instances it included both. But regardless of the form of discrimination, the important point is that from the 1630's up until slavery clearly appeared in the statutes in the 1660's, the Negroes were being set apart and discriminated against as compared with the treatment accorded Englishmen, whether servants or free.

The colonists of the early seventeenth century were well aware of a distinction between indentured servitude and slavery.[11] This is quite clear from the evidence in the very early years of the century. The most obvious means the English colonists had for learning of a different treatment for Negroes from that for white servants was the slave trade[12] and the slave systems of the Spanish and Portuguese colonies. As early as 1623, a voyager's book published in London indicated that Englishmen knew of the Negro as a slave in the South American colonies of Spain. The book told of the trade in "blacke people" who were "sold unto the Spaniard for him to carry into the West Indies, to remaine as slaves, either in their Mines or in any other servile uses, they in those countries put them to."[13] In the phrase "remaine as slaves" is the element of unlimited service.

The Englishmen's treatment of another dark-skinned, non-Christian people — the Indians — further supports the argument that a special and inferior status was accorded the Negro virtually from the first arrival. Indian slavery was practised in all of the English settlements almost from the beginning[14] and, though it received its impetus from the perennial wars between the races, the fact that an inferior and onerous service was established for the Indian makes it plausible to suppose that a similar status would be reserved for the equally different and pagan Negro.

The continental English could also draw upon other models of a differentiated status for Negroes. The earliest English colony to experiment with large numbers of Negroes in its midst was the shortlived settlement of Providence island, situated in the western Caribbean, just off the Mosquito Coast. By 1637, long before Barbados and the other British sugar islands utilized great numbers of Negroes, almost half of the population of this Puritan venture was black. Such a disproportion of races caused great alarm among the directors of the Company in London and repeated efforts were made to restrict the influx of blacks.[15] Partly because of its large numbers of Negroes, Old Providence became well known to the mainland colonies of Virginia and New England.[16] A. P. Newton has said that Old Providence

> forms the connecting link between almost every English colonising enterprise in the first half of the seventeenth century from Virginia and Bermuda to New England and Jamaica, and thus it is of much greater importance than its actual accomplishments would justify.[17]

Under such circumstances, it was to be expected that knowledge of the status accorded Negroes by these Englishmen would be transmitted to those on the mainland with whom they had such close and frequent contact.

Though the word "slave" is never applied to the Negroes on Providence, and only rarely the word "Servant," "Negroes," which was the term used, were obviously *sui generis*; they were people apart from the English. The Company, for example, distrusted them. "Association [Tortuga island] was deserted thro' their mutinous conduct," the Company told the Governor of Old Providence in 1637. "Further trade for them prohibited, with exceptions, until Providence be furnished with English."[18] In another communication the Company again alluded to the dangers of "too great a number" of Negroes on the island and promised to send 200 English servants over to be exchanged for as many Negroes.[19] A clearer suggestion of the difference in status between an English servant and a

Negro is contained in the Company's letter announcing the forwarding of the 200 servants. As a further precaution against being overwhelmed by Negroes, it was ordered that a "family of fourteen" — which would include servants—was not to have more than six Negroes. "The surplusage may be sold to the poor men who have served their apprenticeship."[20] But the Negroes, apparently, were serving for life.

Other British island colonies in the seventeenth century also provide evidence which is suggestive of this same development of a differing status for Negroes, even though the word "slave" was not always employed. Though apparently the first Negroes were only brought to Bermuda in 1617,[21] as early as 1623 the Assembly passed an "Act to restrayne the insolencies of Negroes." The blacks were accused of stealing and of carrying "secretly cudgels, and other weapons and working tools." Such weapons, it was said, were "very dangerous and not meete to be suffered to be carried by such Vassals . . ." Already, in other words, Negroes were treated as a class apart. To reinforce this, Negroes were forbidden to "weare any weapon in the daytyme" and they were not to be outside or off their master's land during "any undue hours in the night tyme. . . ."[22]

During the 1630's there were other indications that Negroes were treated as inferiors. As early as 1630 some Negroes' servitude was already slavery in that it was for life and inheritable. One Lew Forde possessed a Negro man, while the Company owned his wife; the couple had two children. Forde desired "to know which of the said children properly belong to himself and which to the Company." The Council gave him the older child and the Company received the other.[23] A letter of Roger Wood in 1634 suggests that Negroes were already serving for life, for he asked to have a Negro, named Sambo, given to him, so that through the Negro "I or myne may *ever* be able" to carry on an old feud with an enemy who owned Sambo's wife.[24]

There is further evidence of discrimination against Negroes in later years. A grand jury in 1652 cited one Henry Gaunt as being "suspected of being unnecessarily conversant with negro women" — he had been giving them presents. The presentment added that "if he hath not left his familiarity with such creatures, it is desired that such abominations be inquired into, least the land mourne for them."[25] The discrimination reached a high point in 1656 when the Governor proclaimed that "any Englishman" who discovered a Negro walking about at night without a pass, was empowered to "kill him then and theire without mercye." The proclamation further ordered that all free Negroes "shall be banished from these Islands, never to return eyther by purchase of any man, or otherwise. . . ."[26] When some Negroes asked the Governor for their freedom in 1669, he denied they had any such claim, saying that they had been "purchased by" their masters "without condition or limitation. It being likewise soe practised in these American plantations and other parts of the world."[27]

In Barbados Negroes were already slaves when Richard Ligon lived there in 1647-50. "The Iland," he later wrote, "is divided into three sorts of men, viz: Masters, servants, and slaves. The slaves and their posterity, being subject to their masters for ever," in contrast to the servants who are owned "but for five years. . . ."[28] On that island as at Bermuda it was reported that Negroes were not permitted "to touch or handle any weapons."[29]

On Jamaica, as on the other two islands, a clear distinction was made between the status of the Negro and that of the English servant. In 1656 one resident of the island wrote the Protector in England urging the importation of African Negroes because then, he said, "the planters would have to pay for them" and therefore "they would have an interest in preserving their lives, *which was* wanting in the case of bond servants. . . ."[30]

It is apparent, then, that the colonists on the mainland had ample opportunity before 1660 to learn of a different status for black men from that for Englishmen, whether servants or free.

III

From the evidence available it would seem that the Englishmen in Virginia and Maryland learned their lesson well. This is true even though the sources available on the Negro's position in these colonies in the early years are not as abundant as we would like. It seems quite evident that the black man was set apart from the white on the continent just as he was being set apart in the island colonies. For example, in Virginia in 1630, one Hugh Davis was "soundly whipped before an Assembly of Negroes and others for abusing himself to the dishonor of God and the shame of Christians, by defiling his body in lying with a negro."[31] The unChristian-like character of such behavior was emphasized ten years later when Robert Sweet was ordered to do penance in Church for "getting a negro with child."[32] An act passed in the Maryland legislature in 1639 indicated that at that early date the word "slave" was being applied to non-Englishmen. The act was an enumeration of the rights of "all Christian inhabitants (slaves excepted)."[33] The slaves referred to could have been only Indians or Negroes,[34] since all white servants were Christians. It is also significant of the differing treatment of the two races that though Maryland and Virginia very early in their history enacted laws fixing limits to the terms for servants who entered without written contracts, Negroes were never included in such protective provisions.[35] The first of such laws were placed upon the books in 1639 in Maryland and 1643 in Virginia; in the Maryland statute, it was explicitly stated: "Slaves excepted."[36]

In yet another way, Negroes and slaves were singled out for special status in the years before 1650. A Virginia law of 1640 provided that "all masters" should try to furnish arms to themselves and "all those of their families which shall be capable of arms" — which would include servants — "(excepting negros)."[37] Not until 1648 did Maryland get around to such a prohibition, when it was provided that no guns should be given to "any Pagan for killing meate or to any other use," upon pain of a heavy fine.[38] At no time were white servants denied the right to bear arms; indeed, as these statutes inform us, they were enjoined to possess weapons.[39]

One other class of discriminatory acts against Negroes in Virginia and Maryland before 1660 also deserves to be noticed. Three different times before 1660 — in 1643, 1644 and 1658 — the Virginia assembly (and in 1654, the Maryland legislature) included Negro and Indian women among the "tithables." But white servant women were never placed in such a category,[40] inasmuch as they were not expected to work in the fields. From the beginning, it would seem, Negro women, whether free or bond, were treated by the law differently from white women servants.[41]

It is not until the 1640's that evidence of a status for Negroes akin to slavery, and, therefore, something more than mere discrimination begins to appear in the sources. Two cases of punishment for runaway servants in 1640 throw some light on the working out of a differentiated status for Negroes. The first case concerned three runaways, of whom two were white men and the third a Negro. All three were given thirty lashes, with the white men having the terms owed their masters extended a year, at the completion of which they were to work for the colony for three more years. The other, "being a Negro named John Punch shall serve his said master or his assigns for the time of his natural Life here or elsewhere."[42] Not only was the Negro's punishment the most severe, and for no apparent reason, but he was, in effect, reduced to slavery. It is also clear, however, that up until the issuing of the sentence, he must have had the status of a servant.

The second case, also of 1640, suggests that by that date some Negroes were already slaves. Six white men and a Negro were implicated in a plot to run away. The punishments meted out varied, but Christopher Miller "a dutchman" (a prime agent in the business) "was given the harshest treatment of all": thirty stripes, burning with an "R" on the cheek, a shackle placed on his leg for a year "and longer if said master

shall see cause" and seven years of service for the colony upon completion of his time due his master. The only other one of the seven plotters
to receive the stripes, the shackle and the "R" was the Negro Emanuel,
but, significantly, he did not receive any sentence of work for the colony.
Presumably he was already serving his master for a life-time — *i.e.*, he
was a slave.[43] About this time in Maryland it does not seem to have been
unusual to speak of Negroes as slaves, for in 1642 one "John Skinner
mariner" agreed "to deliver unto . . . Leonard Calvert, fourteen negro-
men-slaves and three women-slaves."[44]

From a proceeding before the House of Burgesses in 1666 it appears
that as early as 1644 that body was being called upon to determine who
was a slave. The Journal of the House for 1666 reports that in 1644 a
certain "mulata" bought "as a slave for Ever" was adjudged by the
Assembly "no slave and but to serve as other Christian servants do and
was freed in September 1665."[45] Though no reason was given for the
verdict, from the words "other Christian servants" it is possible that
he was a Christian, for it was believed in the early years of the English
colonies that baptism rendered a slave free. In any case, the Assembly
uttered no prohibition of slavery as such and the owner was sufficiently
surprised and aggrieved by the decision to appeal for recompense from
the Assembly, even though the Negro's service was twenty-one years,
an unheard of term for a "Christian servant."[46]

In early seventeenth century inventories of estates, there are two
distinctions which appear in the reckoning of the value of servants and
Negroes. Uniformly, the Negroes were more valuable, even as children,
than any white servant. Secondly, the naming of a servant is usually
followed by the number of years yet remaining to his service; for the
Negroes no such notation appears. Thus in an inventory in Virginia in
1643, a 22-year old white servant, with eight years still to serve, was
valued at 1,000 pounds of tobacco, while a "negro boy" was rated at
3,000 pounds and a white boy with seven years to serve was listed as
worth 700 pounds. An eight-year old Negro girl was calculated to be
worth 2,000 pounds. On another inventory in 1655, two good men
servants with four years to serve were rated at 1,300 pounds of tobacco,
and a woman servant with only two years to go was valued at 800
pounds. Two Negro boys, however, who had no limit set to their terms,
were evaluated at 4,100 pounds apiece, and a Negro girl was said to be
worth 5,500 pounds.[47]

These great differences in valuation of Negro and white "servants"
strongly suggest, as does the failure to indicate term of service for the
Negroes, that the latter were slaves at least in regard to life-time service.
Beyond a question, there was some service which these blacks were

rendering which enhanced their value — a service, moreover, which was not or could not be exacted from the whites. Furthermore, a Maryland deed of 1649 adumbrated slave status not only of life-time term, but of inheritance of status. Three Negroes "and all their issue both male and female" were deeded.[48]

Russell and Ames culled from the Virginia court records of the 1640's and 1650's several instances of Negroes held in a status that can be called true slavery. For example, in 1646 a Negro woman and a Negro boy were sold to Stephen Charlton to be of use to him and his "heyers etc. for ever." A Negro girl was sold in 1652 "with her Issue and pro- duce . . . and their services forever." Two years later a Negro girl was sold to one Armsteadinger "and his heyers . . . forever with all her in- crease both male and female."[49] For March 12, 1655 the minutes of the Council and General Court of Virginia contain the entry, "Mulatto held to be a slave and appeal taken."[50] Yet this is five years before Negro slavery is even implied in the statutes and fifteen before it is declared. An early case of what appears to be true slavery was found by Miss Ames on the Virginia eastern shore. In 1635 two Negroes were brought to the area; over twenty years later, in 1656, the widow of the master was bequeathing the child of one of the original Negroes and the other Negro and her children.[51] This was much more than mere servitude — the term was longer than twenty years and apparently the status was inheritable.

Wesley Frank Craven, in his study of the seventeenth-century Southern colonies, has concluded that in the treatment of the Negro "the trend from the first was toward a sharp distinction between him and the white servant."[52] In view of the evidence presented here, this seems a reason- able conclusion.

Concurrently with these examples of onerous service or actual slavery of Negroes, there were of course other members of the race who did gain their freedom.[53] But the presence of Negroes rising out of servitude to freedom[54] does not destroy the evidence that others were sinking into slavery; it merely underscores the unsteady evolution of a slave status. The supposition that the practice of slavery long antedated the law is strengthened by the tangential manner in which recognition of Negro slavery first appeared in the Virginia statutes.[55] It occurred in 1660 in a law dealing with punishments for runaway servants, where casual ref- erence was made to those "negroes who are incapable of making satis- faction by addition of time,"[56] since they were already serving for life.

Soon thereafter, as various legal questions regarding the status of Negroes came to the fore, the institution was further defined by statute law. In 1662 Virginia provided that the status of the offspring of a white man and a Negro would follow that of the mother — an interesting and unexplained departure from the common law and a reversion to Roman law. The same law stated that "any christian" fornicating "with a negro man or woman . . . shall pay double the fines imposed by the former act." Two years later Maryland prescribed service for Negroes "durante vita" and provided for hereditary status to descend through the father. Any free white woman who married a slave was to serve her hubsand's master for the duration of the slave's life, and her children would serve the master until they were thirty years of age. Presumably, no penalty was to be exacted of a free white man who married a Negro slave.[57]

As early as 1669 the Virginia law virtually washed its hands of protecting the Negro held as a slave. It allowed punishment of refractory slaves up to and including accidental death, relieving the master, explicitly, of any fear of prosecution, on the assumption that no man would "destroy his owne estate."[58]

In fact by 1680 the law of Virginia had erected a high wall around the Negro. One discerns in the phrase "any negro or other slave" how the word "negro" had taken on the meaning of slave. Moreover, in the act of 1680 one begins to see the lineaments of the later slave codes. No Negro may carry any weapon of any kind, nor leave his master's grounds without a pass, nor shall "any negroe or other slave . . . presume to lift his hand in opposition against any christian," and if a Negro runs away and resists recapture it "shalbe lawful for such person or persons to kill said negroe or slave. . . ."[59]

Yet it would be a quarter of a century before Negroes would comprise even a fifth of the population of Virginia. Thus long before slavery or black labor became an important part of the Southern economy, a special and inferior status had been worked out for the Negroes who came to the English colonies. Unquestionably it was a demand for labor which dragged the Negro to American shores, but the status which he acquired here cannot be explained by reference to that economic motive. Long before black labor was as economically important as unfree white labor, the Negro had been consigned to a special discriminatory status which mirrored the social discrimination Englishmen practised against him.[60]

IV

In the course of the seventeenth century New Englanders, like Southerners, developed a system of slavery which seemed permanently to fasten its stigma upon the Negro race. But because of the small number of Negroes in the northern provinces, the development of a form of slavery, which left a caste in its wake, cannot be attributed to pressure from increasing numbers of blacks, or even from an insistent demand for cheap labor. Rather it seems clearly to be the consequence of the general social discrimination against the Negro. For in the northern region, as in the southern, discrimination against the Negro preceded the evolution of a slave status and by that fact helped to shape the form that institution would assume.

References to the status of the Negroes in New England in this period are scattered, but, as was true of the Southern provinces, those references which are available suggest that from the earliest years a lowly, differential status, if not slavery itself, was reserved and recognized for the Negro — and the Indian, it might be added. The earliest date asserted in the sources for the existence of Negro slavery in Massachusetts is that of 1639. John Josselyn tells of a Negro woman held on Noddles Island in Boston harbor. Her master sought to mate her with another Negro, Josselyn says, but she kicked her prospective lover out of the bed, saying that such behavior was "beyond her slavery. . . ."[61] Though the first legal code of Massachusetts, the Body of Liberties of 1641, prohibited "bond-slavery" for the inhabitants, it clearly permitted enslavement of those who are "sold to us,"[62] which would include Negroes brought in by the international slave trade.[63]

Such use of Negroes was neither unknown nor undesirable to the Puritans. Emanuel Downing wrote to John Winthrop in 1645 about the desirability of a war against the Indians so that captives might be taken who, in turn, could be exchanged

> for Moores, which wilbe more gayneful pilladge for us then [*sic*] wee conceive, for I doe not see how wee can thrive untill wee gett into a stock of slaves sufficient to doe all our business, for our children's children will hardly see this great Continent filled with people, soe that our servants will still desire freedome for themselves, and not stay but for verie great wages. And I suppose you know verie well how we shall maynteyne 20 Moores cheaper than one English servant.[64]

The following year the Commissioners of the United Colonies recommended that in order to spare the colonies the cost of imprisoning contumacious Indians they should be given over to the Englishmen whom they had damaged or "be shipped out and exchanged for Negroes as the cause will justly serve."[65] Negroes were here being equated with Indians who were being bound out as prisoners: this was treatment decidedly a cut lower than that visited upon white servants.[66] That enslavement of Negroes was well known in New England by the middle of the century at the latest is revealed by the preamble to an act of Warwick and Providence colonies in 1652. It was said that it "is a common course practised amongst Englishmen to buy negers, to that end they may have them for service or slaves forever. . . ."[67]

By mid-century, Negroes were appearing in the inventories of estates and, significantly, the valuation placed upon them was very close to that found in Virginia inventories of the same period. Their worth is always much more than that of a white servant. Thus in 1650 "a neager Maide" was valued at £ 25; in 1657 the well-known merchant, Robert Keayne left "2 negros and a negro child" estimated to be worth £ 30. "A negro boy servant" was set at £ 20 in an estate of 1661.[68] A further indication of the property character of Negroes was the attachment by the constable of Salem in 1670 of a Negro boy "Seasar" as the "proper goods of the said Powell."[69]

Despite the small numbers of Negroes in New England in this early period, the colonies of that region followed the example of the Southern and insular provinces in denying arms to the blacks in their midst — a discrimination which was never visited upon the English servant. In 1652 Massachusetts provided that Indians and Negroes could train in the militia the same as whites, but this apparently caused friction. The law was countermanded in 1656 by the statement "henceforth no negroes or Indians, altho servants of the English, shalbe armed or permitted to trayne."[70] Although as late as 1680 it was officially reported to London that there were no more than thirty "slaves" in Connecticut, that colony in 1660 excluded Indians and "negar servants" from the militia and "Watch and Ward."[71]

Edward Randolph in 1676 reported that there were a few indentured servants in Massachusetts "and not above two hundred slaves," by which he meant Negroes, for he said "they were brought from Guinea and Madagascar."[72] But it was not until 1698 that the phrase "Negro slave" actually appeared in the Massachusetts statutes.[73] The practice of slavery was preceding the law in Massachusetts precisely as it had in the South. Though an official report to London in 1680 distinguished between Negro slaves and servants in Connecticut,[74] the law of that colony did not bother to define the institution of slavery. Indeed, as late as 1704, the Governor gave it as his opinion that all children born of "negro bond-women are themselves in like condition, i.e., born in servitude," though he admitted that there was no statute which said so. His contention was, however, that such legislation was "needless, because of the constant practice by which they are held as such. . . ."[75]

During the last years of the seventeenth century, laws of Connecticut and Massachusetts continued to speak of Negroes as "servants," but it was very clear that the Negro's status was not being equated with that of the white servant. The General Court of Connecticut observed in 1690 that "many persons of this Colony doe . . . purchase negroe servants" and, since these servants run away, precautions have to be taken against such eventualities. It was therefore laid down that all "negroe or negroes shall" be required to have a pass in order to be outside the town bounds. Any inhabitant could stop a Negroe, free or slave, and have him brought before a magistrate if the black man were found to be without such a pass. Moreover, all ferrymen, upon pain of fine, were to deny access to their ferries to all Negroes who could not produce a pass.[76] Massachusetts in 1698 forbade trade with "any Indian, or negro servant or slave, or other known dissolute, lewd, and disorderly person, of whom there is just cause of suspicion."[77]

By the early years of the eighteenth century, the laws of Connecticut and Massachusetts had pretty well defined the Negro's subordinate position in society. Massachusetts acted to restrict the manumission of slaves by providing in 1703 that "molatto or negro slaves" could be freed only if security was given that they would not be chargeable upon the community. Another law set a curfew upon Indians, mulattoes and Negroes for nine o'clock each night. In 1705 Massachusetts became the only New England province to prohibit sexual relations between Negroes and mulattoes and Englishmen or those of "any other Christian nation."[78] Moreover, "any negro or mulatto" presuming to "smite or strike" an English person or any of another Christian nation would be "severely whipped."[79] In 1717 Negroes were barred from holding land in Connecticut.[80]

Thus, like the colonists to the South, the New Englanders enacted into law, in the absence of any prior English law of slavery, their recognition of the Negroes as different and inferior. This was the way of the seventeenth century; only with a later conception of the brotherhood of all men would such legal discrimination begin to recede; but by then, generations of close association between the degraded status of slavery and black color would leave the same prejudice against the Negro in the North that it did in the South.

It would seem, then, that instead of slavery being the root of the discrimination visited upon the Negro in America, slavery was itself molded by the early colonists' discrimination against the outlander. In the absence of any law of slavery or commandments of the Church to the contrary — as was true of Brazil and Spanish-America — the institution of slavery into which the African was placed in the English colonies inevitably mirrored that discrimination and, in so doing, perpetuated it.

Once the English embodied their discrimination against the Negro in slave law, the logic of the law took over. Through the early eighteenth century, judges and legislatures in all the colonies elaborated the law along the discriminatory lines laid down in the amorphous beginnings. In doing so, of course, especially in the South, they had the added incentive of perpetuating and securing a labor system which by then had become indispensable to the economy. The cleavage between the races was in that manner deepened and hardened into the shape which became quite familiar by the nineteenth century. In due time, particularly in the South, the correspondence between the black man and slavery would appear so perfect that it would be difficult to believe that the Negro was fitted for anything other than the degraded status in which he was almost always found. It would also be forgotten that the discrimination had begun long before slavery had come upon the scene.

Notes

1. *Democracy in America* (New York, 1948), I, 358-60.

2. Most recently, Oscar and Mary Handlin, "The Origins of the Southern Labor System," *William and Mary Quarterly,* 3rd Series, VII (April, 1950), 199-222.

3. *Slave and Citizen; The Negro in the Americas* (New York, 1947).

4. Gilberto Freyre, *Brazil: An Interpretation* (New York, 1945), pp. 96-101; Donald Pierson, *Negroes in Brazil* (Chicago, 1942), pp. 330-6.

5. Handlin, "Origins of Southern Labor," p. 203.

6. Virtually all historians of the institution agree on this. See U. B. Phillips, *American Negro Slavery* (New York, 1933), pp. 74-77; J. C. Ballagh, *History of Slavery in Virginia* (Baltimore, 1902), pp. 28-35. More recently, however, Susie Ames, *Studies of the Virginia Eastern Shore in the Seventeenth Century* (Richmond, 1940), pp. 101-10 and W. F. Craven, *Southern Colonies in the Seventeenth Century, 1607-1689* (Baton Rouge, 1949), pp. 217-9 have more than suggested that it is possible that slavery existed in Virginia almost from the very beginning of the Negro's history in America.

7. *Maryland Archives,* I, 451.

8. *Ibid.,* II, 335.

9. W. W. Hening, *Statutes at Large; being a Collection of all the Laws of Virginia* ... (Richmond, 1809), II, 266.

10. John C. Hurd, *Law of Freedom and Bondage in the United States* (Boston, 1858-61), I, 163, points out that the trade "in negroes as merchandise was . . . recognized as legitimate by European governments, without any direct sanction from positive legislation, but rested on the general customs among nations, known both in municipal and international private law." Furthermore, he reported that none of the colonies ever found it necessary to pass laws legalizing slavery. He quotes from the Connecticut Code of 1821: "Slavery was never directly established by statute; but has been indirectly sanctioned by various statutes and frequently recognized by courts, so that it may be said to have been established by law." I, 212 n.

11. The Handlins, "Origins of Southern Labor," pp. 203-4, have argued that in the early years slavery meant nothing more than a low form of labor and that it

had no basis in law. This is true insofar as statute law is concerned, but, as will appear later, in practice quite a different situation obtained.

12.   The Handlins, "Origins of Southern Labor," pp. 203-4, argue that the continental colonies could not have learned about a different status for Negroes from that of white servants from the slave trade because, they say, "the company of Royal Adventurers referred to their cargo as 'Negers,' 'Negro-servants,' 'Servants . . . from Africa,' or 'Negro Persons' but rarely as slaves." They overlook, however, abundant references to Negro slaves in the correspondence of the contemporary Royal African Company. Thus in 1663 a warrant for that company refers to "negro slaves" as a part of its monopoly. *Calendar of State Papers, Colonial,* V, 121; see also p. 204. In that same year the Privy Council wrote that the Spanish were "seeking to trade with our island of Barbada for a supply of Negro Slaves . . . ." And then the letter referred to a "supply of Negro Servants," and later still "for every Negro Person a Slave" and then "all such Negro Slaves." K. Donnan, *Documents Illustrative of the History of the Slave Trade,* (Washington, 1930), I, 161-2.

13.   Quoted in Donnan, *Slave Trade,* I, 125.

14.   See particularly, Almon Lauber, *Indian Slavery in Colonial Times Within the Present Limits of the United States* (New York, 1913), Chap. IV.

15.   A. P. Newton, *The Colonising Activities of the English Puritans* (New Haven, 1914), p. 258.

16.   *Ibid.,* p. 260.

17.   A. P. Newton, *The European Nations in the West Indies, 1493-1688* (London, 1933), pp. 173-4.

18.   *Calendar of State Papers, Colonial,* I, 249.

19.   *Ibid.,* pp. 277-8.

20.   *Ibid.,* pp. 278-9.

21.   J. H. Lefroy, *Memorials of the Discovery and Early Settlement of the Bermudas or Somers Islands, 1515-1685* (London, 1877), I, 127.

22.   *Ibid.,* I, 308-9.

23.   *Ibid.,* I, 505. Cases in 1676 and 1685 indicate that this practice of dividing the children became the standard practice under slavery in a colony where the parcels of slaves were so small that few masters could have a spouse on their plantations for each of his adult Negroes. *Ibid.,* II, 427, 547-8.

24.   *Ibid.,* I, 539. Emphasis added.

25.   *Ibid.,* II, 30.

26.   *Ibid.,* II, 95-6.

27.   *Ibid.,* II, 293. As late as 1662 the perpetual character of slavery for Negroes was being obscured by their serving for ninety-nine years. See *Ibid.,* II, 166, 184.

28.   Richard Ligon, *A True and Exact History of the Island of Barbados* (London, 1657), p. 43.

29.   *Ibid.,* p. 46.

30.   Quoted in Richard B. Morris, *Government and Labor in Early America* (New York, 1946), p. 499. As early as 1633, on the island of Tortuga, the separation of whites, servants or no, from Negroes was in evidence. At a time of anarchy on the island, "The eighty-odd Englishmen in the island had formed a council among themselves for the government of the colony and to keep in subjection the one hundred and fifty negroes, twenty-seven of whom were the company's property." Newton, *Colonising Activities,* p. 214.

31. Hening, *Statutes,* I, 146.

32. *Ibid.,* I, 552.

33. *Maryland Archives,* I, 80.

34. It is not known whether there were any Negroes in Maryland at that date. J. R. Brackett, *The Negro in Maryland* (Baltimore, 1889), p. 26 found no evidence of Negroes before 1642.

35. Handlin, "Origins of Southern Labor," p. 210; Hening, *Statutes,* I, 411, 539. This is not to say that some Negroes were not indentured servants, for there is evidence to show that limited service was enjoyed by some black men. This was true even during the period after the recognition of slavery in the statutes. In October, 1673, for instance, the Council and General Court of Virginia ordered that "Andrew Moore A Servant Negro," who asserted he was to serve only five years, and who had the support of several "oathes," was declared free. Moreover, his erstwhile master was compelled to "pay him Corne and Clothes According to the custome of the country" and 400 pounds of tobacco and cask for the Negro's service since his time expired and to "pay costs." *Minutes of the Council and General Court of Colonial Virginia,* edited by H. R. McIlwaine (Richmond, 1924), p. 354.

36. Hening, *Statutes,* I, 257; *Maryland Archives,* I, 80.

37. *William and Mary Quarterly,* Second Series, IV (July, 1924), 147.

38. *Maryland Archives,* I, 233.

39. Handlin, "Origins of Southern Labor," p. 209, implies that these early restrictions were later repealed. "Until the 1660's," the Handlins write, "the statutes on the Negroes were not at all unique. Nor did they add up to a decided trend." In substantiation of this point they instance the "fluctuations" in the Negro's right to bear arms. Their cited evidence, however, does not sustain this generalization. Four references to the statutes of Virginia are made; of these four, only two deal with arms bearing. The first one, that referred to in the text above, indicates that Negroes were not to be armed. The other reference is at best an ambiguous statement about who is taxable and which of the taxables are to serve in the militia. It in no wise constitutes either a repeal or even a contradiction of the earlier statute, which, therefore, must be presumed to be controlling. Their evidence for "fluctuations" in the right of Indians to bear arms suffers from the same weakness of sources. The two statutes they cite merely confirm the right of certain Indians to possess guns and deny them to other Indians. No "fluctuation" in rights is involved.

40. Hening, *Statutes,* I, 242, 292, 455; *Maryland Archives,* I, 342. The statement in Handlin, "Origins of Southern Labor," p. 217 n, that the "first sign of discrimination was in 1668 when white but not Negro women were exempt," is therefore erroneous.

41. In his well-known emigrant pamphlet, *Leah and Rachel* (London, 1656), p. 12, John Hammond casts some interesting light on contemporary opinion regarding women who worked in the fields in Virginia. "The Women are not (as is reported) put into the ground to work, but occupie such domestique imployments and housewifery as in England . . . yet some wenches that are nasty, beastly and not fit to be so imployed are put into the ground . . ."

42. *Minutes of the Council,* p. 466.

43. *Ibid.,* p. 467.

44. Catterall, *Judicial Cases,* I, 57 n. Mrs. Catterall does not think any Negroes came under this agreement, but the language itself testifies to an accepted special status for Negroes at that time.

45. *Journals of the House of Burgesses of Virginia,* edited by H. R. McIlwaine (Richmond, 1914), II, 34.

46. *Ibid.,* II, 34-5. His plea, however, was turned down, the Assembly not knowing "any Reason why the Publick should be answerable for the inadvertency of the Buyer . . ."

47. John H. Russell, *The Free Negro in Virginia, 1619-1865* (Baltimore, 1913), p. 36. Russell concludes from his survey of inventories of estates for this early period that Negroes were valued from 20 to 30 pounds sterling, "while white servants of the longest term . . . receive a valuation of not more than £ 15 sterling." *Ibid.,* p. 35. Catterall, *Judicial Cases,* I, 58 n, upon concluding her investigation of inventories of estates, picked 1644 as the date at which " 'servant' standing alone, had generally become synonomous with 'white servant' and 'negro' with 'negro slave', . . ."

48. Catterall, *Judicial Cases,* IV, 9.

49. Russell, *Free Negro in Virginia,* pp. 34-5. He also reports the instance of a Negro by the name of John Casor who was claimed, in 1655, as a "Negro for his life," but he was rescued from such a status by two witnesses testifying that he had an indenture. *Ibid.,* pp. 32-3.

50. *Minutes of the Council,* p. 504. Handlin, "Origins of Southern Labor," p. 216, in arguing the late development of a different status for Negroes as compared with whites in Virginia, says: "As late as the 1660's the law had not even a word to describe the children of mixed marriages. But two decades later, the term mulatto is used . . ." Such a statement is obviously misleading, for though the Handlins presumably mean statute law, the decisions of the General Court were also "law." The *Oxford English Dictionary* cites references for the word "mulatto" for 1595, 1613 and 1657.

51. Ames, *Eastern Shore,* p. 105.

52. Craven, *Southern Colonies,* p. 219.

53. See especially Russell, *Free Negro in Virginia,* pp. 36-9. See also Brackett, *Negro in Maryland,* p. 37.

54. An indication that even freedom for the Negro carried certain disabilities is afforded by an instance reported by Ames, *Eastern Shore,* p. 107 from the Northampton County court records of 1654. For contempt of authority and abuse of certain persons, Anthony Longoe, a Negro, was ordered, almost twenty years after his release from service, to receive "thirty lashes now applied, and tomorrow morning thirty lashes more."

55. A year earlier, 1659/60, a statute dealing with trade with the Dutch promised remission of a ten shilling tax if "the said Dutch or other forreiners shall import any negro slaves . . . ." This is the first reference in the Virginia statutes to Negroes as slaves. Hening, *Statutes,* I, 540.

56. Hening, *Statutes,* II, 26. The equivalent Maryland statute (1663) referred to "Negroes and other Slaves, who are incapeable of makeing Stisfaction [*sic*] by Addition of Tyme . . ." *Maryland Archives,* I, 489.

57. Hening, *Statutes,* II, 170; *Maryland Archives,* I, 533-4. Handlin, "Origins of Southern Labor," p. 215 sees the genesis of these prohibitions in concern over status rather than in objection to racial intermarriage. This seems to be true for Maryland. But in speaking of the Virginia circumstances they write: "It was to guard against the complications of status that the laws after 1691 forbade 'spurious' or illegitimate mixed marriages of the slave and the free . . ." Actually, however, the Virginia statute of 1691 (Hening, *Statutes,* III, 87) clearly aimed at the prevention of "abominable mixture and spurious issue" by forbidding marriage of

"English or other white man or woman being free" with "a negro, mulatto or Indian man or women *bond or free.*" (Emphasis added.)

58. Hening, *Statutes,* II, 270. The working out of the exact legal status of slave property, however, was a slow one. A Virginia law of 1705 (Hening, *Statutes,* III, 333-4), declared "Negro, Mulatto and Indian Slaves . . . to be real estate," but there were a number of exceptions which suggest the later chattel nature of property in slaves. In South Carolina slaves were decreed to be real estate in 1690 and not until 1740 were they said to be legally chattels. Hurd, *Law of Freedom,* I, 297, 303.

59. Hening, *Statutes,* II, 481-2.

60. Like Virginia, Maryland developed its slave law and status long before the Negroes had become an important aspect of the labor force. As late as 1712, Negroes made up only slightly more than 20 per cent of the population. Brackett, *Negro in Maryland,* pp. 38-9. If Virginia was slow in bringing her slave practices out into the open air of the statute books, the same could not be said of Carolina. In the Fundamental Constitutions, drawn up in 1669, it is stated in article CX that "Every freeman of Carolina shall have absolute power and authority over his negro slaves, of what opinion or religion so ever."

61. Massachusetts Historical Society, *Collections,* Third Series, III, 231. There is no doubt that there were Negroes at this time in Massachusetts, for in 1638 Winthrop reported that Capt. Peirce brought back from Old Providence "some cotton, and tobacco and negroes . . ." John Winthrop, *History of New England,* James Savage, ed. (Boston, 1853), I, 305.

62. Some events of 1645 indicate that those few words were of crucial importance to the Puritans. That year some Negroes were brought to Massachusetts by a Captain Smith and they were ordered by the General Court to be returned to Africa on the ground that their importation constituted "the hainous and crying sinn of man-stealing." But this was man-stealing only because Smith and his men had captured the Negroes in a raid, instead of buying them from traders. *Records of Massachusetts,* III, 48, 58, 84.

63. Very early in New England history the concept of perpetual servitude — one of the distinguishing marks of slavery — appears in the records. In 1637 Roger Williams, in pleading for the lives of the captured Indians during the Pequot War, alludes to "pcrpetuall slaverie" as an alternative to their execution. Massachusetts Historical Society, *Collections,* Fourth Series, VI, 214. The will of John Winthrop, written in 1639, deeded to his son Adam "my island" and "also my Indians there and my boat and such household as is there." Robert C. Winthrop, *Life and Letters of John Winthrop* (Boston, 1869), II, 252. Though at least three white men were sentenced to "slavery" in Massachusetts in the early years, in at least two cases this did not, in fact, amount to perpetuity, for they appear to have been released in a short time. The use of the word as a special form of service, however, is most interesting. *Records of Massachusetts,* I, 246, 310, 269.

64. Massachusetts Historical Society, *Collections,* Fourth Series, VI, 65.

65. *Records of the Colony of Plymouth* (Boston, 1859), IX, 71.

66. John Cotton in 1651 clearly distinguished between slavery and servitude. He wrote Cromwell in that year in regard to the Scottish prisoners sent to New England, that "we have been desirous . . . to make their yoke easy . . . They have not been sold for slaves to perpetuall servitude, but for 6, or 7 or 8 years, as we do our owne." Quoted in George H. Moore, *Notes on the History of Slavery in Massachusetts* (New York, 1866), p. 17 n.

67. *Records of the Colony of Rhode Island . . .* (Providence, 1856), I, 243.

68. Quoted in William B. Weeden, *Economic and Social History of New England* (Boston, 1891), p. 149 n. It was officially reported in 1680 by Connecticut colony that three or four "Blacks" were imported each year from the Barbados, and that they usually sold for £22 apiece. This was much more than the going price for servants. *Public Records of the Colony of Connecticut* (Hartford, 1850-90), III, 298.

69. Quoted in Lorenzo Greene, *The Negro in Colonial New England, 1620-1776* (New York, 1942), p. 172.

70. *Records of Massachusetts,* III, 268, 397.

71. *Records of Connecticut,* III, 298, I, 349.

72. Quoted in Palfrey, *History of New England,* III, 298.

73. Hurd, *Law of Freedom,* I, 262. Greene, *Negro in New England,* pp. 65-6, says that in 1670 slavery in Massachusetts became legally inheritable, for in that year the word "strangers" was dropped from the Body of Liberties as a description of those who might be enslaved.

74. *Records of Connecticut,* III, 298.

75. Quoted in Bernard C. Steiner, *History of Slavery in Connecticut* (Baltimore, 1893), p. 18.

76. *Records of Connecticut,* IV, 40.

77. Hurd, *Law of Freedom,* I, 262-3.

78. *Ibid.,* I, 263, Massachusetts had prohibited marriages between whites and Negroes, mulattoes and Indians in 1692. Lauber, *Indian Slavery,* p. 253.

79. Hurd, *Law of Freedom,* I, 263. Rhode Island, too, in 1728, provided that before a Negro or mulatto could be manumitted, security had to given that he would not become a public charge. Hurd, *Law of Freedom,* I, 276.

80. Greene, *Negro in New England,* p. 312.

MODERN TENSIONS AND THE ORIGINS OF AMERICAN SLAVERY

Winthrop D. Jordan

Although Jordan provides additional fragments of data regarding the status of blacks in the earliest decades of the American colonies, he stresses that the evidence is simply insufficient to reach a firm conclusion about the degree of difference in the initial status of blacks and indentured whites.[1] This, however, has not prevented scholars, past and present, from taking definite positions on the issue. Jordan perceptively suggests that the position taken is intimately related to the prospects for change in American race relations. The position and the prospects — or, more precisely, the individual's optimism or pessimism regarding the prospects for changing the prevailing pattern of discrimination — are linked via the individual's conception of the causal relation between slavery and prejudice. Those who are pessimistic about change see innate prejudice as the primary cause of a rapidly emergent new world slavery. Conversely, those of an optimistic bent — or writing at a time when the prospects for change were particularly promising — are inclined to see slavery as the dominant cause of racial antagonism and to view the first black Americans as essentially similar in status to indentured whites. To be aware of the biasing influence of existent conditions upon historical analysis is a vital first step toward neutralizing this influence.

Noting that the first signs of slavery and other forms of racial discrimination appeared at about the same time, Jordan modifies earlier analyses of the causal relation between slavery and prejudice by concluding that both were consequents of a general debasement of blacks. From this perspective slavery and prejudice are seen to have fed upon each other more or less equally in a continuous process of mutual causation. This is a sociologically sophisticated analysis but its validity is seriously called into doubt on two counts. First, although reciprocal causation prevails throughout the social world, this need not mean that

81

interrelated variables are *equally* cause and effect. (Palmer has in effect challenged this aspect of Jordan's analysis in noting that "in the attempt to balance a variety of viewpoints he gives too much credence to some of the arguments for early racial antipathy."[2]) Either slavery or prejudice might exert causal *primacy* despite the fact that their relationship is, undeniably, reciprocal to some degree. Second, Jordan's dismissal of the possibility that slavery preceded and caused prejudice is based upon the faulty assumption that prejudice necessarily precedes and causes discrimination (i.e., "invidious distinctions concerning working in the fields, bearing arms, and sexual union").[3] In making this assumption, Jordan also violates his conclusion that equal reciprocal causality was the original relation between slavery and prejudice. Slavery is a gross form of discrimination and if prejudice must precede lesser forms of discrimination so it must also precede slavery. In short, the critical weakness of Jordan's analysis is that he simply does not make the conceptual distinctions essential to determination of the primary direction of causality.

Despite these serious sociological deficiencies, Jordan's work constitutes a very useful contribution both for its additional data and for its sensitivity to reciprocal causation. His analysis has been elaborated in the award-winning *White Over Black,* but the analysis is not significantly different from the earlier article. Thus the article is chosen for inclusion in the present reader because it is more succinct.

Notes

1. Indeed, Jordan has subsequently suggested that the *process* by which blacks became chattel slaves is unlikely to ever be adequately reconstructed: "there is simply not enough evidence (and very little chance of more to come) to show precisely when and how and why Negroes came to be treated so differently from white men, though there is just enough to make historians differ as to its meaning." *White Over Black* (Chapel Hill: University of North Carolina Press, 1968), p. 44.

2. Paul C. Palmer, "Servant into Slave: The Evolution of the Legal Status of the Negro Laborer in Colonial Virginia," *South Atlantic Quarterly* 65 (1966): 355-70 (quotation at p. 369n). Palmer continues: "This is particularly true when he asserts that the identification of some persons simply as 'a negro' rather than by name is evidence that persons so identified had some peculiar status. There are several instances of court decisions from the period wherein Negroes are identified by name and whites merely as Dutchmen, Scots, etc."

3. See p. 90, below. The inadequacy of the assumption that prejudice must precede discrimination is documented in the concluding essay in this reader.

Thanks to John Smith we know that Negroes first came to the British continental colonies in 1619.[1] What we do not know is exactly when Negroes were first enslaved there. This question has been debated by historians for the past seventy years, the critical point being whether Negroes were enslaved almost from their first importation or whether they were at first simply servants and only later reduced to the status of slaves. The long duration and vigor of the controversy suggest that more than a simple question of dating has been involved. In fact certain current tensions in American society have complicated the historical problem and greatly heightened its significance. Dating the origins of slavery has taken on a striking modern relevance.

During the nineteenth century historians assumed almost universally that the first Negroes came to Virginia as slaves. So close was their acquaintance with the problem of racial slavery that it did not occur to them that Negroes could ever have been anything but slaves. Philip A. Bruce, the first man to probe with some thoroughness into the early years of American slavery, adopted this view in 1896, although he emphasized that the original difference in treatment between white servants and Negroes was merely that Negroes served for life. Just six years later, however, came a challenge from a younger, professionally trained historian, James C. Ballagh. His *A History of Slavery in Virginia* appeared in the *Johns Hopkins University Studies in Historical and Political Science,* an aptly named series which was to usher in the new era of scholarly detachment in the writing of institutional history. Ballagh offered a new and different interpretation; he took the position that the first Negroes served merely as servants and that enslavement did not begin until around 1660, when statutes bearing on slavery were passed for the first time.[2]

There has since been agreement on dating the statutory establishment of slavery, and differences of opinion have centered on when enslavement began in actual practice. Fortunately there has also been general agreement on slavery's distinguishing characteristics: service for life and inheritance of like obligation by any offspring. Writing on the free Negro in Virginia for the Johns Hopkins series, John H. Russell in 1913 tackled the central question and showed that some Negroes were indeed servants but concluded that "between 1640 and 1660 slavery was fast becoming an established fact. In this twenty years the colored population was divided, part being servants and part being slaves, and some who were servants defended themselves with increasing difficulty from the encroach-

Reprinted from *Journal of Southern History* 28 (February 1962): 18-30. Copyright 1962 by the Southern Historical Association. Reprinted by permission of the Managing Editor. A modified and much more complete description of the origin of American slavery is in Winthrop D. Jordan, *White Over Black: American Attitudes Toward the Negro, 1550-1812* (Chapel Hill: University of North Carolina Press, 1968).

ments of slavery."[3] Ulrich B. Phillips, though little interested in the matter, in 1918 accepted Russell's conclusion of early servitude and transition toward slavery after 1640. Helen T. Catterall took much the same position in 1926. On the other hand, in 1921 James M. Wright, discussing the free Negro in Maryland, implied that Negroes were slaves almost from the beginning, and in 1940 Susie M. Ames reviewed several cases in Virginia which seemed to indicate that genuine slavery had existed well before Ballagh's date of 1660.[4]

All this was a very small academic gale, well insulated from the outside world. Yet despite disagreement on dating enslavement, the earlier writers — Bruce, Ballagh, and Russell — shared a common assumption which, though at the time seemingly irrelevant to the main question, has since proved of considerable importance. They assumed that prejudice against the Negro was natural and almost innate in the white man. It would be surprising if they had felt otherwise in this period of segregation statutes, overseas imperialism, immigration restriction, and full-throated Anglo-Saxonism. By the 1920's, however, with the easing of these tensions, the assumption of natural prejudice was dropped unnoticed. Yet only one historian explicitly contradicted that assumption: Ulrich Phillips of Georgia, impressed with the geniality of both slavery and twentieth-century race relations, found no natural prejudice in the white man and expressed his "conviction that Southern racial asperities are mainly superficial, and that the two great elements are fundamentally in accord."[5]

Only when tensions over race relations intensified once more did the older assumption of natural prejudice crop up again. After World War II American Negroes found themselves beneficiaries of New Deal politics and reforms, wartime need for manpower, world-wide repulsion at racist excesses in Nazi Germany, and growingly successful colored anticolonialism. With new militancy Negroes mounted an attack on the citadel of separate but equal, and soon it became clear that America was in for a period of self-conscious reappraisal of its racial arrangements. Writing in this period of heightened tension (1949) a practiced and careful scholar, Wesley F. Craven, raised the old question of the Negro's original status, suggesting that Negroes had been enslaved at an early date. Craven also cautiously resuscitated the idea that white men may have had natural distaste for the Negro, an idea which fitted neatly with the suggestion of early enslavement. Original antipathy would mean rapid debasement.[6]

In the next year (1950) came a sophisticated counterstatement, which contradicted both Craven's dating and implicitly any suggestion of early prejudice. Oscar and Mary F. Handlin in "Origins of the Southern Labor System" offered a case for late enslavement, with servitude as the status of Negroes before about 1660. Originally the status of both Negroes and white servants was far short of freedom, the Handlins maintained, but Negroes failed to benefit from increased freedom for servants in mid-century and became less free rather than more.[7] Embedded in this description of diverging status were broader implications: Late and gradual enslavement undercut the possibility of natural, deep-seated antipathy toward Negroes. On the contrary, if whites and Negroes could share the same status of half freedom for forty years in the seventeenth century, why could they not share full freedom in the twentieth?

The same implications were rendered more explicit by Kenneth M. Stampp in a major reassessment of Southern slavery published two years after the Supreme Court's 1954 school decision. Reading physiology with the eye of faith, Stampp frankly stated his assumption "that innately Negroes *are,* after all, only white men with black skins, nothing more, nothing less."[8] Closely following the Handlins' article on the origins of slavery itself, he almost directly denied any pattern of early and inherent racial antipathy: ". . . Negro and white servants of the seventeenth century seemed to be remarkably unconcerned about their visible physical differences." As for "the trend toward special treatment" of the Negro, "physical and cultural differences provided handy excuses to justify it."[9] Distaste for the Negro, then, was in the beginning scarcely more than an appurtenance of slavery.

These views squared nicely with the hopes of those even more directly concerned with the problem of contemporary race relations, sociologists and social psychologists. Liberal on the race question almost to a man, they tended to see slavery as the initial cause of the Negro's current degradation. The modern Negro was the unhappy victim of long association with base status. Sociologists, though uninterested in tired questions of historical evidence, could not easily assume a natural prejudice in the white man as the cause of slavery. Natural or innate prejudice would not only violate their basic assumptions concerning the dominance of culture but would undermine the power of their new Baconian science. For if prejudice was natural there would be little one could do to wipe it out. Prejudice must have followed enslavement, not vice versa, else any liberal program of action would be badly compromised. One prominent social scientist suggested in a UNESCO pamphlet that racial prejudice in the United States commenced with the cotton gin![10]

Just how closely the question of dating had become tied to the practical matter of action against racial prejudice was made apparent by the suggestions of still another historian. Carl N. Degler grappled with the dating problem in an article frankly entitled "Slavery and the Genesis of American Race Prejudice."[11] The article appeared in 1959, a time when Southern resistance to school desegregation seemed more adamant than ever and the North's hands none too clean, a period of discouragement for those hoping to end racial discrimination. Prejudice against the Negro now appeared firm and deep-seated, less easily eradicated than had been supposed in, say, 1954. It was Degler's view that enslavement began early, as a result of white settlers' prejudice or antipathy toward the first Negroes. Thus not only were the sociologists contradicted but the dating problem was now overtly and consciously tied to the broader question of whether slavery caused prejudice or prejudice caused slavery. A new self-consciousness over the American racial dilemma had snatched an arid historical controversy from the hands of an unsuspecting earlier generation and had tossed it into the arena of current debate.

Ironically there might have been no historical controversy at all if every historian dealing with the subject had exercised greater care with facts and greater restraint in interpretation. Too often the debate entered the realm of inference and assumption. For the crucial early years after 1619 there is simply not enough evidence to indicate with any certainty whether Negroes were treated like white servants or not. No historian has found anything resembling proof one way or the other. The first Negroes were sold to the English settlers, yet so were other Englishmen. It can be said, however, that Negroes were set apart from white men by the word *Negroes,* and a distinct name is not attached to a group unless it is seen as different. The earliest Virginia census reports plainly distinguished Negroes from white men, sometimes giving Negroes no personal name; and in 1629 every commander of the several plantations was ordered to "take a generall muster of all the inhabitants men woemen and Children as well *Englishe* as Negroes."[12] Difference, however, might or might not involve inferiority.

The first evidence as to the actual status of Negroes does not appear until about 1640. Then it becomes clear that *some* Negroes were serving for life and some children inheriting the same obligation. Here it is necessary to suggest with some candor that the Handlins' statement to the contrary rests on unsatisfactory documentation.[13] That some Negroes were held as slaves after about 1640 is no indication, however, that American slavery popped into the world fully developed at that time. Many historians, most cogently the Handlins, have shown slavery to have been a gradual development, a process not completed until the eighteenth century. The complete deprivation of civil and personal rights, the legal conversion of the Negro into a chattel, in short slavery as Americans came to know it, was not accomplished overnight. Yet these developments practically and logically depended on the practice of hereditary lifetime service, and it is certainly possible to find in the 1640's and 1650's traces of slavery's most essential feature.[14]

The first definite trace appears in 1640 when the Virginia General Court pronounced sentence on three servants who had been retaken after running away to Maryland. Two of them, a Dutchman and a Scot, were ordered to serve their masters for one additional year and then the colony for three more, but "the third being a negro named John Punch shall serve his said master or his assigns for the time of his natural life here or else where." No white servant in America, so far as is known, ever received a like sentence.[15] Later the same month a Negro was again singled out from a group of recaptured runaways; six of the seven were assigned additional time while the Negro was given none, presumably because he was already serving for life.[16] After 1640, too, county court records began to mention Negroes, in part because there were more of them than previously — about two per cent of the Virginia population in 1649.[17] Sales for life, often including any future progeny, were recorded in unmistakable language. In 1646 Francis Pott sold a Negro woman and boy to Stephen Charlton "to the use of him . . . forever." Similarly, six years later William Whittington sold to John Pott, "one Negro girle named Jowan; aged about Ten yeares and with her Issue and produce duringe her (or either of them) for their Life tyme. And their Successors forever"; and a Maryland man in 1649 deeded two Negro men and a woman "and all their issue both male and Female." The executors of a York County estate in 1647 disposed of eight Negroes — four men, two women, and two children — to Captain John Chisman "to have hold occupy possesse and inioy and every one of the afforementioned Negroes forever[.]"[18] The will of Rowland Burnham of "Rapahanocke," made in 1657, dispensed his considerable number of Negroes and white servants in language which clearly differentiated between the two by specifying that the whites were to serve for their "full terme of tyme" and the Negroes "for ever."[19] Nor did anything in the will indicate that this distinction was exceptional or novel.

In addition to these clear indications that some Negroes were owned for life, there were cases of Negroes held for terms far longer than the normal five or seven years.[20] On the other hand, some Negroes served only the term usual for white servants, and others were completely free.[21] One Negro freeman, Anthony Johnson, himself owned a Negro.[22] Obviously the enslavement of some Negroes did not mean the immediate enslavement of all.

Further evidence of Negroes serving for life lies in the prices paid for them. In many instances the valuations placed on Negroes (in estate inventories and bills of sale) were far higher than for white servants, even those servants with full terms yet to serve. Since there was ordinarily no preference for Negroes as such, higher prices must have meant that Negroes were more highly valued because of their greater length of service. Negro women may have been especially prized, moreover, because their progeny could also be held perpetually. In 1645, for example, two Negro women and a boy were sold for 5,500 pounds of tobacco. Two years earlier William Burdett's inventory listed eight servants (with the time each had still to serve) at valuations ranging from 400 to 1,100 pounds, while a "very anntient" Negro was valued at 3,000 and an eight-year-old Negro girl at 2,000 pounds, with no time-remaining indicated for either. In the late 1650's an inventory of Thomas Ludlow's large estate evaluated a white servant with six years to serve at less than an elderly Negro man and only one half of a Negro woman.[23] The labor owned by James Stone in 1648 was evaluated as follows:

	lb tobo
Thomas Groves, 4 yeares to serve	1300
Francis Bomley for 6 yeares	1500
John Thackstone for 3 yeares	1300
Susan Davis for 3 yeares	1000
Emaniell a Negro man	2000
Roger Stone 3 yeares	1300
Mingo a Negro man	2000[24]

Besides setting a higher value on the two Negroes, Stone's inventory, like Burdett's, failed to indicate the number of years they had still to serve. It would seem safe to assume that the time remaining was omitted in this and similar documents simply because the Negroes were regarded as serving for an unlimited time.

The situation in Maryland was apparently the same. In 1643 Governor Leonard Calvert agreed with John Skinner, "mariner," to exchange certain estates for seventeen sound Negro "slaves," fourteen men and three women between sixteen and twenty-six years old. The total value of these was placed at 24,000 pounds of tobacco, which would work out to 1,000 pounds for the women and 1,500 for the men, prices considerably higher than those paid for white servants at the time.[25]

Wherever Negro women were involved however, higher valuations may have reflected the fact that they could be used for field work while white women generally were not. This discrimination between Negro and white women, of course, fell short of actual enslavement. It meant merely that Negroes were set apart in a way clearly not to their advantage. Yet this is not the only evidence that Negroes were subjected to degrading distinctions not directly related to slavery. In several ways Negroes were singled out for special treatment which suggested a generalized debasing of Negroes as a group. Significantly, the first indications of debasement appeared at about the same time as the first indications of actual enslavement.

The distinction concerning field work is a case in point. It first appeared on the written record in 1643, when Virginia pointedly recognized it in her taxation policy. Previously tithable persons had been defined (1629) as "all those that worke in the ground of what qualitie or condition soever." Now the law stated that all adult men and *Negro* women were to be tithable, and this distinction was made twice again before 1660. Maryland followed a similar course, beginning in 1654.[26] John Hammond, in a 1656 tract defending the tobacco colonies, wrote that servant women were not put to work in the fields but in domestic employments, "yet som wenches that are nasty, and beastly and not fit to be so imployed are put into the ground."[27] Since all Negro women were taxed as working in the fields, it would seem logical to conclude that Virginians found them "nasty" and "beastly." The essentially racial nature of this discrimination was bared by a 1668 law at the time slavery was crystallizing on the statute books:

> Whereas some doubts, have arisen whether negro women set free were still to be accompted tithable according to a former act, *It is declared by this grand assembly* that negro women, though permitted to enjoy their ffreedome yet ought not in all respects to be admitted to a full fruition of the exemptions and impunities of the English, and are still lyable to payment of taxes.[28]

Virginia law set Negroes apart in a second way by denying them the important right and obligation to bear arms. Few restraints could indicate more clearly the denial to Negroes of membership in the white community. This action, in a sense the first foreshadowing of the slave codes, came in 1640, at just the time when other indications first appear that Negroes were subject to special treatment.[29]

Finally, an even more compelling sense of the separateness of Negroes was revealed in early distress concerning sexual union between the races. In 1630 a Virginia court pronounced a now famous sentence: "Hugh Davis to be soundly whipped, before an assembly of Negroes and others for abusing himself to the dishonor of God and shame of Christians, by defiling his body in lying with a negro."[30] While there were other instances of punishment for interracial union in the ensuing years, fornication rather than miscegenation may well have been the primary offense, though in 1651 a Maryland man sued someone who he claimed had said "that he had a black bastard in Virginia."[31] There may have been nothing racial about the 1640 case by which Robert Sweet was compelled "to do penance in church according to laws of England, for getting a negroe woman with child and the woman whipt."[32] About 1650 a white man and a Negro woman were required to stand clad in white sheets before a congregation in Lower Norfolk County for having had relations, but this punishment was sometimes used in ordinary cases of fornication between two whites.[33]

It is certain, however, that in the early 1660's when slavery was gaining statutory recognition, the colonial assemblies legislated with feeling against miscegenation. Nor was this merely a matter of avoiding confusion of status, as was suggested by the Handlins. In 1662 Virginia declared that "if any christian shall commit ffornication with a negro man or woman, hee or shee soe offending" should pay double the usual fine. Two years later Maryland prohibited interracial marriages:

> forasmuch as divers freeborne English women forgetfull of their free Condicōn and to the disgrace of our Nation doe intermarry with Negro Slaves by which alsoe divers suites may arise touching the Issue of such woemen and a great damage doth befall the Masters of such Negroes for prevention whereof for deterring such freeborne women from such shameful Matches . . . ,

strong language indeed if the problem had only been confusion of status. A Maryland act of 1681 described marriages of white women with Negroes as, among other things, "always to the Satisfaccōn of theire Lascivious & Lustfull desires, & to the disgrace not only of the English butt also of many other Christian Nations." When Virginia finally prohibited all interracial liaisons in 1691, the assembly vigorously denounced miscegenation and its fruits as "that abominable mixture and spurious issue."[34]

One is confronted, then, with the fact that the first evidences of enslavement and of other forms of debasement appeared at about the same time. Such coincidence comports poorly with both views on the causation of prejudice and slavery. If slavery caused prejudice, then invidious distinctions concerning working in the fields, bearing arms, and sexual union should have appeared only after slavery's firm establishment. If prejudice caused slavery, then one would expect to find such lesser discriminations preceding the greater discrimination of outright enslavement.

Perhaps a third explanation of the relationship between slavery and prejudice may be offered, one that might fit the pattern of events as revealed by existing evidence. Both current views share a common starting point: They predicate two factors, prejudice and slavery, and demand a distinct order of causality. No matter how qualified by recognition that the effect may in turn react upon the cause, each approach inevitably tends to deny the validity of its opposite. But what if one were to regard both slavery and prejudice as species of a general debasement of the Negro? Both may have been equally cause and effect, constantly reacting upon each other, dynamically joining hands to hustle the Negro down the road to complete degradation. Mutual causation is, of course, a highly useful concept for describing social situations in the modern world.[35] Indeed it has been widely applied in only slightly altered fashion to the current racial situation: Racial prejudice and the Negro's lowly position are widely accepted as constantly reinforcing each other.

This way of looking at the facts might well fit better with what we know of slavery itself. Slavery was an organized pattern of human relationships. No matter what the law might say, it was of different character than cattle ownership. No matter how degrading, slavery involved human beings. No one seriously pretended otherwise. Slavery was not an isolated economic or institutional phenomenon; it was the practical facet of a general debasement without which slavery could have no rationality. (Prejudice, too, was a form of debasement, a kind of slavery in the mind.) Certainly the urgent need for labor in a virgin country guided the direction which debasement took, molded it, in fact, into an institutional framework. That economic practicalities shaped the external form of debasement should not tempt one to forget, however, that slavery was at bottom a social arrangement, a way of society's ordering its members in its own mind.

Notes

1. "About the last of August came in a dutch man of warre that sold us twenty Negars." Smith was quoting John Rolfe's account. Edward Arber and A. G. Bradley (eds.), *Travels and Works of Captain John Smith* . . . (2 vols., Edinburgh, 1910), II, 541.

2. Philip A. Bruce, *Economic History of Virginia in the Seventeenth Century* (2 vols., New York, 1896), II, 57-130; James C. Ballagh, *A History of Slavery in Virginia* (Baltimore, 1902), 28-35.

3. John H. Russell, *The Free Negro in Virginia, 1619-1865* (Baltimore, 1913), 29.

4. *Ibid.*, 23-39; Ulrich B. Phillips, *American Negro Slavery* (New York, 1918), 75-77, and *Life and Labor in the Old South* (Boston, 1929), 170; Helen T. Catterall (ed.), *Judicial Cases Concerning American Slavery and the Negro* (5 vols., Washington, 1926-1937), I, 54-55, 57-63; James M. Wright, *The Free Negro in*

Maryland, 1634-1860 (New York, 1921), 21-23; Susie M. Ames, *Studies of the Virginia Eastern Shore in the Seventeenth Century* (Richmond, 1940), 100-106. See also T. R. Davis, "Negro Servitude in the United States," *Journal of Negro History,* VIII (July 1923), 247-83, and Edgar T. Thompson, "The Natural History of Agricultural Labor in the South" in David K. Jackson (ed.), *American Studies in Honor of William Kenneth Boyd* (Durham, N. C., 1940), 127-46.

5.   Phillips, *American Negro Slavery,* viii.

6.   Wesley F. Craven, *The Southern Colonies in the Seventeenth Century, 1607-1689* (Baton Rouge, 1949), 217-19, 402-403.

7.   *William and Mary Quarterly,* s. 3, VII (April 1950), 199-222.

8.   Kenneth M. Stampp, *The Peculiar Institution: Slavery in the Ante-Bellum South* (New York, 1956), vii-viii, 3-33.

9.   *Ibid.,* 21-22.

10.   Arnold Rose, "The Roots of Prejudice" in UNESCO, *The Race Question in Modern Science* (New York, 1956), 224. For examples of the more general view see Frederick G. Detweiler, "The Rise of Modern Race Antagonisms," *American Journal of Sociology,* XXXVII (March 1932), 743; M. F. Ashley Montagu, *Man's Most Dangerous Myth: The Fallacy of Race* (New York, 1945), 10-11, 19-20; Gunnar Myrdal, *An American Dilemma: The Negro Problem and Modern Democracy* (New York, 1944), 83-89, 97; Paul Kecskemeti, "The Psychological Theory of Prejudice: Does it Underrate the Role of Social History?" *Commentary,* XVIII (October 1954), 364-66.

11.   *Comparative Studies in Society and History,* II (October 1959), 49-66. See also Degler, *Out of Our Past: The Forces that Shaped Modern America* (New York, 1959), 26-39.

12.   H. R. McIlwaine (ed.), *Minutes of the Council and General Court of Colonial Virginia, 1622-1632, 1670-1676* (Richmond, 1924), 196. See the lists and musters of 1624 and 1625 in John C. Hotten (ed.), *The Original Lists of Persons of Quality* . . . (New York, 1880), 169-265.

13.   "The status of Negroes was that of servants; and so they were identified and treated down to the 1660's." ("Origins," 203). The footnote to this statement reads, "For disciplinary and revenue laws in Virginia that did not discriminate Negroes from other servants, see Hening, *Statutes,* I, 174, 198, 200, 243, 306 (1631-1645)." But pp. 200 and 243 of William Waller Hening (ed.), *The Statutes at Large; Being a Collection of All the Laws of Virginia* . . . (2nd ed. of vols. 1-4, New York, 1823), I, in fact contain nothing about either servants or Negroes, while a tax provision on p. 242 specifically discriminates against Negro women. The revenue act on p. 306 lists the number of pounds of tobacco levied on land, cattle, sheep, horses, etc., and on tithable persons, and provides for collection of lists of the above so that the colony can compute its tax program; nothing else is said of servants and tithables. To say, as the Handlins did in the same note, that Negroes, English servants, and horses, etc., were listed all together in some early Virginia wills, with the implication that Negroes and English servants were regarded as alike in status, is hardly correct unless one is to assume that the horses were sharing this status as well. (For complete bibliographical information on Hening [ed.], *Statutes,* see E. G. Swem, *Virginia Historical Index* [2 vols., Roanoke, Va., 1934-1936], I, xv-xvi.)

14.   Latin-American Negroes did not lose all civil and personal rights, did not become mere chattels, yet we speak of "slavery" in Latin America without hesitation. See Frank Tannenbaum, *Slave and Citizen: The Negro in the Americas* (New York, 1947), and Gilberto Freyre, *The Masters and the Slaves: A Study in the Development of Brazilian Civilization* (New York, 1946).

15. "Decisions of the General Court," *Virginia Magazine of History and Biography,* V (January 1898), 236. Abbot Emerson Smith in the standard work on servitude in America, *Colonists in Bondage: White Servitude and Convict Labor in America, 1607-1776* (Chapel Hill, 1947), 171, says that "there was never any such thing as perpetual slavery for any white man in any English colony." There were instances in the seventeenth century of white men sold into "slavery," but this was when the meaning of the term was still indefinite and often equated with servitude.

16. "Decisions of the General Court," 236-37.

17. *A Perfect Description of Virginia . . .* (London, 1649), reprinted in Peter Force (ed.), *Tracts . . .* (4 vols., Washington, 1836-1846), II.

18. These four cases may be found in Northampton County Deeds, Wills &c. (Virginia State Library, Richmond), No. 4 (1651-1654), 28 (misnumbered 29), 124; *Archives of Maryland* (69 vols., Baltimore, 1883-1961), XLI, 261-62; York County Records (Virginia State Library), No. 2 (transcribed Wills & Deeds, 1645-1649), 256-57.

19. Lancaster County Loose Papers (Virginia State Library), Box of Wills, 1650-1719, Folder 1656-1659.

20. For examples running for as long as thirty-five years, see *William and Mary Quarterly,* s. 1, XX (October 1911), 148; Russell, *Free Negro in Virginia,* 26-27; Ames, *Eastern Shore,* 105. Compare the cases of a Negro and an Irish servant in *Calendar of Virginia State Papers . . .* (11 vols., Richmond, 1875-1893), I, 9-10, and *Maryland Archives,* XLI, 476-78; XLIX, 123-24.

21. Russell, *Free Negro in Virginia,* 24-41. See especially the cases in *Virginia Magazine of History and Biography,* V (July 1897), 40; York County Deeds, Wills, Orders, etc. (Virginia State Library), No. 1 (1633-1657, 1691-1694), 338-39.

22. John H. Russell, "Colored Freeman as Slave Owners in Virginia," *Journal of Negro History,* I (July 1916), 234-37.

23. York County Records, No. 2, 63; Northampton County Orders, Deeds, Wills, &c., No. 2 (1640-1645), 224; York County Deeds, Orders, Wills, &c. (1657-1662), 108-109.

24. York County Records, No. 2, 390.

25. Apparently Calvert's deal with Skinner was never consummated. *Maryland Archives,* IV, vii, 189, 320-21. For prices of white servants see *ibid.,* IV, 31, 47-48, 74, 78-79, 81, 83, 92, 98, 108-109, 184, 200, 319.

26. Hening (ed.), *Statutes,* I, 144, 242, 292, 454. The Handlins erroneously placed the "first sign of discrimination" in this matter at 1668 ("Origins," 217n). For Maryland, see *Maryland Archives,* I, 342; II, 136, 399, 538-39; XIII, 538-39.

27. John Hammond, *Leah and Rachel, or, the Two Fruitful Sisters Virginia, and Mary-land: Their Present Condition, Impartially Stated and Related . . .* (London, 1656), reprinted in Force (ed.), *Tracts,* II.

28. Hening (ed.), *Statutes,* II, 267. The distinction between white and colored women was neatly described at the turn of the century by Robert Beverley, *The History and Present State of Virginia,* Louis B. Wright, ed. (Chapel Hill, 1947), 271-72.

29. Hening (ed.), *Statutes,* I, 226, and for the same act in more detail see *William and Mary Quarterly,* s. 2, IV (July 1924), 147. The Handlins discounted this law: "Until the 1660's the statutes on the Negroes were not at all unique. Nor did they add up to a decided trend." ("Origins," 209.) The note added to this statement reads, "That there was no trend is evident from the fluctuations in naming

Negroes slaves or servants and in their right to bear arms. See Hening, *Statutes,* I, 226, 258, 292, 540; Bruce, *Institutional History,* II, 5 ff., 199 ff. For similar fluctuations with regard to Indians, see Hening, *Statutes,* I, 391, 518." But since the terms "servants" and "slaves" did not have precise meaning, as the Handlins themselves asserted, fluctuations in naming Negroes one or the other can not be taken to mean that their status itself was fluctuating. Of the pages cited in Hening, p. 258 is an act encouraging Dutch traders and contains nothing about Negroes, servants, slaves, or arms. Page 292 is an act providing that fifteen tithable persons should support one soldier; Negroes were among those tithable, but nothing was said of allowing them to arm. Page 540 refers to "any negro slaves" and "said negro," but mentions nothing about servants or arms. In the pages dealing with Indians, p. 391 provides that no one is to employ Indian servants with guns, and p. 518 that Indians (not "Indian servants") are to be allowed to use their own guns; the two provisions are not contradictory. Philip A. Bruce, *Institutional History of Virginia in the Seventeenth Century* (2 vols., New York, 1910), II, 5 ff., indicates that Negroes were barred from arming in 1639 and offers no suggestion that there was any later fluctuation in this practice.

30.   Hening (ed.), *Statutes,* I, 146. "Christianity" appears instead of "Christians" in McIlwaine (ed.), *Minutes of the Council,* 479.

31.   *Maryland Archives,* X, 114-15.

32.   Hening (ed.), *Statutes,* I, 552; McIlwaine, *Minutes of the Council,* 477.

33.   Bruce, *Economic History of Virginia,* II, 110.

34.   Hening (ed.), *Statutes,* II, 170; III, 86-87; *Maryland Archives,* I, 533-34; VII, 204. Opinion on this matter apparently was not unanimous, for a petition of several citizens to the Council in 1699 asked repeal of the intermarriage prohibition. H. R. McIlwaine (ed.), *Legislative Journals of the Council of Colonial Virginia* (3 vols., Richmond, 1918-1919), I, 262. The Handlins wrote ("Origins," 215), "Mixed marriages of free men and servants were particularly frowned upon as complicating status and therefore limited by law." Their citation for this, Hening (ed.), *Statutes,* II, 114 (1661/62), and Marcus W. Jernegan, *Laboring and Dependent Classes in Colonial America, 1607-1783* (Chicago, 1931), 55, 180, gives little backing to the statement. In Virginia secret marriage or bastardy between whites of different status got the same punishment as such between whites of the same status. A white servant might marry any white if his master consented. See Hening (ed.), *Statutes,* I, 252-53, 438-39; II, 114-15, 167; III, 71-75, 137-40. See also James C. Ballagh, *White Servitude in the Colony of Virginia* (Baltimore, 1895), 50. For Maryland, see *Maryland Archives,* I, 73, 373-74, 441-42; II, 396-97; XIII, 501-502. The Handlins also suggested that in the 1691 Virginia law, "spurious" meant simply "illegitimate," and they cited Arthur W. Calhoun, *A Social History of the American Family from Colonial Times to the Present* (3 vols., Cleveland, O., 1917-1919), I, 42, which turns out to be one quotation from John Milton. However, "spurious" was used in colonial laws with reference only to unions between white and black, and never in bastardy laws involving whites only. Mulattoes were often labeled "spurious" offspring.

35.   For example, George C. Homans, *The Human Group* (New York, 1950).

RACE RELATIONS IN SEVENTEENTH-CENTURY AMERICA: THE PROBLEM OF THE ORIGINS OF NEGRO SLAVERY

Joseph Boskin

The previous selections have provided the raw data and many of the concepts essential to any meaningful interpretation of the growing alienation between blacks and whites in seventeenth-century America. Boskin compactly arrays, contrasts, and evaluates the interpretations advanced in these selections. In addition, he suggests new lines of research which must be explored in order to achieve a complete understanding of the emergence of American slavery.

In particular, Boskin raises the question of the relative importance of economic and cultural variables in slavery's formative years. Like Degler, he challenges the priority of the economic variable by citing Northern slavery without distinguishing the question of slavery's profitability for the individual slaveowner from the question of its profitability for the colony as a whole.[1] This weakness in Boskin's analysis in no way denies the importance of his call for further research on the causal role of cultural variables, especially ethnocentrism. The economic factor is not a sufficient explanation of slavery's origin. Boskin has not only correctly identified the need for research on noneconomic variables but has elsewhere contributed to its fulfillment by analyzing the dearth of educational opportunities for seventeenth-century black Americans. He suggests that the lack of educational opportunities for blacks reflected the society's low estimation of their social worth.[2] This estimation, rooted in ethnocentrism, probably was a significant factor in the uniformity of the degraded status accorded blacks throughout the colonies. Operating independent of economic interests, ethnocentrism augments the economic explanation of slavery and may have been especially critical in regards to the origin of slavery in the North.

Boskin might also have emphasized the need for more explicit consideration of the role of differential power in formulating a theory of slavery's origin. The power variable is often left implicit or treated as a derivative of economic forces with the result that its independent significance is overlooked or, more commonly, simply assumed. Numerous writers have stressed that white servants were also subjected to harsh treatment in the seventeenth century but they were never successfully enslaved.[3] This probably reflects the role of both ethnocentrism and group power. As compared to the Indians, white indentured servants had a comparable power position and were the objects of less ethnocentric rejection. As compared to the Africans they enjoyed both a superior power position and less rejection. In an economic context where laborers, regardless of race or nationality, were greatly in demand, it seems likely that ethnocentrism and power had decisive significance for the selection of a population to be enslaved. The failure to date to precisely measure either variable[4] prevents a firm conclusion regarding their (relative) significance in determining the differential outcomes of the struggle for status.

Notes

1.   See Arthur Zilversmit, *The First Emancipation: The Abolition of Slavery in the North* (Chicago: University of Chicago Press, 1967), pp. 45-46 and esp. 52-53. A comment from an analysis of the abolition of Northern slavery is highly relevant: "The traditional economic argument of unprofitability is easily refuted since slavery remained profitable *for some,...*." Eugene D. Genovese, *The World the Slaveholders Made* (New York: Random House [Pantheon], 1969), p. 65 (emphasis added).

2.   Joseph Boskin, "The Origins of American Slavery: Education as an Index of Early Differentiation," *Journal of Negro Education* 35 (1966): 125-33.

3.   For example, see Marvin Harris, *Patterns of Race in the Americas* (New York: Walker, 1964), esp. p. 70, and Abbot E. Smith, *Colonists in Bondage: White Servitude and Convict Labor in America, 1607-1776* (Chapel Hill: University of North Carolina Press, 1947).

4.   A useful guide for measurement of and comparative research on ethnocentrism has been proffered by Donald T. Campbell and Robert A. Levine, "A Proposal for Cooperative Cross-Cultural Research on Ethnocentrism," *Journal of Conflict Resolution* 5 (1961): 82-108.

In the introduction to Act I of the play *Porgy* written in 1926, Dubose and Dorothy Heyward set the stage for the curious activities on Catfish Row:

Reprinted from *Sociology and Social Research* 49 (July 1965): 446-55, by permission of the Editor.

As the curtain rises, revealing Catfish Row on a summer evening, the court re-echoes with African laughter and friendly banter in "Gullah," the language of the Charleston Negro, which still retains many African words. The audience understands none of it. Like the laughter and movement, the twanging of a guitar from an upper window, the dancing of an urchin with a loose, shuffling step, it is part of the picture of Catfish Row as it really is — an alien scene, a picture as little known to most Americans as the people of the Congo.[1]

Almost twenty-five years later, in an important work on race relations, Robert Park wrote:

One thing that complicates any attempt to study peasant institutions is the fact that, though the white man and the Negro have lived and worked together in the United States for three hundred years or more, the two races are still in a certain sense strangers to one another.[2]

The estrangement to which the Heywards and Park refer is one of the most consistent themes in the history of the relationship between Whites and Blacks in the United States. Moreover, the factors underlying the origins of the estrangement, and its institutionalization in the form of slavery, are still far from being fully understood. Many facets of the interactive processes in seventeenth century America which resulted in the alienation of the races are yet to be explored. Prior to Frank Tannenbaum's classic work, *Slave and Citizen: The Negro in the Americas,*[3] few historians, sociologists, and social anthropologists tackled the problem of the origins of Negro slavery in the Western Hemisphere.

Within the past generation, however, four significant works have reappraised the problem and have suggested new approaches to the understanding of its origins in the United States. These are Oscar and Mary Handlin, "The Origins of the Southern Labor System"; Stanley M. Elkins, *Slavery: A Problem in American Institutional and Intellectual Life*; Carl N. Degler, "Black Men in a White Man's Country"; and Winthrop D. Jordan, "Modern Tensions and the Origins of American Slavery."[4] It is the dual purpose of this paper to evaluate and contrast the interpretations of these recent works and to suggest briefly those areas of research which must be further explored by social scientists.

The origins of the slave system, in the Handlins' interpretation, lay within a situation which might be described as environmental *tabula rasa:*

An examination of the conditions and status of seventeenth-century labor will show that slavery was not there from the start, that it was not simply imitated from elsewhere, and that it was not a response to any unique qualities in the Negro himself.[5]

How, then, did slavery come into being? "It emerged from the adjustment to American conditions of traditional European institutions."[6]

The traditional European institutions to which the Handlins refer were the system of villenage and involuntary bondage and those laws which defined limitations upon human action. In the seventeenth century the laws of England recognized gradations of servility, the lowest position being not one of slave but one of relative "unfreedom." The term "slave" had no meaning in law; thus no Englishman could be denied a place within society. In the transference of this labor system to the colonies, and abetted by conditions on the coast, these degrees of unfreedom were maintained. The first generation Negroes were accepted into society as relatively "unfree" servants and, as such, enjoyed whatever privileges as were granted to white indentured servants. "These newcomers," the Handlins contend, "like so many others, were accepted, bought, and held as kinds of servants."[7]

Despite the amorphous character of the Negro's legal position, however, the Handlins note that differential treatment was accorded the African. This, they state, was due partly to the settler's own anxieties and insecurities which came in response to a strange environment. In a unique and challenging setting men quickly band together for support and strength; distinctions are made between the familiar and unfamiliar. But it also was due in part, it seems to "unique qualities in the African." In a descriptive paragraph the Handlins undermine their original position *vis-à-vis* the African:

> The rudeness of the Negroes' manners, the strangeness of their languages, the difficulty of communicating to them English notions of morality and proper behavior occasioned sporadic laws to regulate their conduct.[8]

These initial social antagonisms were not crucial, however. "Until the 1660's the statutes on the Negroes were not at all unique. Nor did they add up to a decided trend."[9]

If the Negro was incorporated into society with a status approximately equivalent to that of other white, indentured servants, what factors operated to force him into a caste system? The Handlins point to the process of adjustment — not the adjustment of two cultures coming together for the first time, but the adjustment of the colonist as capitalist to a severe economic need.

Simply stated, there was the desire for a greater labor force to fill the needs of an expanding economy at a time when the migration from England was contracting. To encourage immigration it became necessary to ameliorate the condition of the white, indentured servant by shortening his term and by ensuring his future life as a freeman and landowner. The effect of these actions adversely affected the position of the Negro. He was omitted from these enactments of expectancy and hope.

Concomitantly, there was no one in England or in the colonies to pressure for the curtailment of the Negro's servitude or to fight for his future. By mid-century, the work-term of the Negroes "seems generally lengthier than that of the whites; and thereafter the consciousness dawns that the Blacks will toil for the whole of their lives, not through any particular concern with their status but simply by contrast with those whose years of labor are limited by statute."[10]

Gradually the standing of the Negro deteriorated. With the arrival of increasing numbers from Barbados and Africa came corresponding fears of uprisings, sexual immorality, and mixed marriages. Inevitably, the Handlins argue, color became a sign of slave status and just as inevitably slave status connoted a type of chattel property. "The identical steps that made the slave less a man made him more of a chattel."[11]

When the Handlins turn to the development of the caste system in the northern colonies, they note parallel developments of labor shortages, social distinctions, police regulations, and other factors which helped to define the Negro as chattel property.

In his analysis of the evolvement of slavery, Stanley Elkins concurs with the Handlins' view that there was nothing "natural" about its origins:

> . . . it had no necessary connection with either tropical climate or tropical crops; . . . . It had nothing to do with characteristics which might have made the Negro peculiarly suited either to slavery or to the labor of tobacco culture. . . . Nor was it a matter of common law precedent. . . .[12]

Although Elkins' thesis is similar in essence to that of the Handlins, he does not rule out the possibility of external influences. He rejects the Handlins' statement that Virginians could not have been affected by West Indian Slavery noting that in response to a large influx of Africans into Barbados the Governor's council in 1636 declared that all Negroes and Indians were to serve for life as slaves.[13]

Nevertheless, Elkins' interpretation rests on dynamic internal developments. The state of Negroes' legal indeterminacy to which the Handlins referred, is highly significant to Elkins.[14] For it suggests that the status of the Negro could conceivably have been otherwise. The few examples of free and propertied Negroes are ample enough, he writes,

> . . . to convince one that even so small a margin between automatic lifetime slavery and something else made all the difference. . . . It meant a precious margin of space, not to be discounted, for the conservation of traditional human rights.[15]

That "precious margin of space" which meant the difference between acceptance or rejection of the Negro as a free being crumbled rapidly in the middle of the century under the heavy blows of an expanding large-scale capitalism. In Colonial Virginia, Elkins maintains, an agrarian capitalist organization was "taking on a purity of form never yet seen," in an environment "where no prior traditional institutions, with competing claims of their own, might interfere at any of a dozen points with sufficient power to retard or modify its progress. What happens when such energy meets no limits?"[16]

Elkins concludes that the rising capitalist class, confronted by increasing costs and declining profits in the decades of the 1660's and 1670's, turned to the full use of the Negro in order to stabilize its labor supply. With the maturation of the large-scale, profit-making plantation and in the absence of competing institutions, there was nothing "to prevent unmitigated capitalism from becoming unmitigated slavery. The planter was now engaged in capitalistic agriculture with a labor force entirely under his control."[17]

Unlike the Handlins' approach, cultural differences are subsidiary to the economic hypothesis. It is not that Elkins is unaware of social differences — there is in fact a passage revealing acute sensitivity on his part to African-English relations — it is more that his approach to the problem is primarily an institutional one. Ignored, however, is the northern colonists' reaction to the Negro. In a footnote Elkins dismisses the statutory recognition of slavery with the statement that the number of Negroes being comparatively small, "no effort was made requiring all Negroes to be placed in the condition."[18]

Thus, concludes Elkins, the factors which tipped the scales against the Negro were the dynamics of the unchallenged, expanding institution of capitalism rather than the dynamic effects of labor scarcity as emphasized by the Handlins. There is agreement on one basic and important consideration, namely, that the denial of the Negro as a whole person was a consequence of slavery itself, the badge of an inferior status as labor doomed to perpetuity as chattel property.

Carl Degler reverses this causal relationship. Observing the contradiction in historical development between the American colonies and the Spanish-Portuguese slave system, Degler suggests that

If, instead of assuming that discrimination is a consequence of slavery, we work on the assumption that discrimination preceded slavery and thereby conditioned it, then the contradiction disappears.[19]

The origins of the American racial problem, Degler argues, lay "in the discriminatory social atmosphere of the early seventeenth century,"[20] an atmosphere which reflected a "folk bias" on the part of the early settlers. Differences between the English and the Negro — in terms of race, religion, and culture — were the determinants which initiated the slave system. Given the attitudes toward and treatment of other peoples, the Irish and the American Indian, for example, it was to be expected that the English would reject the African as an equal. The introduction of Africans as slaves into the colonies, in fact, "unquestionably fostered a sense of superiority among Englishmen."[21]

More important, Degler flatly disagrees with the Handlins and goes beyond Elkins in declaring that the colonists on the seaboard had "ample opportunity to learn of discriminatory practices against Negroes from island settlements of Englishmen such as Bermuda and New Providence in the Caribbean."[22] These practices, which restricted movement, trading, and the bearing of arms, were legislated in the 1620's at a time when the number of Negroes was comparatively small.

What Degler alludes to, then, is a *universality of responses on* the part of the English to other cultures, the implication being that this "folk bias" operated wherever Englishmen encountered diverse cultural groups, and, in particular, the African. In this context Degler explains the passage of slave laws in the North:

Thus, like the southern colonists, the New Englanders enacted into law, in the absence of any prior English law of slavery, their recognition of Negroes as different in race, religion, and culture.[23]

So the equations are turned around, in Degler's opinion. Slavery must therefore "be absolved from starting the cycle. It was the discriminatory attitude and behavior which conditioned the form slavery would take."[24]

More recently, a third approach has been propounded. In an article which cleverly correlates the historiographical interpretations of Negro enslavement with racial relations in the twentieth century, Winthrop

Jordan finds the previous approaches unsatisfactory. The question of whether prejudice was the precursor of slavery or slavery the institution which led to prejudicial behavior he finds basically unanswerable. Why, he asks, must it be an either/or proposition? ". . . what if we were to regard both slavery and prejudice as species of a general debasement of the Negro?"[25]

> Both may have been equally cause and effect, constantly reacting upon each other, dynamically joining hands to hustle the Negro down the road to degradation.[26]

Interaction of these two processes began, Jordan maintains, in agreement with Degler, in the early part of the seventeenth century. By the 1640's, slavery's most essential characteristics are to be found in acts which singled out the Negroes for special treatment: longer labor sentences in the general courts for the violation of laws, higher prices paid for Negroes than for white servants, and preference for Negro women as servants. The latter were highly prized because the children could be held for life. Jordan presents statistics contrasting the prices paid for Negro and white labor and concludes that

> In many instances the valuations placed on Negroes (in estate inventories and bills of sale) were far higher than for white servants. . . . Since there was ordinarily no preference for Negroes as such, higher prices must have meant that Negroes were more highly valued because of their greater length of service.[27]

Furthermore, they were specifically prohibited from bearing arms, denied sexual union with whites, and singled out in tax laws. These actions, which demonstrate a singular dislike for the Negro in Maryland and in Virginia, have led Jordan to conclude that slavery was a social arrangement, not an isolated economic institutional phenomenon as the Handlins and Elkins (though, for some reason, Jordan ignores Elkins' work) contend. It was, he states, "the practical facet of a general debasement without which slavery could have no rationality."[28]

Clearly, the four works under consideration are in agreement on one vital point: that the position of the African in the early years of colonial settlement and development was, at best, fairly precarious and tenuous. But in their respective analyses of the causal factors and relationships which determined the ultimate station of the Negro, there is wide variation and divergence.

The Handlins' thesis falls far short of explaining the acceptance of Negro inferiority in the northern colonies. Despite the small number of

Negro laborers, restrictions were placed on their behavior and movement prior to the laws defining their status as slaves. Why were there no groups in either England or in the colonies demanding greater freedom for the Negro at a time when energy was being directed toward improving the white servant position? It is difficult to accept the Handlins' position that this was due to oversight and to the desire to attract new workers to the colonies. Would improvement of the Negroes' lot have made a difference to the potential English servant? What does this say about the attitude of English who had little knowledge or contact with Americans or Indians? Highly questionable is the contention that the growing consciousness in the 1660's that the Negro would labor for life was the result not of "any particular concern with their status but simply by contrast with those whose years of labor are limited by statute." Given the validity of economic need dictating measures to insure a labor supply, the basic question is: why the adoption of the all-depriving condition of slavery with its destructive moral, social and personal ramifications? Would it not follow that there was indeed a deep concern or rather a dilemma regarding the role of the Negro in a purely social sense? The lengthening service for the Negro might well be a product of social unacceptance, as Degler and Jordan have argued; for if the Negro was not fully a human being, then certainly *he* and not the superior Englishman should labor for the longer period.

The dynamics of unopposed agrarian capitalism, while explaining why the plantation as a politico-economic unit became as powerful as it did, also fails to answer the same questions. Despite the paucity of Negro labor in the north, five colonies in the seventeenth century enacted statutes recognizing slavery as the condition of the Negro. Why was it necessary to do so? This aspect of Elkins' thesis, as does the Handlins', raises a more pertinent question: does economics play the primary role in the determination of social status?

Degler and Jordan basically posit that economic status is a reflection of society's view of one's social worth. Thus slavery was effected by an adverse appraisal of the Negro by the English; discriminatory acts preceded the legal definition of the institution. The nature of their argument draws attention back to several basic and still elusive considerations: why did the Englishman react to the African as he did? What cultural traits prevalent in his society or in the colonial settlements motivated his response? It is interesting to note that the English attitude toward the American Indian was quite similar and that the English pioneer sought resolution of the conflict with the alien cultures through a program of destruction of one and enslavement of the other.

It is obvious, then, that this problem of seventeenth century social conflict is subtle, complex, and demanding of additional research by social scientists. An analysis along the lines of what Degler has referred to as "folk bias," what Richard Hofstadter has termed the "feeling for social psychology,"[29] and particularly what Daniel Bell has labeled as the "moral sensibilities and temper" of a people[30] would seem most promising.

Within these contexts certain lines of studies might be pursued: a comparative study of English and African attitudes toward social institutions; the nature and intensity of English ethnocentrism; the field of education in the seventeenth century; and a comparative analysis of the reactions of other colonizing groups to the African, such as the Dutch and Scotch-Irish.

"To see history," Daniel Bell has suggested, "as changes in sensibilities and style or, more, how different classes of people mobilized their emotional energies and adopted different moral postures is relatively novel; yet the history of moral temper is, I feel, one of the most important ways of understanding social change, and particularly the irrational forces at work in men."[31]

Notes

1.   Board of Directors of the Theater Guild, *The Theater Guild Anthology* (New York: Random House, 1936), 517-18.

2.   Robert E. Park, *Race and Culture* (New York: The Free Press, 1950), 76.

3.   Frank Tannenbaum, *Slave and Citizen: The Negro in the Americas* (New York: Alfred A. Knopf, 1946). Tannenbaum's work is a comparative analysis of the Portuguese, Spanish, Dutch, and English systems of slavery.

4.   Oscar and Mary Handlin, "The Origins of the Southern Labor System," *William and Mary Quarterly,* 3rd Series, VII (April, 1950) 199-222; Stanley M. Elkins, *Slavery: A Problem in American Institutional and Intellectual Life* (Chicago: University of Chicago Press, 1959); Carl N. Degler, *Out of Our Past* (Harper and Row, 1959); Winthrop D. Jordan, "Modern Tensions and the Origins of American Slavery," *Journal of Southern History,* 28, No. 1 (February, 1962), 18-32.

5.   Handlin and Handlin, *ibid.,* 199.

6.   *Ibid.*

7.   *Ibid.,* 203 and n. 16.

8.   *Ibid.,* 208.

9.   *Ibid.,* 209 and n. 49.

10.   *Ibid.,* 211.

11.   *Ibid.,* 217.

12.   Elkins, *Slavery,* 37. Unlike the Handlins, however, Elkins contends that the absence of common law precedent had a negative effect: "Not only was there little in the common law, simply as law, to prevent the Negro from being compelled into

a state of slavery, but the very philosophy of the common law would encourage the colonial courts to develop whatever laws appeared necessary to deal with unprecedented conditions" (n. 22).

13. *Ibid.*, 38.

14. *Ibid.*, 41. There is a subtle difference on this point. Elkins supports the position held by Susie M. Ames, *Studies of the Virginia Eastern Shore in the Seventeenth Century* (Richmond: Dietz, 1940); and Wesley Frank Craven, *The Southern Colonies in the Seventeenth Century, 1607-1689* (Baton Rouge: Louisiana State University Press, 1949), who argue that in this "ill-defined" state there were no automatic guarantees for the Negro, one way or the other. Some Negroes remained slaves for life, whereas others were granted freedom and property. The Handlins, placing much import on the lack of differentiation between White servants and Africans, imply that the latter were on an equal footing with the former. In support of their position, the Handlins point to the large body of free Negroes in the colonies; Ames, Craven, Elkins and Degler do not accept the proposition that the existence of free Negroes demonstrates the absence of status differentiation. For an excellent synopsis of the historiographical line-ups of this dispute, see Elkins, 39, n. 16.

15. *Ibid.*, 41-42.

16. *Ibid.*, 43.

17. *Ibid.*, 49. By contrast, the presence of strong, traditional institutions in other capitalistic and noncapitalistic countries in South America prevented the development of slavery unique to the American South. Drawing heavily from the works of Tannenbaum and Gilberto Freyre, Elkins notes that in other countries where slavery took root, the Catholic Church, civil authorities, and the planter-adventurer acted as counterveiling forces to the depersonalization of the Negro.

18. *Ibid.*, 41 n. 19. This statement misses the essential point, however. The question is: why was there uniformity of agreement throughout the colonies when many were only indirectly concerned with the status of the African?

19. Carl Degler, *Out of Our Past,* 30.

20. *Ibid.*

21. *Ibid.*, 31.

22. *Ibid.*

23. *Ibid.*, 38.

24. *Ibid.*

25. Winthrop D. Jordan, "Modern Tensions and the Origins of American Slavery," 29.

26. *Ibid.*

27. *Ibid.*, 25. Degler's argument is identical: "In early seventeenth-century inventories of estates there are two distinctions which appear in the reckoning of the value of servants and Negroes. Uniformly, the Negroes are more valuable, even as children, than any white servant" (33).

28. *Ibid.*, 30.

29. Richard Hofstadter, "U. B. Phillips and the Plantation Legend," *Journal of Negro History,* 29 (April, 1944), 124.

30. Daniel Bell, *The End of Ideology* (New York: The Free Press, 1961), 440 n. 169.

31. *Ibid.*

A THEORY OF THE ORIGIN OF ETHNIC STRATIFICATION

Donald L. Noel

The concluding paper in part two is an attempt to state a theory of the origin of ethnic stratification which will explain the known facts regarding the origin of American slavery. The author draws upon a variety of earlier theories and studies in order to construct a theory which will meet the criticisms leveled at the explanations advanced and critiqued by the preceding selections. Competition, ethnocentrism, and differential power are the critical variables in Noel's theory. These variables describe the necessary and sufficient conditions for the emergence of any system of ethnic stratification and provide the following answers to the three critical theoretical questions. First, one group seeks to permanently subordinate another in order to achieve some scarce value, economic or otherwise. Second, the group selected for subordination is one which is accessible, vulnerable (i.e., *relatively* powerless), and sufficiently different (culturally and/or racially) to be the object of sharp ethnocentric rejection. Third, the form which ethnic stratification takes (e.g., serfdom, slavery, or segregation) is a function of the strength and interaction of the three key variables. The more intense the competition, the greater the (mutual) ethnocentrism and incongruence of critical group values, and the greater the difference in power between the groups involved, the greater the likelihood that slavery, the harshest form of ethnic stratification, will emerge and be institutionalized.

Much more precise measurement of these variables is essential before the theory can demonstrably explain variations in the *form* of ethnic stratification. Despite the present measurement deficiency, the theory is offered as an explanation of the origin of ethnic stratification in general, not just slavery, because it is the purpose of theory to generalize — to seek and state a comprehensive but parsimonious explanation of the myriad expressions of what is, at a higher level, a common social form.

106

Additional research, American and comparative, is definitely needed to firmly establish the validity of the theory and to specify the critical values of the key variables. In the meantime, critical assessment and clarification of the theory are in order.

Willhelm has criticized Noel's theory on the grounds that it under-emphasizes the importance of economic considerations.[1] In sharp contrast to Degler, who argues that economic factors were not crucial to the origin of American slavery, Willhelm argues that the economic variable is primary and, indeed, provides the base for the development of both ethnocentrism and differential power. Clearly the competitive gain to be derived from slavery may have stimulated ethnocentrism and economic variations are undoubtedly an important factor in the initial power differential between Europeans and Africans. However, it is quite another matter to explain ethnocentrism and power solely in economic terms.

Power, for example, is also crucially influenced by social organization (e.g., unity and solidarity) and it influences economic status as well as vice versa. Neither variable can be satisfactorily viewed as entirely a derivative of the other. Nevertheless, it is a plausible hypothesis that the initial preference for white instead of black laborers was a function of economic returns independent of ethnocentrism. The white indentured servants were more culturally similar to their employers and hence could be more efficiently exploited. However, the economic variable is clearly not adequate to account for the specific discriminatory laws and practices which existed prior to the institutionalization of slavery. For example, the desire for economic gain does not explain laws prohibiting blacks (servant or free) from bearing arms nor does it explain why black indentured females were required to work in the fields while white females were not. Ethnocentrism and prestige competition[2] provide much more convincing explanations for these early manifestations of ethnic stratification. The economic variable is vitally important but for the present it — or, more broadly, the condition of competition, whether for economic or other objects — must be viewed as merely *one* of the conditions essential to the emergence of ethnic stratification.

Two additional aspects of Noel's discussion require clarification. First, the elite undoubtedly played a role in the emergence of *de facto* slavery comparable to the critical role they subsequently played in instituting statutory, or *de jure,* slavery. The elite of any society are in a favorable position to secure the establishment of norms and practices beneficial to their interests regardless of whether they benefit the general populace. They may also have been the driving force behind passage of the discriminatory laws enacted prior to statutory slavery. The absence of a compelling motive, other than the ethnocentrism or prestige gain shared by the entire white population, plus the sparseness of the historical record for the critical years (1619–40) leaves this an open question—probably forever. Second, these early laws may be viewed as a separate form of ethnic stratification or simply as the beginning stage of slavery. In either event, the theory which explains the emergence of slavery should also explain the advent of these early laws.

Notes

1. Sidney M. Willhelm, personal communication to the author, dated October 17, 1969. Willhelm's position is forcefully stated in his excellent book *Who Needs the Negro?* (Cambridge, Mass.: Schenkman, 1970).

2. The importance of both the prestige motive ("the desire for aristocratic distinction") and the economic motive in the rise of racism and discrimination is effectively argued by Yves R. Simon, "Secret Sources of the Success of the Racist Ideology" in M. A. Fitzsimons, T. T. McAvoy, and F. O'Malley, eds., *The Image of Man* (Notre Dame, Ind.: University of Notre Dame Press, 1959), pp. 192-219.

While a great deal has been written about the nature and consequences of ethnic stratification, there have been few theoretical or empirical contributions regarding the causes of ethnic stratification.[1] It is the purpose of this paper to state a theory of the origin of ethnic stratification and then test it by applying the theory to an analysis of the origin of slavery in the United States. A number of recent contributions have clarified our knowledge of early Negro-white stratification[2] but there has been no attempt to analyze slavery's origin from the standpoint of a general theoretical framework. The present attempt focuses upon ethnocentrism, competition, and differential power as the key variables which together constitute the necessary and sufficient basis for the emergence and initial stabilization of ethnic stratification.

Ethnic stratification is, of course, only one type of stratification. Social stratification as a generic form of social organization is a structure of social inequality manifested via differences in prestige, power, and/or economic rewards. Ethnic stratification is a system of stratification wherein some relatively fixed group membership (e.g., race, religion, or

Reprinted from *Social Problems* 16 (Fall 1968): 157-72, by permission of The Society for the Study of Social Problems.

It should be emphasized that the present paper attempts only to explain the *origin* of ethnic stratification. The author and Ernest Barth are currently engaged in an effort to construct a general theory of ethnic stratification which answers a number of sociological questions in addition to that of origin.

nationality) is utilized as a major criterion for assigning social positions with their attendant differential rewards.

Prior to the emergence of ethnic stratification there must be a period of recurrent or continuous contact between the members of two or more distinct ethnic groups. This contact is an obvious requisite of ethnic stratification, but it is equally a requisite of equalitarian intergroup relations. Hence, intergroup contact is assumed as given and not treated as a theoretical element because in itself it does not provide a basis for predicting whether ethnic relations will be equalitarian or inequalitarian (i.e., stratified). Distinct ethnic groups can interact and form a stable pattern of relations without super-subordination.[3] Factors such as the nature of the groups prior to contact, the agents of contact, and the objectives of the contacting parties affect the likelihood of an equalitarian or inequalitarian outcome but only as they are expressed through the necessary and sufficient variables.[4]

The Theory and Its Elements

In contrast to intergroup contact *per se,* the presence of ethnocentrism, competition, and differential power provides a firm basis for predicting the emergence of ethnic stratification. Conversely, the absence of any one or more of these three elements means that ethnic stratification will not emerge. This is the essence of our theory. Each of the three elements is a variable but for present purposes they will be treated as attributes because our knowledge is not sufficiently precise to allow us to say what degrees of ethnocentrism, competition, and differential power are necessary to generate ethnic stratification. Recognition of the crucial importance of the three may stimulate greater efforts to precisely measure each of them. We shall examine each in turn.

Ethnocentrism is a universal characteristic of autonomous societies or ethnic groups. As introduced by Sumner the concept refers to that ". . . view of things in which one's own group is the center of everything, and all others are scaled and rated with reference to it."[5] From this perspective the values of the in-group are equated with abstract, universal standards of morality and the practices of the in-group are exalted as better or more "natural" than those of any out-group. Such an orientation is essentially a matter of in-group glorification and not of hostility toward any specific out-group. Nevertheless, an inevitable consequence of ethnocentrism is the rejection or downgrading of all out-groups to a greater or lesser degree as a function of the extent to which they differ from the in-group. The greater the difference the lower will be the relative rank of any given out-group, but any difference at all is grounds for negative evaluation.[6] Hence, English and Canadian immigrants rank very high relative to other out-groups in American society *but* they still rank below old American WASPs.[7]

Ethnocentrism is expressed in a variety of ways including mythology, condescension, and a double standard of morality in social relations. Becker has labeled this double standard a "dual ethic" in which in-group standards apply only to transactions with members of the in-group.[8] The outsider is viewed as fair game. Hence, intergroup economic relations are characterized by exploitation. Similarly, sexual relations between members of different groups are commonplace even when intermarriage is rare or prohibited entirely. The practice of endogamy is itself a manifestation of and, simultaneously, a means of reinforcing ethnocentrism. Endogamy is, indeed, an indication that ethnocentrism is present in sufficient degree for ethnic stratification to emerge.[9]

Insofar as distinct ethnic groups maintain their autonomy, mutual ethnocentrism will be preserved. Thus Indians in the Americas did not automatically surrender their ethnocentrism in the face of European technological and scientific superiority. Indeed, if the cultural strengths (including technology) of the out-group are not relevant to the values and goals of the in-group they will, by the very nature of ethnocentrism, be negatively defined. This is well illustrated in the reply (allegedly) addressed to the Virginia Commission in 1744 when it offered to educate six Indian youths at William and Mary:

> Several of our young people were formerly brought up at Colleges of the Northern Provinces; they were instructed in all your sciences; but when they came back to us, they were bad runners, ignorant of every means of living in the woods, unable to bear either cold or hunger, knew neither how to build a cabin, take a deer, or kill an enemy, spoke our language imperfectly, were therefore neither fit for hunters, warriors, or counsellors; they were totally good for nothing. We are, however, not the less obliged by your kind offer, though we decline accepting it; and to show our grateful Sense of it, if the Gentlemen of Virginia will send us a Dozen of their Sons we will take great care of their education, instruct them in all we know, and make Men of them.[10]

Ethnocentrism in itself need not lead to either interethnic conflict or ethnic stratification, however. The Tungus and Cossacks have lived in peace as politically independent but economically interdependent societies for several centuries. The groups remain racially and culturally dissimilar and each is characterized by a general ethnocentric preference for the in-group. This conflict potential is neutralized by mutual respect and admission by each that the other is superior in certain specific respects, by the existence of some shared values and interests, and by the absence of competition due to economic complementarity and low population density.[11]

The presence of competition, structured along ethnic lines, is an additional prerequisite for the emergence of ethnic stratification. Antonovsky has suggested that a discriminatory system of social relations requires both shared goals and scarcity of rewards,[12] and competition here refers to the interaction between two or more social units striving to achieve *the same scarce goal* (e.g., land or prestige). In the absence of shared goals members of the various ethnic groups involved in the contact situation would have, in the extreme case, mutually exclusive or nonoverlapping value hierarchies. If one group is not striving for a given goal, this reduces the likelihood of discrimination partly because members of that group are unlikely to be perceived as competitors for the goal. In addition, the indifference of one group toward the goal in effect reduces scarcity — i.e., fewer seekers enhance the probability of goal attainment by any one seeker. However, if the goal is still defined as scarce by members of one group they may seek to establish ethnic stratification in order to effectively exploit the labor of the indifferent group and thereby maximize goal attainment. In such a situation the labor (or other utility) of the indifferent group may be said to be the real object of competition. In any event the perceived scarcity of a socially valued goal is crucial and will stimulate the emergence of ethnic stratification *unless* each group perceives the other as: 1) disinterested in the relevant goal, *and* 2) nonutilitarian with respect to its own attainment of the goal.

In actuality the various goals of two groups involved in stable, complex interaction will invariably overlap to some degree and hence the likelihood of ethnic stratification is a function of the arena of competition. The arena includes the shared object(s) sought, the terms of the competition, and the relative adaptability of the groups involved.[13] Regarding the objects (or goals) of competition the greater the number of objects subject to competition, the more intense the competition. Moreover, as Wagley and Harris observe, "It is important to know the objects of competition, for it would seem that the more vital or valuable the resource over which there is competition, the more intense is the conflict between the groups."[14] Barring total annihilation of one of the groups, these points can be extended to state that the more intense the competition or conflict the greater the likelihood — other things being equal — that it will culminate in a system of ethnic stratification. In other words, the number and significance of the scarce, common goals sought determine the degree of competition which in turn significantly affects the probability that ethnic stratification will emerge.

The terms of the competition may greatly alter the probability of ethnic stratification, however, regardless of the intensity of the competition. The retention of a set of values or rules which effectively regulates — or moderates — ethnic interrelations is of particularly crucial significance. If a framework of regulative values fails to emerge, or breaks down, each group may seek to deny the other(s) the right to compete with the result that overt conflict emerges and culminates in annihilation, expulsion, or total subjugation of the less powerful group. If, in contrast, regulative values develop and are retained, competition even for vital goals need not result in ethnic stratification — or at least the span of stratification may be considerably constricted.[15]

Even where the groups involved are quite dissimilar culturally, the sharing of certain crucial values (e.g., religion or freedom, individualism, and equality) may be significant in preventing ethnic stratification. This appears to have been one factor in the enduring harmonious relations between the Cossacks and the Tungus. The influence of the regulative values upon the span of ethnic stratification is well illustrated by Tannenbaum's thesis regarding the differences between North American and Latin American slavery.[16] In the absence of a tradition of slavery the English had no established code prescribing the rights and duties of slaves and the racist ideology which evolved achieved its ultimate expression in the Dred Scott decision of 1857. This decision was highly consistent with the then widely held belief that the Negro "had no rights which the white man was bound to respect. . . ." By contrast the Iberian code accorded certain rights to the Latin American slave (including the right to own property and to purchase his freedom) which greatly restricted the extent of inequality between free man and slave.[17]

In addition to the regulative values, the structural opportunities for or barriers to upward mobility which are present in the society may affect the emergence and span of ethnic stratification. Social structural barriers such as a static, nonexpanding economy are a significant part of the terms of competition and they may be more decisive than the regulative values as regards the duration of the system. Finally, along with the goals and the terms of competition, the relative adaptive capacity of the groups involved is an aspect of competition which significantly affects the emergence of ethnic stratification.

Wagley and Harris assume that ethnic stratification is given and focus their analysis on the adaptive capacity of *the minority group* in terms of its effect upon the span and the duration of ethnic stratification. Thus they view adaptive capacity as:

> those elements of a minority's cultural heritage which provide it with a basis for competing more or less effectively with the dominant group, which afford protection against exploitation, which stimulate or retard its adaptation to the total social environment, and which facilitate or hinder its upward advance through the socio-economic hierarchy.[18]

We shall apply the concept to an earlier point in the intergroup process — i.e., prior to the emergence of ethnic stratification — by broadening it to refer to those aspects of any ethnic group's sociocultural heritage which affect its adjustment to a given social and physical environment. The group with the greater adaptive capacity is apt to emerge as the dominant group[19] while the other groups are subordinated to a greater or lesser degree — i.e., the span of the stratification system will be great or slight — dependent upon the extent of their adaptive capacity relative to that of the emergent dominant group.

The duration, as well as the origin and span, of ethnic stratification will be markedly influenced by adaptive capacity. Once a people have become a minority, flexibility on their part is essential if they are to efficiently adjust and effectively compete within the established system of ethnic stratification and thereby facilitate achievement of equality. Sociocultural patterns are invariably altered by changing life conditions. However, groups vary in the alacrity with which they respond to changing conditions. A flexible minority group may facilitate the achievement of equality or even dominance by readily accepting modifications of their heritage which will promote efficient adaptation to their subordination *and* to subsequent changes in life conditions.

Competition and ethnocentrism do not provide a sufficient explanation for the emergence of ethnic stratification. Highly ethnocentric groups involved in competition for vital objects will not generate ethnic stratification *unless* they are of such unequal power that one is able to impose its will upon the other.[20] Inequality of power is the defining characteristic of dominant and minority groups, and Lenski maintains that differential power is the foundation element in the genesis of any stratification system.[21] In any event differential power is absolutely essential to the emergence of ethnic stratification and the greater the differential the greater the span and durability of the system, other things being equal.

Technically, power is a component of adaptive capacity as Wagley and Harris imply in their definition by referring to "protection against exploitation." Nevertheless, differential power exerts an effect independent of adaptive capacity in general and is of such crucial relevance for ethnic stratification as to warrant its being singled out as a third major causal variable. The necessity of treating it as a distinct variable is amply demonstrated by consideration of those historical cases where one group has the greater adaptive capacity in general but is subordinated because another group has greater (military) power. The Dravidians overrun by the Aryans in ancient India and the Manchu conquest of China are illustrative cases.[22]

Unless the ethnic groups involved are unequal in power, intergroup relations will be characterized by conflict, symbiosis, or a pluralist equilibrium. Given intergroup competition, however, symbiosis is unlikely and conflict and pluralism are inevitably unstable. Any slight change in the existing balance of power may be sufficient to establish the temporary dominance of one group and this can be utilized to allow the emerging dominant group to perpetuate and enhance its position.[23] Once dominance is established the group in power takes all necessary steps to restrict the now subordinated groups, thereby hampering their effectiveness as competitors,[24] and to institutionalize the emerging distribution of rewards and opportunities. Hence, since power tends to beget power, a slight initial alteration in the distribution of power can become the basis of a stable inequalitarian system.

We have now elaborated the central concepts and propositions of a theory of the emergence and initial stabilization of ethnic stratification. The theory can be summarized as follows. When distinct ethnic groups are brought into sustained contact (via migration, the emergence and expansion of the state, or internal differentiation of a previously homogeneous group), ethnic stratification will invariably follow if — and only if — the groups are characterized by a significant degree of ethnocentrism, competition, *and* differential power. Without ethnocentrism the groups would quickly merge and competition would not be structured along ethnic lines. Without competition there would be no motivation or rationale for instituting stratification along ethnic lines. Without differential power it would simply be impossible for one group to achieve dominance and impose subordination to its will and ideals upon the other(s).

The necessity of differential power is incontestable but it could be argued that either competition or ethnocentrism is dispensable. For example, perhaps extreme ethnocentrism independent of competition is sufficient motive for seeking to impose ethnic stratification. Certainly ethnocentrism could encourage efforts to promote continued sharp differentiation, but it would not by itself motivate stratification unless we assume the existence of a *need* for dominance or aggression. Conversely, given sociocultural differences, one group may be better prepared for and therefore able to more effectively exploit a given environment. Hence, this group would become economically dominant and might then perceive and pursue the advantages (especially economic) of ethnic stratification quite independent of ethnocentrism. On the other hand, while differential power and competition alone are clearly sufficient to generate stratification, a low degree of ethnocentrism could readily forestall *ethnic* stratification by permitting assimilation and thereby eliminating differential adaptive capacity. Ethnocentrism undeniably heightens awareness of ethnicity and thereby promotes the formation and retention of ethnic competition, but the crucial question is whether or not some specified degree of ethnocentrism is *essential* to the emergence of ethnic stratification. Since autonomous ethnic groups are invariably ethnocentric, the answer awaits more precise measures of ethnocentrism which will allow us to test hypotheses specifying the necessary degree of ethnocentrism.[25]

Given the present state of knowledge it seems advisable to retain both competition and ethnocentrism, as well as differential power, as integral elements of the theory. Our next objective, then, is to provide an initial test of the theory by applying it to an analysis of the genesis of slavery in the seventeenth century mainland North American colonies.

The Origin of American Slavery

There is a growing consensus among historians of slavery in the United States that Negroes were not initially slaves but that they were gradually reduced to a position of chattel slavery over several decades.[26] The historical record regarding their initial status is so vague and incomplete, however, that it is impossible to assert with finality that their status was initially no different from that of non-Negro indentured servants.[27] Moreover, while there is agreement that the statutory establishment of slavery was not widespread until the 1660's, there is disagreement regarding slavery's emergence in actual practice. The Handlins maintain that "The status of Negroes was that of servants; and so they were identified and treated down to the 1660's."[28] Degler and Jordan argue that this conclusion is not adequately documented and cite evidence indicating that some Negroes were slaves as early as 1640.[29]

Our central concern is to relate existing historical research to the theory elaborated above, *not* to attempt original historical research intended to resolve the controversy regarding the nature and extent of the initial status differences (if any) between white and Negro bondsmen. However, two findings emerging from the controversy are basic to our concern: 1) although the terms servant and slave were frequently used interchangeably, whites were never slaves in the sense of serving for life and conveying a like obligation to their offspring; and 2) many Negroes were not slaves in this sense at least as late as the 1660's. Concomitantly with the Negroes' descent to slavery, white servants gained increasingly liberal terms of indenture and, ultimately, freedom. The origin of slavery for the one group and the growth of freedom for the other are explicable in terms of our theory as a function of differences in ethnocentrism, the arena of competition, and power vis-à-vis the dominant group or class.[30]

Degler argues that the status of the Negro evolved in a framework of discrimination and, therefore, "The important point is not the evolution of the legal status of the slave, but the fact that discriminatory legislation regarding the Negro long preceded any legal definition of slavery."[31] The first question then becomes one of explaining this differential treatment which foreshadowed the descent to slavery. A major element in the answer is implied by the Handlins' observation that "The rudeness of the Negroes' manners, the strangeness of their languages, the difficulty of communicating to them English notions of morality and proper behavior occasioned sporadic laws to regulate their conduct."[32] By itself this implies a contradiction of their basic thesis that Negro and white indentured servants were treated similarly prior to 1660. They maintain, however, that there was nothing unique nor decisive in this differential treatment of Negroes, for such was also accorded various Caucasian out-groups in this period.[33] While Jordan dismisses the Handlins' evidence as largely irrelevant to the point and Degler feels that it is insufficient, Degler acknowledges that "Even Irishmen, who were white, Christian, and European, were held to be literally 'beyond the Pale,' and some were even referred to as 'slaves'."[34] Nevertheless, Degler contends that the overall evidence justifies his conclusion that Negroes were generally accorded a lower position than any white, bound or free.

That the English made status distinctions between various out-groups is precisely what one would expect, however, given the nature of ethnocentrism. The degree of ethnocentric rejection is primarily a function of the degree of difference, and Negroes were markedly different from the dominant English in color, nationality, language, religion, and other aspects of culture.[35] The differential treatment of Negroes was by no means entirely due to a specifically anti-Negro *color* prejudice. Indeed, color was not initially the most important factor in determining the relative status of Negroes; rather, the fact that they were non-Christian was of major significance.[36] Although beginning to lose its preeminence, religion was still the central institution of society in the seventeenth century and religious prejudice toward non-Christians or heathens was widespread. The priority of religious over color prejudice is amply demonstrated by analysis of the early laws and court decisions pertaining to Negro-white sexual relations. These sources explicitly reveal greater concern with Christian-non-Christian than with white-Negro unions.[37] During and after the 1660's laws regulating racial intermarriage arose but for some time their emphasis was generally, if not invariably, upon religion, nationality, or some basis of differentiation other than race *per se*. For example, a Maryland law of 1681 described marriages of white women with Negroes as lascivious and "to the disgrace not only of the English butt allso [sic] of many *other Christian* Nations."[38] Moreover, the laws against Negro-white marriage seem to have been rooted much more in economic considerations than they were in any concern for white racial purity.[39] In short, it was not a simple color prejudice but a marked degree of ethnocentrism, rooted in a multitude of salient differences, which combined with competition and differential power to reduce Negroes to the status of slaves.[40]

Degler has noted that Negroes initially lacked a status in North America and thus almost any kind of status could have been worked out.[41] Given a different competitive arena, a more favorable status blurring the sharp ethnic distinctions could have evolved. However, as the demand for labor in an expanding economy began to exceed the supply, interest in lengthening the term of indenture arose.[42] This narrow economic explanation of the origin of slavery has been challenged on the grounds that slavery appeared equally early in the Northern colonies although there were too few Negroes there to be of economic significance.[43] This seemingly decisive point is largely mitigated by two considerations.

First, in the other colonies it was precisely *the few* who did own slaves who were not only motivated by vested interests but were also the men of means and local power most able to secure a firm legal basis for slavery.[44] The distribution of power and motivation was undoubtedly similar and led to the same consequences in New England. For the individual retainer of Negro servants the factual and legal redefinition of Negroes as chattel constitutes a vital economic interest whether or not the number of slaves is sufficient to vitally affect the economy of the colony. Our knowledge of the role of the elite in the establishment of community mores suggests that this constitutes at least a partial explanation of the Northern laws.[45] In addition, the markedly smaller number of Negroes in the North might account for the fact that "although enactments in the Northern colonies recognized the legality of lifetime servitude, no effort was made to require all Negroes to be placed in that condition."[46] We surmise that the laws were passed at the behest of a few powerful individuals who had relatively many Negro servants and were indifferent to the status of Negroes in general so long as their own vested interests were protected.

The explanation for the more all-encompassing laws of the Southern colonies is rooted in the greater homogeneity of interests of the Southern elite. In contrast to the Northern situation, the men of power in the Southern colonies were predominantly planters who were unified in their need for large numbers of slaves. The margin of profit in agricultural production for the commercial market was such that the small land-holder could not compete and the costs of training and the limitations on control (by the planter) which were associated with indentured labor made profitable exploitation of such labor increasingly difficult.[47] Hence, it was not the need for labor *per se* which was critical for the establishment of the comprehensive Southern slave system but rather the requirements of the emerging economic system for a particular kind of labor. In short, the Southern power elite uniformly needed slave labor while only certain men of power shared this need in the North and hence the latter advocated slave laws but lacked the power (or did not feel the need) to secure the all-encompassing laws characteristic of the Southern colonies.

There is a second major consideration in explaining the existence of Northern slavery. Men do not compete only for economic ends. They also compete for prestige and many lesser objects, and there is ample basis for suggesting that prestige competition was a significant factor in the institutionalization of slavery, North and South. Degler calls attention to the prestige motive when he discusses the efforts to establish a feudal aristocracy in seventeenth century New York, Maryland, and the Carolinas. He concludes that these efforts failed because the manor was "dependent upon the scarcity of land."[48] The failure of feudal aristocracy in no way denies the fundamental human desire for success or prestige. Indeed, this failure opened the society. It emphasized success and mobility for "it meant that wealth, rather than family or tradition, would be the primary determinant of social stratification."[49] Although the stress was on economic success, there were other gains associated with slavery to console those who did not achieve wealth. The desire for social prestige derivable from "membership in a superior caste" undoubtedly provided motivation and support for slavery among both Northern and Southern whites, slaveholders and nonslaveholders.[50]

The prestige advantage of slavery would have been partially undercut, especially for nonslaveholders, by enslavement of white bondsmen, but it is doubtful that this was a significant factor in their successfully eluding hereditary bondage. Rather the differential treatment of white and Negro bondsmen, ultimately indisputable and probably present from the very beginning, is largely attributable to differences in ethnocentrism and relative power. There was little or no ethnocentric rejection of the majority of white bondsmen during the seventeenth century because most of them were English.[51] Moreover, even the detested Irish and other non-English white servants were culturally and physically much more similar to the English planters than were the Africans. Hence, the planters clearly preferred white bondsmen until the advantages of slavery became increasingly apparent in the latter half of the seventeenth century.[52]

The increasing demand for labor after the mid-seventeenth century had divergent consequences for whites and blacks. The colonists became increasingly concerned to encourage immigration by counteracting "the widespread reports in England and Scotland that servants were harshly treated and bound in perpetual slavery" and by enacting "legislation designed to improve servants' conditions and to enlarge the prospect of a meaningful release, a release that was not the start of a new period of servitude, but of life as a freeman and landowner."[53] These improvements curtailed the exploitation of white servants without directly affecting the status of the Africans.

> Farthest removed from the English, least desired, [the Negro] communicated with no friends who might be deterred from following. *Since his coming was involuntary, nothing that happened to him would increase or decrease his numbers.* To raise the status of Europeans by shortening their terms would ultimately increase the available hands by inducing their compatriots to emigrate; to reduce the Negro's term would produce an immediate loss and no ultimate gain. By mid-century the servitude of Negroes seems generally lengthier than that of whites; and thereafter, the consciousness dawns that the blacks will toil for the whole of their lives. . . .[54]

The planters and emerging agrarian capitalism were unconstrained in a planter-dominated society with no traditional institutions to exert limits. In this context even the common law tradition helped promote slavery.[55]

Ethnocentrism set the Negroes apart but their almost total lack of power and effective spokesmen, in contrast to white indentured servants, was decisive in their enslavement. Harris speaks directly to the issue and underscores the significance of (organized) power for the emergence of slavery:

> The facts of life in the New World were such . . . that Negroes, being the most defenseless of all the immigrant groups, were discriminated

against and exploited more than any others. . . . Judging from the very nasty treatment suffered by white indentured servants, it was obviously not sentiment which prevented the Virginia planters from enslaving their fellow Englishmen. They undoubtedly would have done so had they been able to get away with it. But such a policy was out of the question as long as there was a King and a Parliament in England.[56]

The Negroes, in short, did not have any organized external government capable of influencing the situation in their favor.[57] Moreover, "there was no one in England or in the colonies to pressure for the curtailment of the Negro's servitude or to fight for his future."[58]

The Negroes' capacity to adapt to the situation and effectively protest in their own behalf was greatly hampered by their cultural diversity and lack of unification. They did not think of themselves as "a kind." They did not subjectively share a common identity and thus they lacked the group solidarity necessary to effectively "act as a unit in competition with other groups."[59] Consciousness of shared fate is essential to effective unified action but it generally develops only gradually as the members of a particular social category realize that they are being treated alike despite their differences. "People who find themselves set apart eventually come to recognize their common interests," but for those who share a subordinate position common identification usually emerges only after "repeated experiences of denial and humiliation."[60] The absence of a shared identification among seventeenth century Negroes reflected the absence of a shared heritage from which to construct identity, draw strength, and organize protest. Hence, Negroes were easily enslaved and reduced to the status of chattel. This point merits elaboration.

We have defined adaptive capacity in terms of a group's sociocultural heritage as it affects adjustment to the environment. Efficient adaptation may require the members of a group to modify or discard a great deal of their heritage. A number of factors, including ethnocentrism and the centrality of the values and social structures requiring modification, affect willingness to alter an established way of life.[61] Even given a high degree of willingness, however, many groups simply have not possessed the cultural complexity or social structural similarity to the dominant group necessary to efficient adaptation. Many Brazilian and United States Indian tribes, for example, simply have not had the knowledge (e.g., of writing, money, markets, etc.) or the structural similarity to their conquerors (e.g., as regards the division of labor) necessary to protect themselves from exploitation and to achieve a viable status in an emerging multi-ethnic society.[62]

By comparison with most New World Indians the sociocultural heritage of the Africans was remarkably favorable to efficient adaptation.[63] However, the discriminatory framework within which white-Negro relations developed in the seventeenth century ultimately far outweighed the cultural advantages of the Negroes vis-à-vis the Indians in the race for status.[64] The Negroes from any given culture were widely dispersed and their capacity to adapt *as a group* was thereby shattered. Like the Negroes, the Indians were diverse culturally but they retained their cultural heritage and social solidarity, and they were more likely to resist slavery because of the much greater probability of reunion with their people following escape. Hence, Negroes were preferred over Indians as slaves both because their cultural background had better prepared them for the slave's role in the plantation system (thus enhancing the profits of the planters) and because they lacked the continuing cultural and group support which enabled the Indians to effectively resist slavery.[65] By the time the Africans acquired the dominant English culture and social patterns *and* a sense of shared fate, their inability to work out a more favorable adaptation was assured by the now established distribution of power and by the socialization processes facilitating acceptance of the role of slave.[66]

Conclusion

We conclude that ethnocentrism, competition, and differential power provide a comprehensive explanation of the origin of slavery in the seventeenth century English colonies. The Negroes were clearly more different from the English colonists than any other group (*except* the Indians) by almost any criterion, physical or cultural, that might be selected as a basis of social differentiation. Hence, the Negroes were the object of a relatively intense ethnocentric rejection from the beginning. The opportunity for great mobility characteristic of a frontier society created an arena of competition which dovetailed with this ethnocentrism. Labor, utilized to achieve wealth, and prestige were the primary objects of this competition. These goals were particularly manifest in the Southern colonies, but our analysis provides a rationale for the operation of the same goals as sources of motivation to institutionalize slavery in the Northern colonies also.

The terms of the competition for the Negro's labor are implicit in the evolving pattern of differential treatment of white and Negro bondsmen prior to slavery and in the precarious position of free Negroes. As slavery became institutionalized the moral, religious, and legal values of the society were increasingly integrated to form a highly consistent complex which acknowledged no evil in "the peculiar institution."[67] Simultaneously, Negroes were denied any opportunity to escape their position of lifetime, inheritable servitude. Only by the grace of a generous master, not by any act of his own, could a slave achieve freedom and, moreover, there were "various legal strictures aimed at impeding or discouraging the process of private manumission."[68] The rigidity of "the peculiar institution" was fixed before the Negroes acquired sufficient common culture, sense of shared fate, and identity to be able to effectively challenge the system. This lack of unity was a major determinant of the Africans' poor adaptive capacity as a group. They lacked the social solidarity and common cultural resources essential to organized resistance and thus in the absence of intervention by a powerful external ally they were highly vulnerable to exploitation.

The operation of the three key factors is well summarized by Stampp:

> Neither the provisions of their charters nor the policy of the English government limited the power of colonial legislatures to control Negro labor as they saw fit. . . . Their unprotected condition encouraged the trend toward special treatment, and their physical and cultural differences provided handy excuses to justify it . . . . [T]he landholders' growing appreciation of the advantages of slavery over the older forms of servitude gave a powerful impetus to the growth of the new labor system.[69]

In short, the present theory stresses that *given* ethnocentrism, the Negroes' lack of power, and the dynamic arena of competition in which they were located, their ultimate enslavement was inevitable. The next task is to test the theory further, incorporating modifications as necessary, by analyzing subsequent accommodations in the pattern of race relations in the United States and by analyzing the emergence of various patterns of ethnic stratification in other places and eras.

Notes

1.   The same observation regarding social stratification in general has recently been made by Gerhard Lenski, *Power and Privilege,* New York: McGraw-Hill, 1966, p. ix.

2.   See Joseph Boskin, "Race Relations in Seventeenth Century America: The Problem of the Origins of Negro Slavery," *Sociology and Social Research,* 49 (July, 1965), pp. 446-455, including references cited therein; and David B. Davis, *The Problem of Slavery in Western Culture,* Ithaca: Cornell U., 1966.

3.   A classic example is provided by Ethel John Lindgren, "An Example of Culture Contact Without Conflict: Reindeer Tungus and Cossacks of Northwest Manchuria," *American Anthropologist,* 40 (October-December, 1938), pp. 605-621.

4.   The relevance of precontact and of the nature and objectives of the contacting agents for the course of intergroup relations has been discussed by various scholars including Edward B. Reuter in his editor's "Introduction" to *Race and Culture Contacts,* New York: McGraw-Hill, 1934, pp. 1-18; and Clarence E. Glick, "Social Roles and Types in Race Relations," in Andrew W. Lind, editor, *Race Relations in World Perspective,* Honolulu: U. of Hawaii, 1955, pp. 239-262.

5.   William G. Sumner, *Folkways,* Boston: Ginn, 1940, p. 13. The essence of ethnocentrism is well conveyed by Catton's observation that "Ethnocentrism makes us see out-group behavior as deviation from in-group mores rather than as adherence to out-group mores." William R. Catton, Jr., "The Development of Sociological Thought" in Robert E. L. Faris, editor, *Handbook of Modern Sociology,* Chicago: Rand McNally, 1964, p. 930.

6.   Williams observes that "in various *particular* ways an out-group may be seen as superior" insofar as its members excel in performance vis-à-vis certain norms that the two groups hold in common (e.g., sobriety or craftsmanship in the production of a particular commodity). Robin M. Williams, Jr., *Strangers Next Door,* Englewood Cliffs, N.J.: Prentice-Hall, 1964, p. 22 (emphasis added). A similar point is made by Marc J. Swartz, "Negative Ethnocentrism," *Journal of Conflict Resolution,* 5 (March, 1961), pp. 75-81. It is highly unlikely, however, that the out-group will be so consistently objectively superior in the realm of shared values as to be seen as generally superior to the in-group unless the in-group is subordinate to or highly dependent upon the out-group.

7.   Emory S. Bogardus, *Social Distance,* Yellow Springs: Antioch, 1959.

8.   Howard P. Becker, *Man in Reciprocity,* New York: Praeger, 1956, Ch. 15.

9.   Endogamy is an overly stringent index of the degree of ethnocentrism essential to ethnic stratification and is not itself a prerequisite of the emergence of ethnic stratification. However, where endogamy does not precede ethnic stratification, it is a seemingly invariable consequence. Compare this position with that of Charles Wagley and Marvin Harris who treat ethnocentrism and endogamy as independent structural requisites of intergroup hostility and conflict. See *Minorities in the New World,* New York: Columbia, 1958, pp. 256-263.

10.   Quoted in T. Walter Wallbank and Alastair M. Taylor, *Civilization: Past and Present,* Chicago: Scott, Foresman, 1949, rev. ed., Vol. 1, pp. 559-560. The offer and counter-offer also provide an excellent illustration of mutual ethnocentrism.

11.   Lindgren, *op. cit.*

12.   Aaron Antonovsky, "The Social Meaning of Discrimination," *Phylon,* 21 (Spring, 1960), pp. 81-95.

13.   This analysis of the arena of competition is a modification of the analysis by Wagley and Harris, *op. cit.,* esp. pp. 263-264. These authors limit the concept "arena" to the objects sought *and* the regulative values which determine opportunity to compete and then partly confound their components by including the regulative values, along with adaptive capacity and the instruments necessary to compete, as part of the "terms" of competition.

14.   *Ibid.,* p. 263. They suggest that competition for scarce subsistence goals will produce more intense conflict than competition for prestige symbols or other culturally defined goals.

15.   Discussing the ideological aspect of intergroup relations, Wagley and Harris note that equalitarian creeds have generally not been effective in *preventing* ethnic stratification. *Ibid.,* pp. 280 ff. The operation of ethnocentrism makes it very easy for the boundaries of the in-group to become the boundaries of adherence to group values.

16. Frank Tannenbaum, *Slave and Citizen: The Negro in the Americas,* New York: Random House, 1963.

17. *Ibid.,* esp. pp. 49 ff. Marvin Harris has criticized Tannenbaum's thesis by arguing that the rights prescribed by the Iberian code were largely illusory and that there is no certainty that *slaves* were treated better in Latin America. Harris in turn provides a functional (economic necessity) explanation for the historical difference in treatment of *free* Negroes in the two continents. See Marvin Harris, *Patterns of Race in the Americas,* New York: Walker, 1964, esp. Chs. 6 and 7.

18. Wagley and Harris, *op. cit.,* p. 264.

19. This point is explicitly made by Tamotsu Shibutani and Kian M. Kwan, *Ethnic Stratification: A Comparative Approach,* New York: Macmillan, 1965, p. 147; see also Ch. 9.

20. This point is made by Antonovsky, *op. cit.,* esp. p. 82, and implied by Wagley and Harris in their discussion of the role of the state in the formation of minority groups, *op. cit.,* esp. pp. 240-244. Stanley Lieberson's recent modification of Park's cycle theory of race relations also emphasizes the importance of differential power as a determinant of the outcome of intergroup contacts. See "A Societal Theory of Race and Ethnic Relations," *American Sociological Review,* 26 (December, 1961), pp. 902-910.

21. Lenski, *op. cit.,* esp. Ch. 3.

22. See Wallbank and Taylor, *op. cit.,* p. 95; and Shibutani and Kwan, *op. cit.,* pp. 129-130.

23. See *ibid.,* esp. Chs. 6, 9, and 12; and Richard A. Schermerhorn, *Society and Power,* New York: Random House, 1961, pp. 18-26.

24. Shibutani and Kwan observe that dominance rests upon victory in the competitive process and that competition between groups is eliminated or greatly reduced once a system of ethnic stratification is stabilized, *op. cit.,* pp. 146 and 235, and Ch. 12. The extent to which competition is actually stifled is highly variable, however, as Wagley and Harris note in their discussion of minority adaptive capacity and the terms of competition, *op. cit.,* pp. 263 ff.

25. The issue is further complicated by the fact that the necessary degree of any one of the three elements may vary as a function of the other two.

26. The main relevant references in the recent literature include Carl N. Degler, *Out of Our Past,* New York: Harper and Row, 1959 and "Slavery and the Genesis of American Race Prejudice," *Comparative Studies in Society and History,* 2 (October, 1959), pp. 49-66; Stanley M. Elkins, *Slavery: A Problem in American Institutional and Intellectual Life,* Chicago: U. of Chicago, 1959; Oscar and Mary F. Handlin, "Origins of the Southern Labor System," *William and Mary Quarterly,* 3rd Series, 7 (April, 1950), pp. 199-222; and Winthrop D. Jordan, "Modern Tensions and the Origins of American Slavery," *The Journal of Southern History,* 28 (February, 1962), pp. 18-30, and *White over Black,* Chapel-Hill: U. of North Carolina, 1968. See also Boskin, *op. cit.,* and "Comment" and "Reply" by the Handlins and Degler in the cited volume of *Comparative Studies . . . ,* pp. 488-495.

27. Jordan, *The Journal . . . ,* p. 22.

28. Handlin and Handlin, *op. cit.,* p. 203.

29. Degler, *Comparative Studies . . . ,* pp. 52-56 and Jordan, *The Journal . . . ,* pp. 23-27 and *White over Black,* pp. 73-74. Also see Elkins, *op. cit.,* pp. 38-42 (esp. fns. 16 and 19).

30. Our primary concern is with the emergence of Negro slavery but the theory also explains how white bondsmen avoided slavery. Their position vis-à-vis the dominant English was characterized by a different "value" of at least two of the key variables.

31. Degler, *Out of Our Past,* p. 35. Bear in mind, however, that slavery was not initially institutionalized in law or in the mores.

32. Handlin and Handlin, *op. cit.,* pp. 208-209.

33. *Ibid.* They note that "It is not necessary to resort to racialist assumptions to account for such measures; . . . [for immigrants in a strange environment] longed . . . for the company of familiar men and singled out to be welcomed those who were most like themselves." See pp. 207-211 and 214.

34. Jordan, *The Journal* . . . , esp. pp. 27 (fn. 29) and 29 (fn. 34); and Degler, *Out of Our Past,* p. 30.

35. Only the aboriginal Indians were different from the English colonists to a comparable degree and they were likewise severely dealt with via a policy of exclusion and annihilation after attempts at enslavement failed. See Boskin, *op. cit.,* p. 453; and Jordan, *White over Black,* pp. 85-92.

36. The priority of religious over racial prejudice and discrimination in the early seventeenth century is noted in *ibid.,* pp. 97-98 and by Edgar J. McManus, *A History of Negro Slavery in New York,* Syracuse: Syracuse U., 1966, esp. pp. 11-12.

37. Jordan, *The Journal* . . . , p. 28 and *White Over Black,* pp. 78-80.

38. Quoted in *ibid.,* pp. 79-80 (emphasis added). Also see pp. 93-97, however, where Jordan stresses the necessity of carefully interpreting the label "Christian."

39. See Handlin and Handlin, *op. cit.,* pp. 213-216; and W. D. Zabel, "Interracial Marriage and the Law," *The Atlantic* (October, 1965), pp. 75-79.

40. The distinction between ethnocentrism (the rejection of out-groups *in general* as a function of in-group glorification) and prejudice (hostility toward the members of a *specific* group because they are members of that group) is crucial to the controversy regarding the direction of causality between discrimination, slavery, and prejudice. Undoubtedly these variables are mutually causal to some extent but Harris, *op cit.,* esp. pp. 67-70, presents evidence that prejudice is primarily a consequence and is of minor importance as a cause of slavery.

41. Degler, *Comparative Studies* . . . , p. 51. See also Boskin, *op. cit.,* pp. 449 and 454 (esp. fn. 14); Elkins, *op. cit.,* pp. 39-42 (esp. fn. 16); and Kenneth M. Stampp, *The Peculiar Institution,* New York: Knopf, 1956, p. 21. The original indeterminacy of the Negroes' status is reminiscent of Blumer's "sense of group position" theory of prejudice and, in light of Blumer's theory, is consistent with the belief that there was no widespread prejudice toward Negroes prior to the institutionalization of slavery. See Herbert Blumer, "Race Prejudice as a Sense of Group Position," *Pacific Sociological Review,* 1 (Spring, 1958), pp. 3-7.

42. Handlin and Handlin, *op. cit.,* p. 210. Differential power made this tactic as suitable to the situation of Negro bondsmen as it was unsuitable in regard to white bondsmen.

43. Degler acknowledges that the importance of perpetuating a labor force indispensable to the economy later became a crucial support of slavery but he denies that the need for labor explains the origin of slavery. His explanation stresses prior discrimination which, in the terms of the present theory, was rooted in ethnocentrism and differential power. See *Comparative Studies* . . . , including the "Reply" to the Handlins' "Comment;" and *Out of Our Past,* pp. 35-38 and 162-168.

44. Elkins, *op. cit.*, pp. 45 (esp. fn. 26) and 48.

45. Historical precedent is provided by the finding that "The vagrancy laws emerged in order to provide the powerful landowners with a ready supply of cheap labor." See William J. Chambliss, "A Sociological Analysis of the Law of Vagrancy," *Social Problems,* 12 (Summer, 1964), pp. 67-77. Jordan, *White over Black,* pp. 67 and 69, provides evidence that the economic advantages of slavery were clearly perceived in the Northern colonies.

46. Elkins, *op. cit.*, p. 41 (fn. 19).

47. By the 1680's "The point had clearly passed when white servants could realistically, on any long-term appraisal, be considered preferable to Negro slaves." *Ibid.*, p. 48.

48. Degler, *Out of Our Past,* p. 3. Also see Hubert M. Blalock, Jr., *Toward a Theory of Minority Group Relations,* New York: Wiley, 1967, pp. 44-48.

49. Degler, *Out of Our Past,* p. 5; see also pp. 45-50. Elkins, *op. cit.*, esp. pp. 43-44, also notes the early emphasis on personal success and mobility.

50. Stampp, *op. cit.*, pp. 29-33, esp. 32-33. Also see J. D. B. DeBow, "The Interest in Slavery of the Southern Non-Slaveholder," reprinted in Eric L. McKitrick, editor, *Slavery Defended: The Views of the Old South,* Englewood Cliffs, N.J.: Prentice-Hall, 1963, pp. 169-177.

51. Stampp, *op. cit.*, p. 16: and Degler, *Out of Our Past,* pp. 50-51. Consistent with the nature of ethnocentrism, "The Irish and other aliens, less desirable, at first received longer terms. But the realization that such discrimination retarded 'the peopling of the country' led to an extension of the identical privilege to all Christians." Handlin and Handlin, *op. cit.*, pp. 210-211.

52. Elkins, *op. cit.*, pp. 40 and 48; and Handlin and Handlin, *op. cit.*, pp. 207-208.

53. *Ibid.*, p. 210.

54. *Ibid.*, p. 211 (emphasis added). That the need for labor led to improvements in the status of white servants seems very likely but Degler in *Comparative Studies . . .* effectively challenges some of the variety of evidence presented by the Handlins, *op. cit.*, pp. 210 and 213-214 and "Comment."

55. Elkins, *op. cit.*, pp. 38 (fn. 14), 42 (fn. 22), 43 and 49-52; and Jordan, *White over Black,* pp. 49-51.

56. Harris, *op. cit.*, pp. 69-70.

57. The effectiveness of intervention by an external government is illustrated by the halting of Indian emigration to South Africa in the 1860's as a means of protesting "the indignities to which indentured 'coolies' were subjected in Natal, ..." See Pierre L. van den Berghe, *South Africa, A Study in Conflict,* Middletown: Wesleyan U., 1965, p. 250.

58. Boskin, *op. cit.*, p. 448. Also see Stampp, *op. cit.*, p. 22; and Elkins, *op. cit.*, pp. 49-52.

59. Shibutani and Kwan, *op. cit.*, p. 42. See also William O. Brown, "Race Consciousness Among South African Natives," *American Journal of Sociology,* 40 (March, 1935), pp. 569-581.

60. Shibutani and Kwan, *op. cit.*, Ch. 8, esp. pp. 202 and 212.

61. See the discussions in Brewton Berry, *Race and Ethnic Relations,* Boston: Houghton-Mifflin, 1965, 3rd ed., esp. pp. 147-149; Shibutani and Kwan, *op. cit.*, esp. pp. 217f; and Wagley and Harris, *op. cit.*, pp. 40-44.

62. *Ibid.,* pp. 15-86 and 265-268.

63. *Ibid.,* p. 269; Harris, *op. cit.,* p. 14; and Stampp, *op. cit.,* pp. 13 and 23.

64. The Indians were also discriminated against but to a much lesser extent. The reasons for this differential are discussed by Jordan, *White over Black,* pp. 89-90; and Stampp, *op. cit.,* pp. 23-24.

65. Harris, *op. cit.,* pp. 14-16, an otherwise excellent summary of the factors favoring the enslavement of Negroes rather than Indians, overlooks the role of sociocultural support. The importance of this support is clearly illustrated by the South African policy of importing Asians in preference to the native Africans who strenuously resisted enslavement and forced labor. Shibutani and Kwan, *op. cit.,* p. 126. Sociocultural unity was also a significant factor in the greater threat of revolt posed by the Helots in Sparta as compared to the heterogeneous slaves in Athens. Alvin W. Gouldner, *Enter Plato,* New York: Basic Books, 1965, p. 32.

66. Shibutani and Kwan, *op. cit.,* esp. Chs. 10-12. Stampp observes that the plantation trained Negroes to be slaves, not free men, *op. cit.,* p. 12. Similarly, Wagley and Harris note that the Negroes were poorly prepared for survival in a free-market economic system even when they were emancipated, *op. cit.,* p. 269.

67. Davis asserts that while slavery has always been a source of tension, "in Western culture it was associated with certain religious and philosophical doctrines that gave it the highest sanction." *Op. cit.,* p. ix.

68. Wagley and Harris, *op. cit.,* p. 124.

69. Stampp, *op. cit.,* p. 22.

PART III

The Origin of American Racism

Part three, containing essays by Nash and Noel, shifts the focus of our analysis to a consideration of the origin and causes of racism. Nash's essay is an excellent summary of seventeenth-century attitudes toward red men and black men and of the factors which shaped these evolving attitudes.[1] He perceptively analyzes the context of race relations, especially the power framework, to account for the emergence of significant differences in the attitudes of whites toward Indians and Africans. In particular he stresses the differences in the economic, political, and sexual[2] contacts of whites and Indians as compared to whites and blacks to explain the divergent attitudes.

Nash also spotlights the causal relationship between racial attitudes and slavery. Unfortunately his analysis of this relationship falls victim to the same weakness which has beset many earlier analyses. He confuses racial prejudice with racism and ethnocentrism and thereby obscures the very causal process he is seeking to clarify.

Noel's concluding essay on slavery and the rise of racism is specifically addressed to the task of differentiating these and related concepts in order to refine analysis and thereby clarify the causal relationship between slavery and racism. In addition, Noel presents a tentative theory of the origin of racism and suggests several lines of research which, if pursued with the appropriate conceptual distinctions, should advance our understanding of the emergence of racism and its relation to slavery.

Notes

1. Louis Ruchames's essay on "The Sources of Racial Thought in Colonial America" in L. Ruchames, ed., *Racial Thought in America* (Amherst: University of Massachusetts Press, 1969) is also an excellent source on this topic. Also see Wilcomb E. Washburn, ed., *The Indian and the White Man* (Washington Square: New York University Press, 1964).

2. While Nash's analysis of the role of sexual contacts as a factor in race relations is sensible, the significance of sex in this area has so often been distorted and exaggerated that it is imperative to recommend the sobering caution proffered by Marvin Harris, *Patterns of Race in the Americas* (New York: Walker and Company, 1964), pp. 68-69.

RED, WHITE AND BLACK: THE ORIGINS OF RACISM IN COLONIAL AMERICA

Gary B. Nash

Racial attitudes in America have their origins in the culture of Elizabethan England, for it was in the closing decades of the sixteenth century
that the English people, who were on the verge of creating an overseas
empire in North America and the Caribbean, began to come into frequent contact with peoples whose culture, religion, and color was markedly different from their own. In the early responses of Englishmen to
Indians and Africans lay the seeds of what would become, four centuries
later, one of the most agonizing social problems in American history —
the problem of racial prejudice.

I

Englishmen did not arrive at Jamestown, Virginia, in 1607, or at Plymouth, Massachusetts, in 1620, with minds barren of images and pre-
conceptions of the native occupiers of the land. A mass of reports and
stories concerning the Indians of the New World, many of them based
upon the Spanish and Portuguese experience in Mexico, Peru, and Brazil,
were available in printed form or by word of mouth for curious Englishmen crossing the Atlantic. From this literature ideas and fantasies concerning the Indians gradually entered the English consciousness.

These early accounts seem to have created a split image of the Indian
in the English mind. On the one hand, the native was imagined to be a

From Chapter One, "Red, White and Black: The Origins of Racism in Colonial
America" by Gary B. Nash, from *The Great Fear: Race in the Mind of America,*
edited by Gary B. Nash and Richard Weiss. Copyright © 1970 by Gary B. Nash
and Richard Weiss. Reprinted by permission of Holt, Rinehart and Winston, Inc.

savage, hostile, beastlike creature who inhabited the animal kingdom rather than the kingdom of men. In 1585, prospective adventurers to the New World could read one description of the natives of North America which depicted them as naked, lascivious individuals who cohabited "like beasts without any reasonableness." Another account described them as men who "spake such speech that no men coulde understand them, and in their demeanour like to bruite beastes."[1] But Englishmen also entertained another more positive version of the New World native. Richard Hakluyt, the great propagandist for English colonization, described the Indians in 1585 as "simple and rude in manners, and destitute of the knowledge of God or any good lawes, yet of nature gentle and tractable, and most apt to receive the Christian Religion, and to subject themselves to some good government."[2] Many other reports spoke of the native in similarly optimistic terms.

This dual vision of the native matched the two-sided image of the New World refracted through the prism of the sixteenth-century European mind. In some ways prospective colonists fantasized the New World as a Garden of Eden, a land abounding with precious minerals, health foods, and exotic wildlife. The anti-image was of a barbarous land filled with a multitude of unknown dangers — a "howling wilderness" capable of dragging man down to the level of beasts.

In a rough way the two images of the Indian not only matched English visions of the New World, but coincided with the intentions of prospective settlers. In the early stages of colonization, when trade with the Indians was deemed important and the hope existed that the natives would lead the settlers to gold and silver — perhaps even to the fabled Northwest Passage to the Orient — the Indians were seen as primitive but winsome, as ignorant but receptive individuals. If treated kindly, they could be wooed and won to the advantages of trade and copperation with the English. Only a friendly or malleable Indian *could* be a trading or assisting Indian. Thus, when thoughts of conducting trade and exploration from small trading stations on the coast were uppermost in the English mind, as they were between 1580 and 1610, the colonial leaders frequently portrayed the Indian in relatively gentle hues. Though the natives could be wary and "fearful by nature," wrote George Peckham in 1585, "courtesie and myldnes" along with a generous supply of "prittie merchaundizes and trifles" would win them over and "induce theyr Barbarous natures to a likeing and mutuall society with us."[3] Also important in this optimistic view of the native was the need to quiet the fears of prospective colonists by assuring them that the Indians were not waiting to destroy them or drive them back into the sea.

When permanent settlement became the primary English concern, however, and land the object of desire, the image of the Indian as a hostile savage became ascendant in the English mind. Beginning with the Jamestown settlement of 1607 and intensifying with the great Puritan migration of the 1630s, Englishmen coming to the New World thought less about Indian trade, the Northwest Passage, and fabled gold mines and more about land. As the dreams of El Dorado evaporated, English attention centered on the less glamorous goal of permanent settlement. Now land became all-important, for without land how could there be permanent settlement? The Indian, who had been important when trade and exploration were the keys to overseas involvement, became an inconvenient obstacle. One Englishman went to the heart of the difficulty in 1609: "by what right or warrant can we enter into the land of these Savages, take away their rightfull inheritance from them, and plant ourselves in their places, being unwronged or unprovoked by them?"[4] It was a cogent question to ask, for Englishmen, like other Europeans, had organized their society around the concept of private ownership of land. They regarded it, in fact, as an important characteristic of their superior culture. Colonists were not blind to the fact that they were invading the land of another people, who by prior possession could lay sole claim to the whole of mainland America. The resolution of this moral and legal problem was accomplished by an appeal to logic and to higher powers. The English claimed that they came to share, not appropriate, the trackless wilderness. The Indians would benefit because they would be elevated far above their present condition through contact with a richer culture, a more advanced civilization, and most importantly, the Christian religion. Samuel Purchas, a clerical promoter of English expansion, gave classic expression to this idea: "God in wisedome . . . enriched the Savage Countries, that those riches might be attractive for Christian suters, which there may sowe spirituals and reape temporals." Spirituals, to be sown, of course, meant Christianity; temporals to be reaped meant land. Purchas went on to argue that to leave undeveloped a sparsely settled land populated only by a few natives was to oppose the wishes of God who would not have showed Englishmen the way to the New World if he had not intended them to possess it.[5] Moreover, if the English did not occupy North America, Spain would; and the Indians would then fall victim to Catholicism.

Land was the key to English settlement after 1620. It was logical to assume in these circumstances that the Indian would not willingly give up the ground that sustained him, even if the English offered to purchase land, as they did in most cases. For anyone as property conscious as the

English, the idea that people would resist the invasion of their land with all the force at their disposal came almost as a matter of course. Thus the image of the hostile, savage Indian began to triumph over that of the receptive, friendly Indian. Their own intentions had changed from establishing trade relations to building permanent settlements. A different conception of the Indian was required in these altered circumstances.

The image of a treacherous, uncooperative Indian caused great confusion in the English mind during the first years of the Virginia settlement when the Indians still entertained notions of profiting from the English presence. When Christopher Newport, the leader of the 1607 Jamestown expedition, made the first exploratory trip up the newly named James River, he was puzzled by what he encountered. The Indians, he wrote to his superiors in London, "are naturally given to trechery howbeit we could not finde it in our travell up the river, but rather a most kind and loving people."[6] Every new act of generosity — there is much evidence that the Indians provided the food that kept the struggling settlement alive over the first winter — was taken as another indication of Indian guile and treachery. Hospitality, eagerness to trade, curiosity at the newcomers, and the desire of some tribal leaders to use English support to defeat their enemies were all taken as evidence of the sly, treacherous qualities inherent in Indians.

What we see here is a subconscious attempt to manipulate the world in order to make it conform to the English definition of it. The evidence also suggests that the English stereotype of the hostile savage helped assuage a sense of guilt which inevitably arose when men whose culture was based on the concept of private property embarked on a program to dispossess another people of their land. To type-cast the Indian as a brutish savage was to solve a moral dilemma. If the Indian was truly cordial, generous, and eager to trade, what justification could there be for taking his land? But if he was a savage, without religion or culture, perhaps the colonists' actions were defensible. The English, we might speculate, anticipated hostility and then read it into the Indian's character because they recognized that they were embarking upon an invasion of land to which the only natural response could be violent resistance. Having created the conditions in which the Indian could only respond violently, the Englishmen defined the native as brutal, beastly, savage, and barbarian and then used that as a justification for what he was doing.

This concept had a self-fulfilling quality to it. The more violence was anticipated, the more violence occurred. This is not to argue that hostility would have been avoided if the settlers had seen the native in a different light, since opportunities for mutual mistrust and hostility abounded. But certainly the chances of conflict were greatly enhanced by misperceiving the intentions of the Indian as he struggled within his own society to adapt to the presence of the Europeans.

There was hostility. In Virginia, after a period of uneasy relations punctuated with outbreaks of violence, the Indians mounted a concerted attack on the white settlements with the intention of driving the white man back into the sea. The Massacre of 1622 wiped out one third of the Chesapeake colony. The Indian victory was costly, however, for it left the English colonists with the excuse to set aside the old claim, frequently mentioned in the early years of settlement, of devoting themselves to civilizing and converting the natives. After 1622, most Virginians felt at liberty to attack the natives at will. A no-holds-barred approach was taken to what became known as the "Indian problem." Whereas before, the settlers had engaged in reprisals against the natives whenever they had been attacked, the English now put aside all restraint. As a leader in Virginia wrote revealingly after the Indian attack of 1622,

> Our hands, which before were tied with gentleness and faire usage, are now set at liberty by the treacherous violence of the Savages so that We may now by right of Warre and law of Nations invade the Country, and destroy them who sought to destroy us. . . . Now their cleared grounds in all their villages, (which are situate in the fruitfullest places of the land) shall be inhabited by us, whereas heretofore the grubbing of woods caused us the greatest labour.[7]

A note of grim satisfaction that the Indians had conducted an all-out attack can be detected. Hereafter one was entitled to devastate Indian villages and take, rather than buy, the best land of the area. It was a policy so profitable that the Virginia Council in 1629 reneged on a peace treaty that had been recently negotiated and proclaimed that on second thought a policy of "perpetual enmity" toward the natives was best for the colony.

After 1622 the stereotype of the Indian became less ambivalent. Little in his culture was found worthy of respect—in fact, he was deemed almost cultureless. More and more abusive words crept into English descriptions of Indian society. Negative qualities were newly found and projected onto the natives. Whereas John Smith and other early leaders of the Virginia colony had written lengthy descriptions of the political organization, religion, and customs of the natives, Edward Waterhouse, writing after the Massacre of 1622, could only describe the Indians as "by nature sloathfull and idle, vitious, melancholy, slovenly, of bad conditions, lyers, of small memory, of no constancy or trust . . . by nature of all people the most lying and most inconstant in the world, sottish and sodaine, never looking what dangers may happen afterwards, lesse capable then children of sixe or seaven years old, and less apt and ingenious. . . ."[8] Samuel Purchas, writing in 1625 of the Virginia Indians, described them as "bad people, having little of Humanitie but shape, ignorant of Civilitie, of Arts, of Religion; more brutish then [sic] the beasts they hunt, more wild and unmanly then [sic] that unmanned wild Countrey which they range rather than inhabite; captivated also to Satans tyranny in foolish pieties, mad impieties, wicked idleness, busie and bloudy wickednesse. . . . ."[9] After the Indian attack of 1622 Englishmen in Virginia no longer needed to restrain their impulses or remind themselves of their obligation to convert the Indian.

In New England, despite the many differences in motives and means of colonization, attitudes evolved in much the same manner. In the first two attempts at settlement, on the coast of Maine in 1607 and at Plymouth in 1620, Anglo-Indian relations followed a pattern of initial wariness by the Indians, petty acts of violence and plunder by the white settlers, and then reciprocating and escalating hostility. When the great Puritan migration to New England began in 1630, the Indians were naturally apprehensive, though not hostile. John Winthrop, who led the Massachusetts Bay Colony throughout the 1630s, often mentioned the Puritans' obligation to convert the natives, giving the impression that he felt a real compulsion to "save their souls for Christ." But a careful reading of early New England literature suggests that with significant exceptions such as Roger Williams, the Puritans held the natives in contempt and would have preferred them all dead or removed from the region where they were building their "city on the hill." Winthrop remarked in his journal that the smallpox epidemic of 1617, communicated to the Indians by visiting fishermen, was God's way of "thinning out" the native population to make room for the Puritans. Another prominent Puritan referred to the epidemic, which ravaged the New England natives, as a "wonderful Plague." Later Winthrop wrote that the Indians "are neere all dead of the small Poxe, so the Lord hathe cleared our title to what we possess."[10] Rather than civilize or proselytize the natives, it was easier to see them eliminated by European diseases and then to interpret this as God's wish.

In the Puritan mind there was always a tension between the inclusionist and exclusionist impulse, between the evangelical desire to convert the heathen and others who followed "false Gods," and the desire to keep the community pure by excluding deviant types. Despite many professions of concern for converting the natives, New England ministers made only a few perfunctory efforts in this direction. The same impulse which led to the expulsion of theologically deviant Puritans such as Anne Hutchinson and Roger Williams, or to the persecution of Quakers in Boston in the 1650s, was at the heart of the unwillingness to assimilate the New England Indians, even on the few occasions when they were converted to Christianity. Before the end of the first decade of Puritan settlement, the Indian had come to stand for Satanic opposition to the divine experiment being conducted in the Bay Colony. An Indian, when he attacked a white man, indirectly attacked God whose hand the Puritans saw in all that they did. In this sense, the Indians came to represent followers of Satan, savages pitting themselves against the Puritans' "errand into the wilderness." With the drama of colony building invested with divine guidance, with the hand of God seen in every act, to kill an Indian who had demonstrated his resistance or opposition to the Massachusetts Bay Colony, was only to destroy an opponent of God. When hostility with the Pequot Indians flared in 1637, and spread into a general war, the Puritans again saw evidence of divine intervention. The climax of the war came when the Puritans surrounded 500 Pequot men, women, and children in Mystic Fort and burned them to death. The Massachusetts leaders, suffused with a sense of mission, recorded that God "had laughed at his Enemies . . . making them as a fiery oven. . . . Thus did the Lord judge among the Heathen, filling the Place [the fort] with dead bodies."[11] To dehumanize the Indians was one means of justifying one's own inhumanity.

Two important concepts concerning the Indians were left in the English mind after the first period of painful confrontation. First, the image of the native as a hostile and inferior creature became indelibly printed upon the white mind. The Indian was noticeably different in color, though the colonists seemed to have made little of this. Far more important, he was uncivilized, and, it was generally concluded, incapable of civilization as Europeans defined it. As Roy H. Pearce has noted, the Indian was a constant reminder to the colonists of what they must not become. For men who were deeply concerned about the barbarizing effects of the wilderness, the Indian provided a means of measuring their own civility, culture, and self-identity. "The Indian became important for the English mind, not for what he was in and of himself, but rather for what he showed civilized men they were not and must not be."[12] Not to control the Indian, therefore, was to lose control of one's new environment, and ultimately of oneself. This was the psychological importance of the Indian to the colonist.

At a more practical level was the problem of how to control the Indian. Defined as a savage, regarded in most cases as unassimilable, and inconveniently located in the path of English settlement, the Indian posed one of the colonists' most serious problems. At first colonial leaders had hoped that cultural interaction with the Indians would be possible. But it could only be on English terms. When the Indian threatened the white community, control and security became uppermost in the minds of the settlers. With the Indian now conforming to type, the colonists worked with grim determination to isolate this alien and dangerous subgroup and to control it strictly. A special status, inferior and subservient, was created for those Indians who wished to accept European culture and live within it on the white man's terms. The only other alternative for the native was to move out of the path of English settlement.

During the course of the seventeenth century thousands of Indians did choose to live within white society. Over the years they became dependent upon the iron-age implements of the European — the knife, gun, kettle, fishhook — and, most importantly, upon the white man's liquor. Gradually those Indians who chose to remain on the eastern seaboard lost their forest skills. Their culture slowly changed under the pressure of contact with a more technologically advanced society and their lot often was reduced to pathetic subservience as day laborers and sometimes as slaves. For these Indians — tamed, decultured, and utterly dependent — the colonist had only contempt. Unlike his brother on the frontier, the dreaded "savage," the domesticated Indian was looked upon as a despised menial.

The psychological calculus by which intentions governed attitudes can be illuminated further by studying the views of Anglo-Americans who genuinely desired amicable relations with the Indians. The Quakers of Pennsylvania and West New Jersey, who were the most important early practitioners of pacifism in the New World, threatened no violence to the Indians when they arrived in the Delaware River Valley in the last quarter of the seventeenth century. It was pacifism, not violence, that was on the Quaker mind. Though relations with the Indians would deteriorate in the eighteenth century, when Germans and Scotch-Irish streamed into Pennsylvania, it is significant to note that in the early years of settlement the pacifistic Quakers tended to view the Indian differently than their neighbors to the north and south. Though they regarded the native as backward and "under a dark Night in things relating to Religion," they also saw him as physically attractive, generous, mild-tempered, and possessed of many admirable traits. William Penn, the Quaker proprietor of Pennsylvania, revived old speculations that the Indians were the "Jews of America," the descendants of the Lost Tribes of Israel, and found their language "lofty" and full of words "of more sweetness or greatness" than most European tongues.[13]

In other colonies, too, the image of the Indian began to change, at least within the reflective element of society, when the precariousness of the English position declined and when attacks on white communities subsided. In the first half of the eighteenth century a number of colonial observers began to develop a new image of the Indian. Unlike later writers from seaboard cities or European centers of culture, who sentimentalized the native into a "noble savage," these men knew of Indian life from first-hand experience as missionaries, provincial officials, and fur traders. Close to Indian culture, but not pitted against the native in a fight for land or survival, they developed clearer perspectives on aboriginal life. During the earlier period of hostility, the Indian had been regarded as virtually cultureless. Now all of the missing elements in the Indian's cultural make-up—government, social structure, religion, family organization, codes of justice and morality, arts and crafts — were discovered.

Thus, in 1705, thirty years after the last significant Indian attack in Virginia, Robert Beverley described the Indians in terms strikingly different from those employed by preceding generations, whose contacts, even in the best of times, had been highly abrasive. Beverley viewed the Indians not as savages, but as a cultural group whose institutions, modes of living, and values were worthy of examination on their own terms. He found aspects of Indian civilization reminiscent of classical Spartan life and much to be admired. In Beverley's view, the Indians' contact with European civilization, far from advancing their existence, was responsible for the loss of their "Felicity as well as their Innocence."[14]

John Lawson, who traveled extensively among the southeastern tribes in the early eighteenth century, also dwelled on the integrity of native culture and took note of many traits, such as cleanliness, equable temperament, bravery, tribal loyalty, hospitality, and concern for the welfare of the group rather than the individual, that often seemed absent from English society. Like Beverley, Lawson concluded that the Indians of the southern regions were the "freest people from Heats and Passions (which possess the Europeans)." He lamented that contact with the settlers had vitiated what was best in Indian culture.[15] Many other writers who did not covet the Indians' land or were not engaged in the exploitive Indian trade, agreed that the concept of community, which colonial leaders cherished as an ideal but rarely achieved, was best reflected in North America by the natives. As Pearce has noted, "the essential integrity of savage life, for good and bad, became increasingly the main concern of eighteenth-century Americans writing on the Indian."[16]

II

It was in an atmosphere emotionally charged by the tension between English settlers and Indians that the black man made his initial appearance in America. We know that the first Africans arrived in the colonies in 1619, though their status — whether slave or indentured servant — is uncertain. Not until the 1640s do we have any indications that Africans were being consigned to perpetual servitude and even then the evidence is scanty. But certainly by the 1660s, the indeterminate position of the African changed; hereditary slavery took root in the colonies. By the mid-eighteenth century, the black man in most colonies had been stripped of virtually all the rights accorded the white settler under the common law. In many colonies the black man was no longer defined as a legal person, but rather as chattel property — the object of rights, but never the subject of rights. A slave could neither appeal to nor testify in the courts; he had no rights to religion or marriage or parenthood; he could not own or carry arms; he could not buy or sell commodities or engage in any economic activity; he could not congregate in public places with more than two or three of his own race. Even education — the right to literacy — was forbidden slaves in many colonies, for it was thought that if the African was permitted to read, the germ of freedom might grow in him.

Much has been written concerning the evolution of this system of chattel slavery; and much has been learned by comparing it to slavery in the ancient world, where it was not based on race, and in the South American colonies of Spain and Portugal, where a less repressive and closed system of servitude developed than in British North America. But for our purposes the primary question concerns the effect of racial attitudes upon the evolution of slavery, and, conversely, the effects of slavery, once instituted, upon racial attitudes. Was racial prejudice against the African responsible for his consignment to slavery? Or were other factors, such as the great labor shortage in the New World, combined with the availability of Africans and the example of slave trading set much earlier by Spain, Holland, and Portugal, responsible for a system of slave labor which cast the black man in such an inferior and degraded role that racial prejudice against him developed?

Certainly there was little about the first impressions of Africans that Englishmen formed in the late sixteenth century which augured well for the status of the African in English colonial society. Winthrop D. Jordan shows in his recent book *White Over Black: American Attitudes Toward the Negro, 1550–1812,* which is the most probing historical account we have of racial attitudes in early America, that Englishmen responded negatively to Africans even when their contacts were of a casual and exploratory nature. To begin with, the African's blackness was strange, troublesome, and vaguely repugnant. Englishmen were already familiar with people of darker skin than their own, for they had traded with people of the Mediterranean world and come into contact with Moors and occasional traders from the Middle East and North Africa. But they had not met truly black men, though they had probably heard of them. When these Englishmen, among the lightest-skinned people in the world, came face to face with one of the darkest-skinned people of the world, their reaction was strongly negative. Unhappily, blackness was already a means of conveying some of the most ingrained values of English society. Black — and its opposite, white — were emotion-laden words. Black meant foul, dirty, wicked, malignant, and disgraceful. And of course it signified night — a time of fear and uncertainty. Black was a symbol signifying baseness, evil, and danger. Thus expressions filtered into English usage associating black with the worst in human nature: the black sheep in the family, a black mark against one's name, a black day, a black look, to blackball or blackmail. White was all the opposites — chastity, virtue, beauty, and peace. Women were married in white to symbolize purity and virginity. Day was light just as night was black. The angels were white; the devil was black. Thus Englishmen were conditioned to see ugliness and evil in black. In this sense their encounter with the black people of West Africa was prejudiced by the very symbols of color which had been woven into English language and culture over the centuries.

Englishmen also were struck by the religious condition of the African, or what was considered to be his lack of religion. To the English, the Africans were heathens — an altogether Godless people. In an age when religion framed the life of society, this was taken as a grave defect. Though the universalist strain in their own religion emphasized the brotherhood of all men, and though the book of Genesis stressed the point that all men derived from the same act of creation, Englishmen took the Africans' heathenism as an indication of an almost irreparable inferiority.

Englishmen identified a third characteristic interacting with blackness and heathenism — what they called cultural depravity or "savagery." Every new observation of African life added to their belief that the culture of Africans was vastly inferior to that of Europeans. The African's diet, for example, was revolting by European standards. He wore few clothes if any. His habitat was crude. He made war on his fellow men in what was deemed a hideously cruel way. All of this was imprinted on the English consciousness, as Jordan points out, and we find words like "brutish," "savage," and "beastly" creeping into English accounts of Africans. In almost all these respects the image of the African coincided with the image of the Indian after the first period of contact.

Strengthening and vivifying this impression of primitive men in a primitive setting was the extraordinary animal life of Africa. Englishmen were fascinated by the numerous subhuman species they encountered and none so fascinated them as the orangutan or chimpanzee. Though the English were familiar with monkeys and baboons, they had never encountered the tailless, anthropoid ape with his curiously human appearance and behavior, which still makes him a center of attention at zoos. When Englishmen came upon this strangely human creature they began to speculate about possible connections, as Jordan has indicated, between the "beastlike man" —the African—and the "manlike beast"—the orangutan. The logic was tortured, perhaps, but nonetheless Englishmen began discussing the possibility that the African was an intermediate specie between beast and man. To make matters worse, there were speculations about sexual unions between man and beast in Africa, a fantasy of overwrought English imaginations and an idea that probably suggested itself to Englishmen because promiscuity, bestiality, and sodomy were not uncommon in England at this time, and in fact were subjects of some concern.[17]

Thus a number of African characteristics—real and alleged—strongly and negatively impressed English venturers as the New World was opening up: the African's blackness, his heathenism, his cultural inferiority, his sexuality, and his bestiality. Because religion and cultural achievement were the primary reference points for Europeans of this age, it is probable that in this early period of contact the African's skin color was more a matter of curiosity than damning concern. Those who have read sixteenth-century accounts of the Irish, whose ancestral lands were being invaded by the English in this period, will know that the vocabulary of abuse used to describe Africans was applied also to Irishmen. They too were seen as culturally inferior, savage, brutish, and primitive. The blackness of Africans was an additional liability, given the connotations of color in the English mind, but perhaps not a crucially important one. Eventually, of course, blackness would be firmly linked with other negative qualities in the English anatomy of prejudice.

It is important to remember that these early observations of Africans, like those of the Indians, reflect as much about the observer as the observed. We know now from careful research that Africa was not what Englishmen saw and recorded in that age of discovery. West Africa lagged behind western Europe technologically, though the differences were not so great as is usually imagined, but the area had nurtured a highly developed civilization. If art, social organization, and cultural traditions are criteria of advancement, Africa in the sixteenth and seventeenth centuries was far from primitive and backward. Englishmen saw in Africa not what existed there, but what they were psychologically prepared to see. They compared African culture with their own, which they took to be a universal model.

Further insight into the English reaction to Africans and Indians can be gained by comparing it to Spanish and Portuguese attitudes. Though England's colonial competitors regarded the natives of Africa and North America as primitive and inferior, the image they represented in their psychic landscape was far less negative and emotional. Geography explains much of this, for whereas the English of the sixteenth century were noted for their insularity, the Spanish and Portuguese, situated astride Europe and Africa, had been in near continuous contact with peoples of different races and cultures for centuries.

Because of this, Portugal, and to a lesser degree Spain, had an ethnic and cultural diversity not to be found in England. Over the centuries, the Iberian peninsula had been breached again and again: by Muslims between 711 and 1212, by Jews, Berbers, and North African Moors. As usually happens in history, the conquerors and the conquered fraternized, intermarried, and interbred. By the time England was first exposing herself to Africa, her European competitors, especially Portugal, had already amalgamated their bloodstreams with people of darker color and different cultures. This produced a tolerance for diversity in the Spanish and Portuguese cultures that was absent in the English, who had for centuries been relatively isolated from the rest of the world.

It would be unwise to conclude that the long warfare between the Portuguese and Moors and the centuries of contact with a variety of darker-skinned people eliminated racial prejudice among the Spanish and Portuguese in Europe or in their New World colonies. Racial consciousness *did* exist among these people, and with racial consciousness came feelings of racial superiority. There can be little doubt that the lighter one's skin, the greater one's social prestige in Spain and Portugal and in their colonies — a pattern which still exists. And yet because of their ancient exposure to and intermixture with people of darker skin, the Spanish and Portuguese, unlike the English, regarded racial intermixture as inevitable and attached no great moral significance to it. This difference in attitude would lead toward a gradual assimilation of races which in turn increased the tolerance for racial diversity.

A second factor which helps to explain the unusually virulent English reaction to Africans and Indians, not duplicated in Spain and Portugal, was the internal stresses England was undergoing at the time she first exposed herself to the outer world. This period of the late sixteenth and early seventeenth century, called the age of Puritanism, was a "time of troubles" for England — an era in which the traditional feudal society was giving way to a more modern social order. The beginnings of urbanization and industrialization, the breakup of the traditional church, the enclosure of land, and the decay of the guilds were all a part of this process. Englishmen of the late sixteenth century saw poverty and vagabondage on the rise, cities growing faster than they could absorb rural newcomers into the traditional close-knit scheme of life, alehouses and dens of prostitution multiplying, gangs of highwaymen and drifters roaming the country. England was experiencing not only rural dislocation but an associated "urban problem."

Puritanism, a religious reform movement bent on purifying the Church of England, must also be seen as a social response to this crumbling of the old order. Puritans were convinced that England was being threatened by dangerous currents of social change which encouraged the individual to free himself from the old institutionalized restraints. In religion, Puritans attempted to place the individual in a more direct relationship with his God by removing the traditional religious intermediaries — especially the Catholic Church. But individualism in other aspects of life was not greeted with similar enthusiasm, for it threatened to erode all the old symbols of authority, all the old instruments of corporate control in society — the church, the village community, the guild, even the father as patriarchal head of the family. Puritanism was the new religious and social doctrine which some men hoped would re-establish a morally secure and orderly world through new methods of social control, including a work-ethic which stressed industriousness as a way of serving God, and the formation of tight-knit Puritan congregations composed of people who would watch over and discipline themselves and each other. The keynotes of Puritanism were piety, discipline, order, self-restraint, and work.

The rise of Puritanism coincided with England's belated entry into the age of exploration. Puritans, and those around them, were simultaneously participants in an age of self-restraint and social discipline and an age of adventure, exploration, and discovery. As Winthrop Jordan has said, Elizabethan England reverberated with "the twin spirits of adventure and control."[18] Here was a society engaged in voyages of discovery and settlement overseas, as represented by Elizabethans such as John Hawkins, Francis Drake, Humphrey Gilbert, and Walter Raleigh, and simultaneously embarked upon attempts to reform themselves and society, as typified by such colonial leaders as William Bradford, John Winthrop, and Roger Williams.

In this vibrant atmosphere of discovery (a reaching outward) and self-scrutiny (a turning inward), Englishmen tended to use the newly found African black man, and later the Indian, as a foil. For men who were attempting to open up the New World while reorganizing the Old, the African and the Indian came to represent to the Englishman what he was fighting against in himself, what he must never allow himself to become. When we look at the English perceptions of Africans — their blackness, their nakedness, their sexuality — we begin to understand that Englishmen reacted emotionally and negatively because these strangers reminded them, at least at the subconscious level, of problems in themselves and their own society. A negative reaction to blackness stemmed both from the symbology of color in English culture and the awareness of "black deeds" at home; sexuality and bestiality were much on the English mind because of the Puritan emphasis on self-control and the guilt over licentiousness which were widespread in England. When Englishmen called the African bestial and savage, we may conjecture that they were unconsciously projecting onto black men qualities which they had identified and shrank from in themselves. Moreover, by contrasting themselves favorably to Africans or Indians, the English were better able to convince themselves of their own role as God's chosen people, destined to carry their culture and religion to all corners of the earth.

Of course not every settler who came to America in the early seventeenth century harbored deeply negative thoughts about Africans and Indians. Probably few of the Pilgrims and Puritans who colonized New England or few of the settlers in Virginia had met face to face with natives of Africa or North America or even thought very systematically about the culture and character traits of such people. But Africans and Indians *did* impress English adventurers of the late sixteenth and early seventeenth centuries in certain ways, and these impressions were recorded in books which literate men read or knew about. Thus, ideas and attitudes concerning red and black men were entering the collective English consciousness at just that time when England was making its first attempts to compete with Spain, Portugal, Holland, and France for possession of the New World. These first impressions would change under the pressure of circumstances in the New World. But the colonists first met these men from other continents with ideas and notions already in their heads, though the images were vague and half formed.

It is only with an understanding of these early attitudes and a knowledge of early Anglo-Indian relations that we can comprehend the connection between prejudice and slavery. No doubt the early English image of the African as a heathen, primitive creature made it easier for Englishmen to cast him into slavery. However, the Indian also was depicted in unfavorable terms as were the Irish and even the dregs of white English society. But among those seen in such a light, it was the Africans who were most vulnerable to economic exploitation because only they could be wrenched from their homeland in great numbers, often with the active participation of other Africans. Moreover, they were unusually helpless once transported to a distant and unfamiliar environment where they were forced into close association with a people whose power they could not contest. Certainly a latent and still forming prejudice against people with black skin was partially responsible for the subjugation of Africans. But the chronic labor shortage in the colonies and the almost total failure to mold the Indians into an agricultural labor force were probably more important factors. Winthrop Jordan has taken a middle position on this vexing question, writing that "rather than slavery causing 'prejudice,' or vice versa, they seem rather to have generated each other. . . . Slavery and 'prejudice' may have been equally cause and effect, continuously reacting upon each other, dynamically joining hands to hustle the Negro down the road to complete degradation."[19]

The effect of slavery on racial attitudes is less complicated. Once in-stitutionalized in the American colonies, slavery cast the Negro in such a lowly role that the initial bias against him could only be confirmed and vastly strengthened. It was hardly possible for one people to enslave another without developing strong feelings against them. While initially unfavorable impressions of Africans and economic conditions which en-couraged their exploitation led to the mass enslavement of men with black skins, it required slavery itself to harden negative racial feelings into a deep and almost unshakable prejudice which continued to grow for centuries to come. A labor system was devised which kept the African in America at the bottom of the social and economic pyramid. By mid-eighteenth century, when black codes had been legislated to ensure that slaves were totally and unalterably caught in the web of perpetual servi-tude, no further opportunity remained to prove the white stereotype wrong. Socially and legally defined as less than a man, kept in a degraded and debased position, virtually without power in his relationships with his white master, the African became a truly servile, ignoble, degraded creature in the perception of white men. In the long evolution of racial attitudes in America nothing was of greater importance than the enslave-ment of Africans in a land where freedom, equality, and opportunity were becoming the foundations of a new social order.

Whereas the white colonist almost always encountered the black man as a slave after about 1660, and thus came to think of him as a slavelike creature by nature, the English settler met the Indian, especially after 1675 when the last large-scale Indian wars until the nineteenth century occurred, far less frequently. When he did interact with the Indian, it was rarely in a master-slave context. The English settler learned how difficult it was to enslave the native in his own habitat. Thus, if the Indian had survived the coming of white civilization, he usually maintained a certain freedom to come and go, and, more significantly, the capacity to attack and kill the white encroacher. Though he was hated for this, it earned him a grudging respect. The Anglo-Indian relationship in the eighteenth century was rarely that of master and slave, with all rights and power concentrated on one side.

In fact, the Indian and the white man were involved in a set of power relationships in which each side, with something to offer the other, maneuvered for the superior position. That the Indian was the ultimate loser in almost all these interchanges should not obscure the fact that for several hundred years the Anglo-American confronted the native as an adversary rather than a chattel.

The Anglo-Indian economic relationship illustrates the point. In almost every colony the Indian trade was of importance to the local economy in the early stages of development. Trade implied a kind of equality; each side bargained in its own interest; and in each exchange agreement had to be reached between buyer and seller. The long-term effect of the trade was attritional for the Indians because it fostered a dependence upon alcohol and the implements of European civilization, especially the gun. But even while their culture was transformed by this contact with a technologically advanced society, and even though they often were exploited by unscrupulous traders, the Indians maintained considerable power in the trade nexus. Just as the provincial government of South Carolina could bring a recalcitrant tribe to terms by threatening to cut off trade, the Iroquois tribes of New York could obtain advantages from the English by threatening to transfer their allegiance and their trade to the French. New York and Pennsylvania competed for decades for the Indian trade of the Susquehanna River Valley, a fact of which the Indians were well apprised and able to use to their own advantage.

In land transactions, though the Indian was again the ultimate loser, power was also divided between red and white. The Indian, unlike the African, possessed a commodity indispensable to the English settlers. Throughout the colonial period, provincial governments acknowledged an obligation to purchase rather than appropriate land. For several hundred years the two cultural groups negotiated land purchases, signed treaties, registered titles, and determined boundaries. These transactions had symbolic as well as legal meaning for they served as reminders that the Indian, though often despised and exploited, was not without power.

As in matters of land and trade, so it was in political relationships. Between 1652 and 1763, North America was a theater of war in four international conflicts involving the English, French, Spanish, and Dutch. In each of these wars the Indians played a significant role since the contending European powers vied for alliances with them and attempted to employ them against their enemies. Whether it was the English and French competing for the support of the Iroquois in New York or the English and Spanish wooing the Creeks of the Carolina region, the Indians were entitled to the respect which only an autonomous and powerful group could command.

Thus, throughout the colonial period, the Indians alternately traded, negotiated, allied, and fought with the English. In each case power was divided between the two parties and shifted back and forth with time, location, and circumstances. Though he was exploited, excluded, and sometimes decimated in his contacts with European civilization, the Indian always maneuvered from a position of strength which the African, devoid of tribal unity, unaccustomed to the environment, and relatively defenseless, never enjoyed. The African in America was rarely a part of any political or economic equation. He had only his labor to offer the white man and even that was not subject to contractual agreement. He was never in a position to negotiate with the colonist and was only occasionally capable of either retaliating against his oppressors or escaping from them. This relative powerlessness, as compared with the Indian, could not help but effect attitudes. Unlike the native, the African was uniquely unable to win the respect of the white man because his situation was rarely one where respect was required or even possible. Tightly caught in a slave-master relationship, with virtually all the power on the other side, the African could only sink lower and lower in the white man's estimation. Meanwhile, the Indian, though hated, was often respected for his fighting ability, his dignity, solemnity, and even his oratorical ability. American colonists may have scoffed at the Enlightenment portrait of the "noble savage," but their image of the Indian came to have a positive side. The sociology of red-white and black-white relations differed; and from these variations evolved distinct white attitudes, in both cases adverse, but in significantly different ways.

The sociology of red-white and black-white contact differed in another important way — and in differing gave further shape to white attitudes. This was the area of sexual contact. White attitudes toward the black man cannot be dissociated from the fact that sexual relations, especially between white men and black women, were frequent and coercive throughout the eighteenth century, as graphically illustrated by the large mulatto population in America by 1800. The classic case of racial intermixture in the British colonies was in the West Indies where blacks made up as much as 80 percent of the population and white women were relatively unavailable. But in the mainland colonies, especially in the South, black women also became the object of extensive sexual exploitation by white slaveowners.

As Winthrop Jordan has explained in detail, the acceptance of interracial sex and the degree of guilt it engendered depended very heavily upon the availability of white women and the stability of family life in a particular area. In the West Indies, where sugar planters came to make a quick fortune and then return to "civilized" life in England, sexual relations with black women were extensive, but conducted without much guilt. No West Indian colony banned extramarital miscegenation and only the tiny island of Montserrat prohibited racial intermarriage. A Jamaica planter summed up this unembarrassed view of interracial sex by writing in 1774: "He who should presume to shew any displeasure against such a thing as simple fornication [with a black woman], would for his pains be accounted a simple blockhead; since not one in twenty can be persuaded, that there is either sin; or shame in cohabiting with his slave."[20]

In English America, however, the situation was different. Colonists had come to plant white civilization as well as money crops, and interracial sex, given the strong prejudice that had developed against the Negro, was seen as a danger to individual morality, family life, and cultural integrity. In South Carolina and Georgia, where white women were greatly outnumbered by white men in the early years and where black women were plentiful, miscegenation was practiced frequently. But as the white female population grew, such sexual liaisons became socially unacceptable. Farther north, where slaves were proportionately fewer and white women more available, interracial sex was practiced less and condemned more. By the time of the American Revolution all the colonies had banned interracial marriage, although it is significant that South Carolina was the last to do so. That, of course, did not stop sexual contact outside of marriage between white men and black women (the reverse was rare for obvious reasons). To ban racial intermarriage was a way of stating with legal finality that the Negro, even when free, was not the equal of the white man. But by the same logic, to allow white men to exploit black women sexually outside of marriage was a way of permitting the white colonist to act out the concept of white social dominance. Racial intermingling outside of marriage, so long as it involved white men and black women, was no admission of equality but rather an intimate and often brutal proclamation of the superior rights of the white man.

The extensive sexual contact which white men had with black women, especially in the South, had no parallel in the case of Indian women. In the first place, they were not readily available except to an occasional fur trader or frontiersman in remote areas. Moreover, when accessible, it was not as a slave who was defenseless to resist the advances of a master with power of life and death over her. If an Indian women chose to submit to a white man, it was usually on mutually agreeable terms. Thus the frequency and the nature of sexual relationships between white men and red women contrasted sharply with the liaison between the white man and black woman. In these differences we can find the source and meaning of a fear which has preoccupied white America for three hundred years — the fear of the black male lusting after the white woman. This vision of the "black rapist," so enduring in contemporary attitudes and literature, runs through the accounts of the slave uprisings which occurred sporadically from 1712, when slaves revolted in New York, to the 1830s when Nat Turner led the bloodiest of all black insurrections. In large part this fear of the black man seems to have stemmed from feelings of guilt originating in the sexual exploitation of black women and an associated fear of the black avenger, presumably filled with anger and poised to retaliate against the white man. White attitudes toward the Indian only occasionally contain this element of sexual fear. Guilt seldom was aroused by the occasional and noncoercive contact with Indian women; thus the white man, when he encountered the hostile Indian male, rarely pictured his adversary as a sexual avenger. In eighteenth-century literature the Indian rarely is pictured as a frenzied rapist, lurking in the bush or stalking white women. Sometimes the Indian was viewed as a peculiarly asexual creature, which in turn created a confused image in the white mind of a hostile, and yet sexually passive, savage. It is further indicative of this fundamental difference in attitudes that in the colonial period miscegenation with Indians was prohibited only in North Carolina and briefly in Virginia, though sexual contact with Negroes was being banned everywhere in the colonies. A number of prominent colonial figures, including Robert Beverley, John Lawson, and William Byrd, publicly advised intermarriage of whites and Indians — a social policy unthinkable in the realm of black and white.

Arising from the fear of the black slave bent upon sexual revenge was the common perception of the Negro as a hypersexual creature, another view which has transited the centuries so enduringly as to suggest that it fills a need in the white psyche. In part, this myth originated in the vivid imprint which the African first made upon the English mind as a savage, naked, creature of the animal world where sexual urges went unrestrained. A century later in colonial America this image was intensified through the white settler's frequent sexual contact with black women.

Little evidence can be found to show that the black woman *was* physiologically a more sexually responsive person. Instead, the white man *made* her into a symbol of sexuality because he could thus act out with her all of the repressed libidinal desires which were proscribed by his own moral code, and because by assigning to her a promiscuous nature he could assuage his own guilt that festered inevitably as a result of his illicit and exploitative activities.

Thus the degree and nature of contact between red and white and between black and white differed substantially in colonial America. In these differences lay the origins of distinct sets of attitudes toward the African and the Indian. The Englishman in America was constantly reminded by his contacts with the Indians of the advantages and the supposed superiority of his own civilization; likewise, he learned much about the control and coercion of a cultural subgroup within his midst. Through contact with the Indian, he worked out some of the problems of his own identity and destiny. Many of these lessons of control and many of these attitudes were transferred initially to the black African who began to trickle into the colonies in the 1620s. As the trickle broadened to a stream and new problems of control arose, the institution of chattel slavery hardened for Africans but not Indians, thus giving rise to new attitudes. The black man was consigned permanently to slavery; he was excluded from the rights upon which society in the New World was allegedly being built; he was incorporated into a system of close, intimate, servile, and inescapable contact. Because of this the black man became the object of a whole new set of attitudes that marked him off from the Indian with whom, initially, he had been loosely equated.

[Nash concludes his essay with a discussion of the impact of the American Revolution upon the racial attitudes of whites.   Ed.]

Notes

1.   Edward Arber, ed., *The First Three English Books on America* (Birmingham, Eng., 1885), p. xxvii; Richard Hakluyt, *Divers Voyages touching the Discovery of America and the Islands Adjacent . . .*, Hakluyt Society Publications, First Series, VII (London, 1850), p. 23.

2.   E. G. R. Taylor, ed., *The Original Writings & Correspondence of the Two Richard Hakluyts,* Hakluyt Society Publications, Second Series, LXXVI (London, 1935), pp. 164-165.

3. "A true reporte of the late discoveries . . ." in David B. Quinn, ed., *The Voyages and Colonizing Enterprises of Sir Humphrey Gilbert,* Hakluyt Society Publications, Second Series, LXXXIV (London, 1940), pp. 451-452.

4. Robert Gray, *A Good Speed to Virginia* (London, 1609), in Wesley F. Craven, "Indian Policy in Early Virginia," *William and Mary Quarterly,* Third Series, I (1944), p. 65.

5. Samuel Purchas, *Hakluytus Posthumus, or Purchas His Pilgrimes* (20 vols.; Glasgow, 1905-1907), XIX, p. 232.

6. Gabriel Archer, "A relatyon . . . written . . . by a gent. of ye Colony," in Philip L. Barbour, ed., *The Jamestown Voyages under the First Charter, 1606-1609,* Hakluyt Society Publications, Second Series, CXXXVI (London, 1969), pp. 103-104.

7. Edward Waterhouse, *A Declaration of the State of the Colonie and Affaires in Virginia* (London, 1622), in Susan M. Kingsbury, ed., *The Records of the Virginia Company of London* (4 vols.; Washington, D.C., 1906-1935), III, pp. 556-557.

8. In Kingsbury, *The Records of the Virginia Company of London,* III, pp. 562-563.

9. *Hakluytus Posthumus,* XIX, p. 231, in Roy Harvey Pearce, *Savagism and Civilization: A Study of the Indian and the American Mind* (Baltimore, 1953), pp. 7-8.

10. In Pearce, *Savagism and Civilization,* p. 19.

11. John Mason, *A Brief History of the Pequot War* (Boston, 1736), in Alden T. Vaughan, *New England Frontier: Puritans and Indians, 1620-1675* (Boston, 1965), p. 145.

12. Pearce, *Savagism and Civilization,* p. 5.

13. William Penn, *A Letter to the Free Society of Traders . . .* (London, 1683), in Albert C. Myers, ed., *Narratives of Early Pennsylvania, West New Jersey and Delaware* (New York, 1912), pp. 230, 234.

14. Robert Beverley, *History of the Present State of Virginia* [London, 1705], ed. by Louis B. Wright (Chapel Hill, N.C., 1947), p. 233.

15. John Lawson, *A New Voyage to Carolina* [London, 1709], ed. by Hugh T. Lefler (Chapel Hill, N.C., 1967), pp. 209, 239.

16. Pearce, *Savagism and Civilization,* p. 45.

17. Winthrop D. Jordan, *White Over Black: American Attitudes Toward the Negro, 1550-1812* (Chapel Hill, N.C., 1968), pp. 28-32.

18. Jordan, *White Over Black,* p. 40.

19. Jordan, *White Over Black,* p. 80.

20. [Edward Long], *The History of Jamaica . . .* (London, 1774), in Jordan, *White Over Black,* p. 140.

SLAVERY AND THE RISE OF RACISM

Donald L. Noel

The causal relationship between the ideology of racism and American slavery as a structure of social relations has been extensively debated. Thus, the present analysis does not start from neutral ground but is guided by the hypothesis that American racism was far more a product than a cause of slavery. Despite subsequent efforts to justify slavery by reference to the "white man's burden" (i.e., the duty to civilize the savage and Christianize the heathen), black people were not enslaved because they were viewed as inferior beings sorely in need of assistance on the road to the good life. They were enslaved because they were needed. More precisely, their labor power was desperately needed to assure economic success in colonial America. Racism arose, in response to slavery, as a means of justifying the extreme economic exploitation of blacks which was the crux of slavery.

The debate over the causal relation between racism and slavery is but a special case of the historical controversy regarding the causal priority of values and interests. There is, of course, no reason beyond theoretical bias to expect either values or interests to uniformly exert causal primacy. Even the same variables may exhibit different causal relations in different places and times. The causal linkage between ethnic stratification and racism, for example, is not universally the same but variable dependent upon the conditions of the given case. There is nothing inconsistent in affirming that racism, as an ideology, is more a consequence than a cause of American slavery but more a cause than a consequence of Jim Crow segregation.[1] Indeed, racism even exhibits different relationships to differ-

---

This is an original essay written by the editor specifically for this reader.

ent types of slavery. They may be unrelated, either variable may cause the other, or they may exhibit a reciprocal causal relationship in which each variable mutually generates and reinforces the other.[2] Reciprocal causation is a common feature of the sociocultural world, but this does not mean that the variables involved are necessarily, or even generally, of equal causal significance. The problem is to determine the primary direction of the causal linkage and the degree of onesidedness in the relationship.

A reciprocal but asymmetrical relation between slavery and racism is acknowledged in the thesis that American slavery is much *more* a cause than a consequence of racism. This does not deny that racist ideas and beliefs existed in the colonies prior to the emergence of slavery nor even that they had some causal significance.[3] Racism, however, is a variable, not an attribute. Thus the critical question is not whether racist ideas existed or were articulated prior to the emergence of slavery but whether racism was sufficiently strong to have been a significant cause, rather than primarily a product, of slavery. The racist ideas and beliefs expressed in the sixteenth and early seventeenth century do not appear to have been either widespread or legitimate in the sense of being closely articulated with and securely supported by the dominant social institutions. Hence, I do not believe that racism was initially present in sufficient degree to have been a significant cause of American slavery.

There would be little difficulty in substantiating this position if quoting present day "authority" was sufficient. For example:

Slavery was not born of racism: rather, racism was the consequence of slavery.[4]

[During the eighteenth century] individual differences in mental traits were sometimes recognized. But so far as groups of people were concerned . . . equality of natural endowment was the general assumption. . . . When the Negro was first enslaved, his subjugation was not justified in terms of his biological inferiority.[5]

. . . the doctrine of racism appears to have developed in relation to the colored races as an ideological and moral justification for a system already established and highly useful to white dominants.[6]

. . . the white man's relationship with the Negro . . . was eventually rationalized into the most powerful racist doctrine this country has known . . . the importance of Negro slavery in generating race theories in this country can hardly be overestimated.[7]

[Those who] err in making racism a direct product of slavery . . . err less than those who would simply invert the relationship.[8]

On the other hand, racism has occasionally been viewed as primarily a cause, if not *the* cause, of slavery, or as equally a cause and an effect of slavery. Both of these positions are expressed by Finley in his assertions that "the slave-outsider formula argues the other way" (i.e., that racism causes slavery) and "the connection between slavery and racism has been a dialectical one, in which each element reinforced the other."[9] Since authority is divided, it is imperative that the historical record be reexamined to establish the causal relationship between American slavery and racism. Even this will not suffice, however, unless we delineate the precise nature of racism by carefully distinguishing it from a series of related concepts. Thus our first concern is to refine our concepts in order to facilitate precise analysis.

Conceptual Clarification: The Nature of Racism

The preceding discussion implies a conception of racism which is more narrow than that often ascribed to the concept. As it is popularly used today racism embraces, and confounds, three major dimensions — attitudinal, behavioral (including individual acts and institutional patterns), and ideological. This lumping together of a number of significantly different phenomena under a single label forestalls careful causal analysis. Racism simply must be differentiated from such related concepts as ethnocentrism, prejudice, racialism, and discrimination.

Racism is an ideology. It is neither behavior nor attitude. As an ideology it is a set of interrelated values which functions to justify a particular *existent or desired* social order.[10] Ideologies vary in generality but they are not global. They are attempts to interpret some greater or lesser aspect of reality in terms of some set of cultural values in a way that will be meaningful, that will enhance the ability of the population in question to make sense of that aspect of the world around them. Racism is distinguished from other ideologies by its racial focus and from other racial ideologies — i.e., other attempts to interpret and define the meaning or significance of real or alleged racial differences — by being rooted in a conception of biological or genetic superiority-inferiority.[11]

This defining characteristic of racism is made explicit by many scholars. For example:

> Racism is the dogma that one ethnic group is condemned by nature to hereditary inferiority and another group is destined to hereditary superiority.[12]

> Racism assumes inherent racial superiority or the purity and superiority of certain races; . . .[13]

> Racism is any set of beliefs that organic, genetically transmitted differ-
> ences (whether real or imagined) between human groups are intrinsically
> associated with the presence or the absence of certain socially relevant
> abilities or characteristics; . . .[14]

At the extreme racism becomes a denial of common humanity. When
this point is reached members of the relevant out-group(s) are not viewed
simply as inferior; they may be seen additionally as only part human, as
members of a different species, or as nonhuman. In any event belief in
the inherent superiority-inferiority of ethnic groups constitutes the basis
of racism.

From this central belief three major propositions have evolved to constitute the ideological foundation of racism. These three propositions are:

1. racial segregation is an inherent part of the natural order;
2. blacks are a different kind of being with a different evolutionary
    history and lesser culture-building capabilities than whites; and,
    therefore,
3. racial mixture must be avoided at all costs.[15]

Implicit in this ideology is a two-pronged defense of a discriminatory
social structure. First, the structure is conceived as part of an immutable
natural order. Second, it is justified via a logic which takes as its major
premise the idea that culture is chiefly, if not solely, a product of biological capabilities. The minor premise is that blacks are biologically
inferior. It follows that "Amalgamation of the two races would, therefore,
result in the rapid deterioration of the culture of the higher race."[16]
Racism is a bulwark against this calamity.

In sum, racism is an ideology based on the conception that racial groups
form a biogenetic hierarchy. Despite clear specification in the scientific
literature, the concept has commonly been confused with ethnocentrism,
prejudice, and discrimination. It is necessary, for reasons that will become clear, that racism now be carefully distinguished from each of these
concepts.

Racism and Ethnocentrism.   Ethnocentrism is preeminently a matter of
in-group glorification. Its inevitable concomitant is generalized rejection
and disparagement of out-groups, but the focus is on the virtues of the
in-group.[17] This in-group adulation or narcissism is a universal characteristic of autonomous societies and takes one or both of two major
forms — cultural and physical. The basic difference between the two
involves their assumptions about the educability of out-group members.
Cultural ethnocentrism assumes that with opportunity and training out-

group members could be acculturated and become the equals of members of the in-group. On the other hand, physical ethnocentrism (i.e., racism) assumes that members of the relevant out-groups are biogenetically incapable of ever achieving intellectual and moral equality with members of the in-group. Where cultural ethnocentrism attributes differences in behavior and culture to historical accident, racism attributes them to differences in innate endowment. Cultural ethnocentrism is far more common than the racist variety. Indeed, while racist societies invariably claim cultural superiority also (attributing this to their superior genetic endowment), the reverse is not ordinarily the case. Racism is only one kind of ethnocentrism and a relatively rare kind at that.[18]

The greater commonality of cultural ethnocentrism is understandable on a number of grounds. It is simply more flattering to rate one's group superior on the basis of cultural achievements than on the basis of ascribed physical characteristics. Creation is generally held in higher esteem than procreation. Moreover, throughout history many human groups have been without contacts with groups which differed from them in any salient physical way and most have possessed virtually no valid knowledge of genetics. Thus:

> The smallest racial unit is usually split up into many mutually death-dealing in-groups. Their antagonism is not racial but cultural. They do not keep their "blood" separate; each tribe may have made a practice of raiding for women in the other group, and their ancestry therefore may be traceable to the despised group almost in the same proportion as to their own vaunted one.[19]

This fine disregard for biological considerations finds its parallel in the early stages of the contacts of much more physically diverse people attendant upon the European swarming of the globe. Cultural differences — religion, in particular — formed the major initial basis for disparaging and enslaving Africans, Indians, and others encountered in this global expansion.[20]

Given this apparent primacy of cultural over physical differentia as a basis for assigning group status, it is essential that we consider the causal relationship of racism and slavery as a question apart from that of ethnocentrism and slavery. Cultural ethnocentrism was a cause of American slavery, but this in no way demonstrates or assures the same relationship between racism and slavery. Thus Finley's "outsider" interpretation of slavery does not necessarily imply the priority of racism but only that some kind of ethnocentrism precedes slavery.[21] The failure to differentiate racism from cultural ethnocentrism thus emerges as primarily responsible for the chicken-and-egg confusion regarding the causal relationship between American slavery and racism. Precise conceptual distinctions are essential to valid testing of causal propositions.

Racism and Discrimination.   In recent years it has become common to use the concept racism as a global term applying to negative beliefs about and discriminatory practices of whatever nature directed toward black Americans. Thus a person, a practice, an organization, an institution, or a society — any or all — may be labelled racist. In particular it is increasingly used to denote not ideology, nor even beliefs, but discriminatory behavior. For example, although Carmichael and Hamilton imply an ideological element in their definition of racism as "the predication of decisions and policies on considerations of race for the purpose of subordinating a racial group and maintaining control over that group," they immediately move to the behavioral plane in analyzing and employing the concept.

> Racism . . . takes two closely related forms: individual whites acting against individual blacks, and acts by the total white community against the black community.[22]

In either form, this is not racism but discrimination — i.e., differential and unequal *treatment* of the members of a specific group solely because they are members of that group.

To identify racism with discriminatory acts in this manner may be adequate to the worthy task of educating the public to the horrors and gross injustice of racism and discrimination, but such conceptual imprecision destroys the possibility of unraveling the causal relationship between a racist ideology and a discriminatory social structure. The central hypothesis of this essay, that slavery caused racism, simply cannot be tested unless racism and discrimination are differentiated. Slavery is an institutionalized form of discrimination and, thus, when racism is defined as discrimination the quest to pinpoint the causal relationship of slavery and racism is reduced to an absurdity. Racism must be rigorously distinguished from concepts which refer to actual behavior if the relationship between the ideology and a given structure of race relations is to be meaningfully explored.

Racism and Prejudice.   Ethnic prejudice is not an ideology but an attitude — a combination of beliefs, perceptions, feelings and motives which orient the prejudiced individual toward the members of a particular class of objects. While it is meaningful to speak of positive attitudes, including positive prejudices, the concept of prejudice generally implies a negative orientation. This is particularly true in the interethnic context. Hence, we can define prejudice as a hostile or negative attitude toward the members of a *specific* group solely because they are members of that group. In contrast to ethnocentrism, with its in-group focus and derivative generalized rejection of out-groups, prejudice is focused on and directed toward a specific out-group.

Aside from the fact that prejudice and a particular expression of racial ethnocentrism may share a common out-group referent, the primary basis for confusing the two is perhaps traceable to the concept of racialism. Racialism has been used almost interchangeably with both racism and prejudice with the result that racism and prejudice tend to be fused by the unwary.[23] From our perspective racialism is another label for race prejudice; and the emotional aversion, dislike, or hostility which is the essence of prejudice is a profoundly different phenomenon from racism with its value-dictated imposition of behavioral restriction and subordination of the members of an allegedly inferior group.[24]

As an attitude prejudice is a characteristic of an individual — not of a cultural structure. It may be a very widespread, common attitude but its locus, nonetheless, remains the individual and it is *not* analyzed in terms of institutional processes but in terms of the psychological processes of categorization, displacement, and rationalization.[25] A racist culture provides a context in which prejudice may be readily acquired and transmitted, but prejudice may also flourish in the absence of such a culture. Intergroup competition for scarce values provides a sufficient basis for prejudice even in the absence of racism.

An individual can be described as prejudiced or racist — or both; but a culture can only be described as racist.[26] However, acceptance of a belief in inherent racial superiority-inferiority by some or even a majority of the members of the society is not sufficient to demonstrate the existence of an ideology of racism. Conversely, a society can be racist even if only a minority of its members are racist.[27] Racism is not an aggregation of individual ideas; it is rather a distinct cultural orientation sustained and expressed by the society's basic institutions.[28] A society is racist — or, more accurately, its structure is supported by a racist ideology — only if the idea of group superiority-inferiority is incorporated into the institutional structure. To the extent that the institutions of society convey the idea *and* function in accord with the assumption that ability is dependent upon race, the society is racist. For example, when school segregation is justified, overtly or covertly, on the grounds that blacks are innately inferior and unable to learn the same material as rapidly as whites, racism has clearly been incorporated into the institutional structure. If segregation is in reality justified on some other grounds, the society may be just as discriminatory but it is not racist in the scientific sense of the term.

Conceptual Interrelations and Thesis Implication. Racism, ethnocentrism, prejudice, and discrimination are not only analytically independent, they are often empirically independent also. Ethnocentrism exists in societies that are not racist although, by definition, racism cannot occur without ethnocentrism. Prejudice and discrimination are often independent of each other and of racism also.

> Discrimination may be caused by other things than an attitude of prejudice. Prejudiced people do not give vent to their feelings in all situations; sometimes the possibility of punishment for doing so appears too threatening, and prejudice does not produce discrimination. Similarly, discriminators and prejudiced people often do not subscribe to a racist ideology, and people who do are not always prejudiced or likely to discriminate. The three factors are often associated in particular situations but they are in principle independent.[29]

What is presently crucial is that a society can be racist without extensive prejudice and individual discrimination among its members and, conversely, prejudice and individual discrimination can be widespread without the environing sociocultural structure being racist.

A number of descriptions indicate that modern Brazil approximates the latter situation,[30] and there are historical examples of the former. Indeed, the paternalistic type of race relations is characterized precisely by widespread acceptance and institutional implementation of the idea of biological superiority-inferiority combined with the absence of hostility or a highly negative attitude toward members of the subordinate group. In paternalistic societies condescension, not hostility, is the characteristic attitude of dominant group members toward their social inferiors.[31] Thus, at the beginning of the nineteenth century, slaves in the United States were characteristically defined as inferior and the institutional structure reflected this definition; but they were also commonly defined as lovable creatures so long as they "knew their place." Racism was rampant but prejudice was at a low ebb.

Given that prejudice and racism are not only different but also independent phenomena, it follows that evidence of prejudice must not be mistaken as evidence for the existence of racism and vice versa. Since neither prejudice nor racism necessarily implies the other, evidence regarding the relationship between prejudice and slavery does not necessarily inform us regarding the relationship between racism and slavery.

Yet, despite the independence of the phenomena denoted by the four concepts discussed, scholars continue to confuse their interrelations to the detriment of reliable causal analysis. For example, Jordan seemingly equates prejudice and racism[32] and he also misconstrues the causal relationship between prejudice and discrimination. This combination of conceptual confusion and faulty causal analysis makes it logically impossible to view slavery as the cause of racism. Jordan notes that certain "forms of debasement" (i.e., discrimination) occurred simultaneously with or even before slavery (itself a form of discrimination) and from this he concludes that prejudice preceded slavery. This conclusion follows only if one assumes that prejudice invariably precedes and causes discrimination. This simply is not a valid assumption. Prejudice and discrimination are independent phenomena (i.e., either may exist without the other); and when they are related, discrimination precedes or causes prejudice at least as often as the reverse.[33]

We may summarize the issue as follows. If (1) racism is equated with prejudice, (2) prejudice is viewed as a necessary cause of discrimination, and (3) lesser forms of discrimination precede slavery, then slavery cannot be logically viewed as the cause of racism. It may *reinforce* racism but it cannot be the primary cause. By contrast, if racism is differentiated from prejudice and discrimination is freed from its causal dependence upon prejudice, the thesis of the present essay becomes logically viable.

The Emergence of Racism

Even with a broadly common definition there is no agreement as to when racism appeared. Puzzo, for example, asserts that racism was absent in the ancient world and adds that "prior to the XVIth century there was virtually nothing in the life and thought of the West that can be described as racist."[34] Jonassen, however, contends that "the central ideas of racism had been part of the intellectual atmosphere of northwestern Europe since the beginning of historical times. . . ."[35] This might be interpreted as meaning that the ingredients of racism were present long before the ideology *per se*. Alternatively, the apparent contradiction between Puzzo and Jonassen might be resolved by positing two distinct types of racism: stock and substock. It is apparent that the Romans did differentiate population groupings *partly* in terms of physical characteristics as did the Egyptians and the Greeks. This, however, was largely on the basis of substock (i.e., intraracial) variations in physical characteristics and, in any event, exclusion was never solely or even largely on the basis of these characteristics. Rather exclusion was dependent upon a combination of characteristics in which cultural attributes predominated.[36]

Indeed, insofar as racism presupposes a concept of race the ideology could not have existed prior to the modern era for the concept itself did not emerge until the sixteenth century and was not widely used until the eighteenth century.[37] "Physical differences were, of course, known to exist between groups of mankind, but what was unfamiliar was the notion that the difference exhibited by such peoples represented anything fundamental."[38] In any event, the existence of classical racism is irrelevant for the present thesis inasmuch as no ancient form of racism, based upon whatever physical criteria, has historical continuity with modern racism with its heavy emphasis upon skin color as the primary indicator of membership in biologically superior or inferior racial groups. Still, confining our attention to modern racism does not resolve the differences of opinion regarding the initial appearance of racism. Even those who agree that racism is largely an after-the-fact rationalization of slavery date its appearance anywhere from the beginning of the sixteenth to the beginning of the twentieth century. Cox and Benedict, like Puzzo, attribute modern racism to the advent of European expansion; but Benedict asserts that even under the harsh conditions accompanying this expansion racism "did not arise for more than three centuries."[39] This would set the date as late eighteenth century. Others view the rise of racism as essentially a nineteenth-century phenomenon. Thus, Arnold Rose flatly states that "there was a certain curiosity about the physical features of Negroes; but racism . . . did not arise until after the year 1800."[40] By positing Darwinian currents of thought as one of the causes of Western racism, van den Berghe obviously sets its genesis at an even later date.[41]

Lieberman summarizes the issue by suggesting that sometime between 1700 and 1900 "the awareness of race was converted into an ideology of racism" which "took a mild form in the course of the eighteenth century and became particularly intense in the second half of the nineteenth century."[42] This rising intensity of racism provides a reasonable explanation for the general disagreement regarding the temporal origin of racism. As theologians and medical practitioners disagree among and between themselves as to the precise point at which the foetus constitutes life and abortion constitutes murder, so social scientists and historians disagree regarding how much racism is essential before a society is accurately described as racist. This disagreement has a qualitative as well as a quantitative dimension. That is, the rising intensity of racism reflects the transition from a purely exploitative to a paternalist slave system. As slavery became ever more clearly the pivotal institution of Southern society, racism was continually strengthened and became an ever more dominant ideology.[43] Its initial function, justification of slavery, ultimately ceased to be the primary concern or, more precisely, the maintenance of slavery *as a viable economic institution* became incidental to the larger task of assuring the survival of a way of life. Racist values increasingly rivaled economic efficiency as the basis for organizing black-white relations. Eventually racism became an autonomous value complex with a significance of its own apart from the institution which generated it. In all likelihood it did not fully achieve this status until the nineteenth century, but it is as absurd to argue that an ideology must be fully developed before it can exert a significant influence on society as to argue oppositely that it has a significant influence from the day that the basic idea is conceived by one or more persons. In short, I view the eighteenth century as the decisive period — the period when racism became firmly embedded in American culture and institutions. In the following century it became *the* principle by which slavery and all subsequent patterns of race relations had to be ordered, but it was institutionalized in the eighteenth century.

This hypothesized period of origin is, of course, consistent with the thesis that American racism was much more a consequence than a cause of slavery. This contention is initially justified by constructing a theory from certain well established facts about colonial America. The theory specifies a set of variables whose interaction provides a *logical* explanation for the emergence of racism.

A Tentative Theory of the Origin of Racism

While a variety of specific factors can be plausibly adduced as causes of any given historic phenomena, they ultimately reduce themselves to two general classes — material conditions and values. These two classes of factors and the interaction between them provide the dynamic context for the development of all sociocultural structures. Thus, in the case of American slavery the material fact of gross exploitation combined with an egalitarian value system to produce racism. The catalytic agent was the emergence of the antislavery movement. The movement sharply pointed up the contradiction between exploitation and the egalitarian creed and thereby necessitated either a muting of exploitation or a racist redefinition of the exploited people in order to resolve the contradiction.

Exploitation is a seemingly necessary cause of racism. Although rigid Marxists have singled out capitalist exploitation as the basis of racism, it is highly probable that one form of exploitation will serve as well as another.[44] As a matter of historical fact, however, it was the exploitation attendant upon the colonial expansion of capitalist Europe which triggered modern racism.[45] The primary purpose of colonization is to exploit the resources (human and otherwise) of the society colonized for the enrichment of the mother country and its members. Benefits to members of the colonized society, "uplift," may be welcomed by the colonizing power — either because they facilitate short-run control or fulfill missionary ideals — but they are entirely incidental to the main purpose.[46] Exploitation is for the benefit of those doing the exploiting. To insure continued benefit, the exploiters seek to institutionalize their advantage. The resulting ethnic stratification, like any "permanent" institution, is far more efficient if it is linked to and justified by group values. Ethnic stratification thus triggers a search for justification which, under certain conditions, terminates in racism.[47]

As the preceding implies, exploitation is not a sufficient cause of racism. Exploitation and slavery have existed without racism.[48] The value context is a critical determinant of whether or not exploitation, or ethnic stratification, will generate racism. Indeed, the causal role of exploitation hardly makes sense except in an equalitarian value context. Why should exploitation cause racism? The answer is that in itself there is no compelling reason why it should. It does so, paradoxically, only if the values of the exploiting society are such that its members have misgivings about the justice of their actions. In the absence of notions of equality, brotherhood, and justice, members of one group can exploit members of other groups with few qualms and no compulsion to construct a unique justifying rationale. If a rationale is desired, cultural ethnocentrism is an adequate justification for a double standard in which out-group members are viewed as "fair game." Hence, far from preventing racism, an egalitarian creed is a requisite for the emergence of such an ideology.

The American egalitarian creed has its roots in the Judaeo-Christian heritage, in the political ideals of democracy, in the Enlightenment (with its emphasis on the natural rights of man and its implicit assumption of equality of ability among different groups of mankind), in the English common law tradition, and even to some extent in capitalism (the principle of individual opportunity) and nationalism ("a nation of immigrants").[49] The values of equality, brotherhood, and justice derived from these sources were of increasing significance in colonial America. The sharp inconsistency — indeed, the blatant clash — between slavery and these values necessitated a racist ideology to justify and thereby assure preservation of a profitable institution which overtly denied these central values. Once the basic societal institutions defined blacks as biologically inferior, perhaps even subhuman, whites would no longer be constrained in their relations with blacks to honor values designed to regulate interaction between peers. By challenging or denying black humanity a profitable institution could be maintained without surrendering or compromising the beloved egalitarian creed. Thus, "the dogma of racial inequality may, in a sense, be regarded as a strange fruit of the Enlightenment."[50]

Part and parcel with the existence of slavery was a flourishing and highly visible slave trade. This open trade in human beings was a continuous and glaring reminder of the blatant contradiction of basic values. Here the slave was most clearly defined as a commodity — a chattel as totally responsive to his master's wishes as any beast of the field. The trade constituted a powerful impetus to racism both by accentuating the necessity to justify such gross violation of basic values[51] and by impelling the emergence of an antislavery movement whose attack upon the institution of slavery in turn triggered the necessity to create a rationale to justify or defend the system. Initially, the abolitionists concentrated on the regulation, curtailment, and ultimate elimination of the slave trade. Even this, of course, was bitterly opposed by the slave owners in the realization that the power to regulate the trade contained the seeds of the power of life and death over the institution.[52]

The attack upon slavery had its inception in the last quarter of the seventeenth century.[53] The appearance of a pamphlet entitled *The Selling of Joseph, A Memorial* at the turn of the century drew an immediate reply which was "probably the first written defense of slavery in American history."[54] This exchange initiated a controversy whose essential positions were fully developed by the close of the colonial period. Emphases shifted to fit the times but the essential arguments in opposition to and in defense of slavery were largely elaborated in the period between 1700 and 1775.[55] The key point in the present context, however, is that the defense of slavery was, in the main, a response to the attack upon slavery. "The first theories of any political and social institution are to be found long after it has first been established, when its validity and justice are first attacked and then defended."[56] Thus, racism emerged from the "necessity" to defend a profitable institution which was under attack because its gross exploitation of human beings was sharply at odds with emerging Western values.

Regardless of the clarity and logical merit the theory sketched here may have, the only decisive test of the thesis that racism is primarily a consequence rather than a cause of slavery requires careful analysis of the evidence provided by the historical record. Accordingly, our final task is to suggest some methodological guidelines and topics for a program of research designed to ferret out and evaluate the relevant historical evidence.

Research Guidelines and Suggestions

Any effort to establish the relative importance of materialistic and idealistic factors in the generation of slavery and racism requires far more precise conceptual distinctions than have heretofore been used. Research based upon the conceptual distinctions suggested in this essay may conclude as Jordan has, that racism and slavery were linked in such a way that each was more or less equally a cause and equally an effect of the other. In short, we may ultimately conclude that slavery and racism were of equal importance in hustling the Negro "down the road to complete degradation."[57] On the other hand, these distinctions may enable us to conclude that slavery was primarily a cause of racism or that racism was primarily a cause of slavery. In any event, we shall have grounds for vastly greater confidence in the conclusions reached when the researcher consistently has sharply differentiated these closely related concepts.

Actually, it seems likely that the ideology of racism rapidly became so intertwined with slavery as a social structure as to be separable only analytically.[58] This complicates the effort to establish the original relationship between the two and necessitates some serious efforts to develop an index, or set of indexes, which will enable us to assess the degree to which a racist ideology — as distinguished from individual beliefs and institutional patterns — existed in colonial America. The difficulty inheres in measuring the strength of racism in the society *independent* of the proportion of individuals who accept the basic racist belief (i.e., the belief that blacks are in fact biogenetically inferior to whites)[59] and of the institutionalized practices (e.g., slavery and lesser forms of discrimination) which reflect and/or create the racist ideology. We shall essay a tentative solution to this difficulty after taking note of a related methodological problem.

If we wish to ascertain slavery's causal relation to racism obviously we must specify the origin of slavery as well as racism. This is not a simple matter either inasmuch as slavery developed gradually over a period of several decades. Blacks did not all become slaves at the same time. The statutory enactment of slavery can be specified for each colony, but the law generally legitimates an already existing institution rather than creating one where none previously existed.[60] Thus, "slavery was not established by law in any American colony, but its development by custom was later recognized by legislation."[61] The available evidence strongly supports the conclusion that slavery was in fact securely institutionalized not later than 1670 and perhaps as early as the 1640s. The crucial question then is whether or not a socially significant ideology of racial superiority-inferiority antedated this period.

A definitive answer to this question, and accordingly a decisive test of the thesis that racism is primarily a consequence rather than a cause of slavery, requires a comprehensive analysis of primary sources in a variety of institutional areas. For present purposes it will have to suffice to suggest a method of procedure for pinpointing racism. This involves making explicit an operationalization of racism which can be applied to each institutional area to determine when an ideology of racism became significant in that area. Operationalized, the crucial question becomes: "When were specific, discriminatory practices directed toward blacks *commonly justified by reference to a racist rationale?*" In short, an ideology — as opposed to beliefs and practices — must be inferred from a careful analysis of institutional documents. An ideology is defined as a *set of values* justifying a particular (existent or desired) social structure, and values are precisely the standards, or criteria, which we invoke in making choices or decisions in the real world.[62] The evidence accumulated from the analysis of legal and religious records, scientific documents and theories, literature, and educational and political documents from the colonial era should provide a reliable basis for estimating the strength of racism at various points in time (e.g., 1650, 1700, 1750, and 1775). This will then provide the necessary data for assessing the causal relationship between slavery and racism.

More specifically, we can establish the advent of racism in the legal institutions — especially the courts and legislatures — by carefully examining the rationale for decisions which adversely affected blacks. If we simply look at the decisions *per se* (or the behavior patterns which follow from these decisions, statutes, etc.) and infer the extent of racism from these data, we are unable to test the relationship between ideology and behavior because our argument is circular. It is only by inferring racism from an independent base such as the rationales underlying discriminatory decisions, statutes, and practices that we can avoid circularity. If we accept the proposition that racism as ideology is analytically distinct from "racism" as belief, attitude (prejudice), or behavior (discrimination) then we must accept the possibility that each of these may exist independently in the real world. Discriminatory decisions could be elicited and implemented for nonracist reasons — e.g., purely for economic gain or for theological orthodoxy. A critical question, then, in terms of the larger thesis regarding the relationship between slavery and racism, is whether or not the early court decisions involving the term of service of blacks were arrived at and justified by reference to racist or nonracist values. I would hypothesize that justification in terms of religion and other doctrines (e.g., the right to captives taken in a just war) far outweighed justification in terms of biogenetic superiority-inferiority in the critical period up to 1670.[63] Indeed, the shift from religious to racist

justification in the latter third of the seventeenth century has been frequently commented upon. Moreover, the shift itself was probably motivated less by genuine racism than by the economic advantages which
accrued from a slave labor force made permanent by the fact that skin
color, in contrast to religion, could not be changed readily.[64]

While there is considerable evidence that religion was initially the
major overt basis for justifying slavery, it is at least possible that racism
was a more significant *but generally concealed* cause of slavery. There
would seem to be very little reason, however, for the colonists to conceal
an ideology which lacked any effective or organized opposition. Throughout the seventeenth century the Christian Church, for example, even
with its institutional primacy and commitment to the unity of mankind,
was primarily concerned with the conversion of slaves, not with the
morality of slavery or its emerging rationale. Indeed, the clergy welcomed the decision that conversion did not alter the slave status as this
reduced planter opposition to conversion.[65] Certainly there was no hesi-
tancy to make racism explicit after slavery's institutionalization as the
rationale for a 1696 South Carolina slave code indicates.[66] The critical
task which remains is to analyze the historical materials in detail to
determine at what point in time the racist rationale became common.

Within the context of the legal institutions the rationale for decisions
pertaining to certain specific issues might be especially enlightening. For
example, decisions on such issues as the length of service, the status of
children, the effect of conversion upon the slave's status, the stripping
away of the legal rights of slaves, and the status of the free blacks would
seem to warrant very careful scrutiny. In most, if not all, of these cases
the problem of ascertaining the degree of racism is complicated by the
constant play of other forces. Thus it might be tempting to argue from
available evidence that the general failure to treat free Negroes differently from slaves is itself indicative of a pervasive racist ideology. However, the intervention of economic factors justifies vast skepticism
regarding such inferences. The elevated status of free Negroes in Brazil
as compared to the United States does not tell us so much about comparative racism as it does about the differential labor requirements of
the two countries. The differential need for nonwhites in intermediate
occupational statuses may be entirely adequate to account for Brazilian
acceptance and American rejection of free Negroes.[67] In short, racism
cannot automatically be inferred from discrimination. Hence, it is imperative to ascertain the rationale which lies behind discriminatory decisions and practices. An ideology is not revealed nearly so well by what
people do as by why they do it.

Conclusion

It is beyond the scope of the present essay to test the theory of the origin of racism sketched herein. Rather our objectives have been:

1. to provide a set of analytic distinctions which are essential to an adequate test of the theory and, in particular, of the proposition that racism is a consequence of slavery rather than the reverse; and
2. to suggest some methodological guidelines and some institutional areas and issues for research intended to test the theory.

The first objective has been given priority because research to date has only spuriously considered the theoretical possibility that racism is largely a product of slavery. Researchers have either simply declared that slavery caused racism or else they have ruled this possibility out by conceptual confusion and error amounting to fiat. With the conceptual distinctions delineated here the issue of the causal relationship between slavery and racism can now be joined with conceptual tools adequate to ultimate proof or disproof of the thesis advanced.

Racism as an ideology cannot exist without an initial racist belief for, by definition, it is a value complex rooted in that belief. The belief, however, can exist without the ideology. Similarly, racism cannot exist independent of discrimination, but discrimination can exist independent of racism — i.e., discrimination may have economic or other nonracist causes. Therefore, the existence of discrimination is not sufficient grounds for inferring racism, and the fact that lesser forms of discrimination preceded slavery does not prove that racism also preceded slavery. The allegedly high correlation between discrimination and racism simply accentuates the need for precision and care in using these and related concepts to establish causal propositions. A program of research guided by the conceptual distinctions outlined here and focused on issues and institutions such as the ones suggested should significantly clarify and advance our understanding of the causal relationship between American slavery and racism.

Notes

1. As Eugene Genovese states, "once an ideology arises it alters profoundly the material reality and in fact becomes a partially autonomous feature of that reality." His analysis is an excellent critique of the interacting role of values and material interests. See "Materialism and Idealism in the History of Negro Slavery in the Americas," in L. Foner and E. D. Genovese, eds., *Slavery in the New World* (Engle-

wood Cliffs, N. J.; Prentice-Hall, 1969), pp. 238-55 (quotation at p. 244 but also see esp. pp. 248-53). The crucial significance of racism as an autonomous cause of post-slavery forms of ethnic stratification is clearly revealed in the trenchant analysis by Sidney M. Willhelm, *Who Needs the Negro?* (Cambridge, Mass.: Schenkman, 1970).

2.   See M. G. Smith, *The Plural Society in the British West Indies* (Berkeley: University of California Press, 1965), esp. chap. 6 and A. Tuden and L. Plotnicov, eds., *Social Stratification in Africa* (New York: Free Press, 1970).

3.   However, the scattered early expressions of racist ideas may themselves have derived from the developing experience with enslavement of blacks in Iberia and Iberian America.

4.   Eric Williams, *Capitalism and Slavery* (Chapel Hill: University of North Carolina Press, 1944), p. 7.

5.   Gunnar Myrdal, *An American Dilemma* (New York: Harper and Bros., 1944), pp. 83, 84.

6.   Charles F. Marden, *Minorities in American Society* (New York: American Book Co., 1952), p. 64.

7.   Thomas F. Gossett, *Race: The History of an Idea in America* (Dallas: Southern Methodist University Press, 1963), pp. 28-29.

8.   Eugene D. Genovese, *The World the Slaveholders Made* (New York: Pantheon, 1969), p. 105.

9.   Moses I. Finley, "The Idea of Slavery," *New York Review of Books* 8 (January 26, 1967) reprinted in Foner and Genovese, pp. 256-61 (quotations at p. 261).

10.   This conception of ideology, as opposed to one which restricts it to justification of an already established order, is not only logical but also essential if the question of whether racism precedes or follows slavery is to be meaningful. For a composite, general definition of ideology see Elliott A. Krause, "Functions of a Bureaucratic Ideology: 'Citizen Participation'," *Social Problems* 16 (1968): 129-43. Also see Chalmers Johnson, *Revolutionary Change* (Boston: Little, Brown and Co., 1966), esp. pp. 81-87. The classic work is Karl Mannheim, *Ideology and Utopia* (New York: Harcourt, Brace and World, 1936).

11.   Manning Nash, "Race and the Ideology of Race," *Current Anthropology* 3 (1962): 285-88.

12.   Ruth Benedict, *Race: Science and Politics* (New York: Viking Press, 1959), p. 98.

13.   Louis L. Snyder, *The Idea of Racialism* (New York: D. Van Nostrand Company, 1962), p. 10.

14.   Pierre L. van den Berghe, *Race and Racism* (New York: John Wiley & Sons, Inc., 1967), p. 11.

15.   These propositions are most closely paraphrased from James Vander Zanden, "The Ideology of White Supremacy," *Journal of the History of Ideas* 20 (1959) 385-402; but also see the similar analyses by Arnold Rose, "Race and Ethnic Relations" in R. K. Merton and R. A. Nisbet, *Contemporary Social Problems* (New York: Harcourt, Brace and World, 1961), esp. p. 356; Marden, pp. 46-48; Nash, esp. pp. 285-86; and Tamotsu Shibutani and Kian Kwan, *Ethnic Stratification* (New York: Macmillan Company, 1965), pp. 243-46. An excellent early discussion is provided by William S. Jenkins, *Pro-Slavery Thought in the Old South* (Chapel Hill: University of North Carolina Press, 1935), chap. 6.

16.   Rose, p. 356. The racist rationale is clearly stated by Schermerhorn but unfortunately he contradicts his own definition of racism by describing cultural ethno-

centrism directed toward members of a cultural out-group who happen also to be members of a different race as a form of racism. R. A. Schermerhorn, *Comparative Ethnic Relations* (New York: Random House, 1970), esp. pp. 73, 74 and 102.

17.   Puzzo correctly observes that ethnocentrism is "the identification of oneself with one's own people as against the rest of mankind," but he is incorrect when he appends the word "indiscriminately." The rejection of out-groups is not indiscriminate; rather it varies as a function of the perceived degree of difference, cultural and physical, between the in-group and the out-group in question. Dante A. Puzzo, "Racism and the Western Tradition," *Journal of the History of Ideas* 25 (1964): 579-86.

18.   van den Berghe, p. 12; also see Schermerhorn, pp. 73-74.

19.   Benedict, p. 101. Also see Ralph Linton, *The Study of Man* (New York: D. Appleton-Century Company, 1936), p. 46.

20.   Benedict, pp. 107-8 and Winthrop D. Jordan, *White Over Black* (Chapel Hill: University of North Carolina Press, 1968), esp. pp. 23-24 and 89-98.

21.   Finley, p. 261. Moreover, Finley asserts in an earlier analysis that the full rights of marriage for Roman freedmen shows that the racial element in the concept of outsider, though not zero, was largely irrelevant. See M. I. Finley, "Between Slavery and Freedom," *Comparative Studies in Society and History* 6 (1964): 233-49. This certainly supports the contention that racism need not precede slavery.

22.   Stokely Carmichael and Charles V. Hamilton, *Black Power* (New York: Vintage, 1967), pp. 3 and 4. Discrimination, thus, can be either individual or structural in contrast to prejudice, which is individual only, and racism, which is cultural only.

23.   Snyder, p. 10, equates racialism and prejudice while Marden, pp. 46-48 and 62n, equates racialism and racism. The former usage predominates but many sociologists occasionally use racialism in the latter sense.

24.   See Daniel P. Moynihan, "The New Racialism," *The Atlantic Monthly* 222 (August 1968): 35-40 (esp. p. 38).

25.   Gordon W. Allport, *The Nature of Prejudice* (Reading, Mass.: Addison-Wesley, 1954), esp. chaps. 2, 12, 20 and 21.

26.   A racist individual is one who believes that there are biologically superior and inferior races. The individual can be racist without being prejudiced since this kind of stereotyped belief is only one component of prejudice. The belief indicates prejudice only if it is resistant to change because the individual is infused with emotional aversion to the out-group in question. Given the failure to differentiate racist beliefs from an ideology of racism, the frequent part-whole relation between racist beliefs and prejudice no doubt contributes to the tendency to equate racism and prejudice.

27.   This simply expresses the proposition that a ruling minority can indelibly place its stamp upon the society at large. Several authors have noted the success of slave-holding minorities in this regard. For example, see Genovese, *The World the Slaveholders Made,* and Moses I. Finley, "Was Greek Civilization Based on Slave Labour?" in M. I. Finley, ed., *Slavery in Classical Antiquity* (W. Heffer and Sons, 1960), esp. p. 58.

28.   The flaws of the existing institutional order commonly generate a counter-ideology which challenges and seeks to replace the existing order even as the presently dominant ideology continues to be sustained and expressed by the existing institutions. Racism and cultural ethnocentrism (e.g., nationalism, patriotism) are commonly taught by many American institutions which also espouse liberty and equality.

29.   Michael Banton, *Race Relations* (New York: Basic Books, 1967), p. 9. Ideologies are cultural structures but, as value complexes, they are either subscribed to or rejected by individuals.

30.   For example, see Genovese, "Materialism and Idealism. . . ," p. 241; Jose H. Rodrigues, *Africa and Brazil* (Berkeley: University of California Press, 1965), chap. 4; and, esp., van den Berghe, chap. 3 (esp. p. 69).

31.   *Ibid.*, esp. pp. 27-28 and Shibutani and Kwan, pp. 258 and 280.

32.   Jordan, esp. p. 80. Actually Jordan does not use the word racism in his entire volume. This curious omission itself strongly implies that he equates racism with prejudice, an implication supported by perusing the pages listed under "prejudice" in the volume's index. Other scholars, sociologists as well as historians, have explicitly equated racism and prejudice at least on occasion. For examples, see Davis, p. 281; Arnold Rose, *Assuring Freedom to the Free* (Detroit: Wayne State University Press, 1963), p. 33; and Schermerhorn, p. 201.

33.   There is a very lengthy literature regarding the relationship between prejudice and discrimination. Among the best recent articles are: M. L. De Fleur and F. R. Westie, "Attitude as A Scientific Concept," *Social Forces* 42 (1963): 17-31; H. J. Ehrlich, "Attitudes, Behavior and the Intervening Variable," *American Sociologist* 4 (1969): 29-34; and L. S. Linn, "Verbal Attitudes and Overt Behavior: A Study of Racial Discrimination," *Social Forces* 43 (1965): 353-364. Also see Earl Raab, *American Race Relations Today* (New York: Doubleday & Company, 1962), pp. 29-55. The implicit assumption that prejudice always causes discrimination may account for Jordan's imperceptive assertion that Marvin Harris's "concluding discussion on the relationship between slavery and prejudice makes very little sense concerning English America." *White Over Black,* p. 606.

34.   Puzzo, p. 579.

35.   Christen T. Jonassen, "Some Historical and Theoretical Bases of Racism in Northwestern Europe," *Social Forces* 30 (December 1951): 155-61.

36.   See David B. Davis, *The Problem of Slavery in Western Culture* (Ithaca, N.Y.: Cornell University Press, 1966), esp. pp. 47-54 and 67-72; Simon Davis, *Race Relations in Ancient Egypt* (Methuen, 1951); Frederick G. Detweiler, "The Rise of Modern Race Antagonisms," *American Journal of Sociology* 37 (1932): 738-47; Gossett, chap. 1; and A. N. Sherwin-White, *Racial Prejudice in Imperial Rome* (Cambridge: Cambridge University Press, 1967).

37.   Leonard Lieberman, "The Debate Over Race: A Study in the Sociology of Knowledge," *Phylon* 29 (1968): 127-41 (esp. p. 132).

38.   Quoted from Ashley Montagu in Marden, p. 63.

39.   O. C. Cox, *Caste, Class and Race* (New York: Monthly Review Press, 1959), pp. 327-35 and 480-82 and Benedict, pp. 106-11.

40.   Rose, *Assuring Freedom. . . ,* p. 33; also see Rose, "Race and Ethnic Relations," pp. 353-54.

41.   van den Berghe, pp. 15-18. His analysis is inconsistent as he says (p. 15) that racism "came of age" before 1840 which is, of course, pre-Darwin. Genovese suggests, more cautiously, that Social Darwinism was required "for a *fully developed* racist ideology to emerge and conquer the Western world." *The World. . . ,* p. 105 (emphasis added). Higham, focusing his analysis on a refined (substock) version of racism, goes so far as to imply that authentic racism came into being only with the twentieth-century maturing of Nordicism. See John Higham, *Strangers in the Land* (New York: Atheneum, 1965), esp. p. 157.

42.   Lieberman, p. 133.

43. Arnold A. Sio, "Society, Slavery, and the Slave" (Review Article), *Social and Economic Studies* 16 (1967): 330-44 (esp. pp. 337-40). See also Eugene D. Genovese, *The Political Economy of Slavery* (New York: Vintage, 1965), esp. chap. 1.

44. Compare the position of Cox, esp. chap. 16, and Williams, passim, with that of Willhelm, pp. 131-33, and of van den Berghe, pp. 12-16, who notes the existence of racism independent of capitalism in widely scattered places and times.

45. See Benedict, pp. 106-11; Puzzo, esp. p. 583; Schermerhorn, p. 104; and van den Berghe, pp. 16-17.

46. See Carmichael and Hamilton, esp. p. 17.

47. Exploitation is defined as a necessary cause of racism by M. Nash, p. 288, Shibutani and Kwan, pp. 241-49, and van den Berghe, pp. 16-17. Racism is not entirely uniform, however, but varies with the nature of the exploitation and the conditions of economic, political, and sexual contact between the groups involved. See the discussion by Gary B. Nash, "Red, White and Black: The Origins of Racism in Colonial America" in G. B. Nash and R. Weiss, eds., *The Great Fear: Race in the Mind of America* (New York: Holt, Rinehart and Winston, 1970), pp. 1-26 (esp. pp. 16-21).

48. Schermerhorn, p. 156 and van den Berghe, p. 17. Witness slavery in the ancient world and, in more recent times, slavery in parts of Africa as described by Tuden and Plotnicov, esp. pp. 11-15 and 47-58.

49. Myrdal, chap. 1 and Marshall B. Clinard, *The Sociology of Deviant Behavior* (New York: Holt, Rinehart and Winston, 1963), pp. 491-93.

50. Myrdal, pp. 83-89 (quotation at p. 89). Also see Davis, chaps. 13 and 14 and pp. 454-59 for a thorough discussion of the impact of the Enlightenment which emphasizes "the ambivalence of rationalism."

51. "With the growth of the international slave trade in the last quarter of the seventeenth century, theories of Negro inferiority apparently gained in popularity." *Ibid.*, p. 453.

52. Eli Ginzberg and Alfred S. Eichner, *The Troublesome Presence* (Mentor, 1966), p. 46.

53. *Ibid.*, p. 43; Jenkins, pp. 7-8; and esp. Thomas E. Drake, *Quakers and Slavery in America* (New Haven: Yale University Press, 1950), chap. 1; Arthur Zilversmit, *The First Emancipation* (Chicago: University of Chicago Press, 1967), chap. 3; and Louis Ruchames, ed., *Racial Thought in America* (Amherst: University of Massachusetts Press, 1969), pp. 36-45.

54. Jenkins, p. 4.

55. *Ibid.*, pp. 39-47; see also pp. 1-2.

56. Robert Schlaifer, "Greek Theories of Slavery from Homer to Aristotle," in Finley, *Slavery in Classical Antiquity,* p. 93. Also see Jenkins, p. 39 and Gossett, p. 29. Davis, pp. 488-89, points out that a mature antislavery movement did not emerge until late eighteenth century but Drake and Zilversmit document continuous criticism of slavery throughout the century. Towner asserts that the early opposition was primarily directed toward the slave trade not toward slavery *per se,* but Jordan states that "there were at least fifteen known written condemnations of slavery in the English colonies before 1750. . . ." See Jordan, *White Over Black,* p. 195 and Lawrence W. Towner, "The Sewell-Saffin Dialogue on Slavery," *William and Mary Quarterly* 21 (1964): 40-52. The Sewell-Saffin documents are included in Ruchames, pp. 46-58 and discussed in Davis, pp. 341-48.

57. Jordan, p. 80.

58.   This point is implied by Genovese in his comment that "once slavery came into being, ethnocentricity and color prejudice passed quickly, although perhaps not immediately, into racism." *The World. . .* , p. 105. The comment also implies an awareness of the crucial conceptual distinctions necessary to accurately assess the relationship between slavery and racism.

59.   Even establishing the prevalence of the racist belief in seventeenth-century America would be very difficult inasmuch as the early colonists were far too busy securing a livelihood to conduct opinion polls or attitude surveys. Diaries and biographies hardly provide a reliable basis for estimating the frequency of beliefs because their authors are not likely to be representative of the total population.

60.   Statutory enactment itself varied greatly by colony, ranging from 1641 in Massachusetts to 1714 in New Hampshire and never in Vermont. See Elkins, p. 41n and William T. Alexander, *History of the Colored Race in America* (Westport, Conn.: Negro Universities Press, 1968), pp. 132-37. The gradual emergence of slavery in custom prior to statute is repeatedly noted in part two of the present reader.

61.   Wilbert Moore, "Slave Law and the Social Structure," *Journal of Negro History* 26 (1941): 171-202 (quotation at p. 171).

62.   For one of the best sociological discussions of values see Robin M. Williams, Jr., *American Society* (New York: Alfred A. Knopf, 1970), chap. 11.

63.   Regarding the early justification of various forms of servitude see Moore, pp. 172-74, and Lawrence W. Towner, " 'A Fondness for Freedom': Servant Protest in Puritan Society," *William and Mary Quarterly* 19 (1962): 201-19 (see esp. pp. 204-5 and 217-19). Also see Wilcomb E. Washburn, "The Moral and Legal Justifications for Dispossessing the Indians," chap. 2 in James M. Smith, ed., *Seventeenth Century America: Essays in Colonial History* (Chapel Hill: University of North Carolina Press, 1959).

64.   Regarding the shift from the religious to the racist justification of slavery, see Moore, pp. 174-84 and Jordan, pp. 93 and 97-98. Jordan specifically stresses the economic factor in noting (p. 93) that the "decision that the slave's religious condition had no relevance to his status as a slave" was "the only one possible if an already valuable economic institution was to be retained. . . ."

65.   Jordan, pp. 92-93 and 179-81. Jordan also discusses the initial primacy of the religious factor in determining the status of blacks; esp. pp. 93-98.

66.   The code's preamble indicates that "special legislation was necessary to govern slaves because Negroes had 'barbarous, wild, savage *Natures'* and were '*naturally* prone and inclined' to 'Disorders, Rapines and Inhumanity.' " M. Eugene Sirmans, "The Legal Status of the Slave in South Carolina, 1670-1740," *Journal of Southern History* 28 (1962): 462-73 (quotation at p. 466; emphasis added).

67.   See Marvin Harris, *Patterns of Race in the Americas* (New York: Walker and Company, 1964), chap. 7.

BIBLIOGRAPHY

Benedict, Ruth. *Race: Science and Politics*. New York: The Viking Press, 1945. A highly informative analysis of the nature and history of racism.

Davis, David B. *The Problem of Slavery in Western Culture*. Ithaca, N. Y.: Cornell University Press, 1966. While this book does not isolate the question of origin, it will undoubtedly achieve the status of a classic for its searching analysis of the history of slavery in the Western world, especially the new world.

Degler, Carl N. *Neither Black nor White*. New York: The Macmillan Company, 1971. An excellent blending of historical and sociological analysis which both summarizes and expands our knowledge of the similarities and differences, historical and contemporary, in slavery and race relations in Brazil and the United States.

Elkins, Stanley M. "Slavery and Ideology," in Ann J. Lane, ed., *The Debate Over Slavery*. Urbana, Ill.: University of Illinois Press, 1971. In this reappraisal of the controversy generated by his earlier analysis of slavery, Elkins stresses the differences between Brazilian and American slavery and cautions against inferring the existence of a cultural tradition, or ideology, from a few isolated instances compatible with the alleged tradition.

Foner, Laura and Eugene D. Genovese, eds. *Slavery in the New World*. Englewood Cliffs, N. J.: Prentice-Hall, Inc., 1969. A series of readings focused upon the debate initiated by Frank Tannenbaum regarding variations in slavery in the new world.

Genovese, Eugene D. *The Political Economy of Slavery*. New York: Random House, 1967 (Vintage edition). Chapters 1 and 10 of this seminal work

are especially helpful in understanding the emerging relationship between slavery and racism.

Genovese, Eugene D. *The World the Slaveholders Made*. New York: Pantheon Books, 1969. Two essays which provide a wealth of detail on
American slave systems and exhibit an uncommon sensitivity to the
differences between ethnocentrism, racism, and prejudice.

Gossett, Thomas F. *Race: The History of an Idea in America*. Dallas: Southern Methodist University Press, 1963. Chapters 1 and 2 provide very
useful material regarding racial ideas in Europe and colonial America.

Goveia, Elsa V. *Slave Society in the British Leeward Islands at the End of the
Eighteenth Century*. New Haven: Yale University Press, 1965. An
illuminating analysis which is especially significant in the present context for its discussion of the role of racism in integrating a particular
type of slave system.

Jonassen, Christen T. "Some Historical and Theoretical Bases of Racism in
Northwestern Europe," *Social Forces* 30 (December 1951): 155-61.
The author argues that the germ of racism has existed in Europe since
the dawn of history.

Jordan, Winthrop D. *White Over Black*. Chapel Hill, N.C.: University of
North Carolina Press, 1968. A valuable and highly detailed examination
of the emergence and growth of slavery and racial ideas in colonial
America.

Lieberman, Leonard. "The Debate Over Race: A Study in the Sociology of
Knowledge," *Phylon* 29 (Summer 1968): 127-41. The author emphasizes the gradual emergence of racism in the centuries following European expansion over the globe.

Moore, Wilbert. "Slave Law and the Social Structure," *Journal of Negro
History* 26 (April 1941): 171-202. A valuable analysis of the transition
from cultural ethnocentrism, based on religion, to racism as a justification for American slavery.

Nash, Manning. "Race and the Ideology of Race," *Current Anthropology*
3 (June 1962): 285-88. A succinct analysis of the nature of race and
racism and the conditions for the emergence of the latter.

Palmer, Paul C. "Servant into Slave: The Evolution of the Legal Status of the
Negro Laborer in Colonial Virginia," *South Atlantic Quarterly* 65 (Summer 1966): 355-70. An informative exposition of the known facts regarding the status of blacks in seventeenth-century Virginia.

Puzzo, Dante A. "Racism and the Western Tradition," *Journal of the History
of Ideas* 25 (October-December 1964): 579-86. The author distinguishes

racism from ethnocentrism and attributes the origin of racism to the period of European expansion.

Ruchames, Louis, ed. *Racial Thought in America*. Amherst, Mass.: University of Massachusetts Press, 1969. An excellent collection of articles and excerpts with an especially valuable introduction by the editor on "The Sources of Racial Thought in Colonial America."

Sio, Arnold A. "Society, Slavery and the Slave," *Social and Economic Studies* 16 (December 1967): 330-44. An outstanding review article which makes a contribution of its own in assessing the contributions of Genovese, Goveia, and Elkins regarding the emerging significance of racism for the integration of a particular type of slave society.

Twombly, Robert C. and Robert H. Moore. "Black Puritan: The Negro in Seventeenth Century Massachusetts," *William and Mary Quarterly* 24 (April 1967): 224-42. This valuable essay provides extensive evidence of equalitarian legal treatment of blacks in Massachusetts until late in the seventeenth century. (If the ideology of racism was not sufficiently strong to significantly influence the legal process, it is highly unlikely that it could have been a significant cause of slavery.)

Weinstein, Allen and Frank O. Gatell, eds. *American Negro Slavery*. New York: Oxford University Press, 1968. An excellent collection of readings on various aspects of slavery in the United States.

Williams, Eric. *Capitalism and Slavery*. Chapel Hill, N.C.: University of North Carolina Press, 1944. A classic which attributes the emergence of slavery to capitalism and posits racism as a consequence of slavery.

INDEX